Salt Cookbook

Over 80 hands-on recipes to efficiently configure and manage your infrastructure with Salt

Anirban Saha

BIRMINGHAM - MUMBAI

Salt Cookbook

First published: July 2015

Production reference: 1210715

Published by Packt Publishing Ltd.
Livery Place
35 Livery Street
Birmingham B3 2PB, UK.

ISBN 978-1-78439-974-0

www.packtpub.com

Credits

Author

Anirban Saha

Reviewer

Robert Fach

Commissioning Editor

Kartikey Pandey

Acquisition Editors

Richard Gall

Sam Wood

Content Development Editor

Siddhesh Salvi

Technical Editor

Prajakta Mhatre

Copy Editors

Charlotte Carneiro

Sameen Siddiqui

Project Coordinator

Nidhi Joshi

Proofreader

Safis Editing

Indexer

Tejal Soni

Production Coordinator

Aparna Bhagat

Cover Work

Aparna Bhagat

About the Author

Anirban Saha has been a system engineer for several years, mostly working with Linux and cloud-based infrastructures. He has worked extensively on large system deployments in data center environments, as well as public and private cloud infrastructures for several organizations in various industries. He is also an open source and technology enthusiast and a speaker at conferences and meetups. Anirban likes and supports anything about technology.

About the Reviewer

Robert Fach has a degree in computer science. He likes building scalable, fault-tolerant, fail-aware, and autonomous systems. Several years ago, he started working in the software integration area of an automotive manufacturer. He introduced SaltStack to that company to manage the complete software integration infrastructure.

www.PacktPub.com

Support files, eBooks, discount offers, and more

For support files and downloads related to your book, please visit www.PacktPub.com.

Did you know that Packt offers eBook versions of every book published, with PDF and ePub files available? You can upgrade to the eBook version at www.PacktPub.com and as a print book customer, you are entitled to a discount on the eBook copy. Get in touch with us at service@packtpub.com for more details.

At www.PacktPub.com, you can also read a collection of free technical articles, sign up for a range of free newsletters and receive exclusive discounts and offers on Packt books and eBooks.

https://www2.packtpub.com/books/subscription/packtlib

Do you need instant solutions to your IT questions? PacktLib is Packt's online digital book library. Here, you can search, access, and read Packt's entire library of books.

Why Subscribe?

- Fully searchable across every book published by Packt
- Copy and paste, print, and bookmark content
- On demand and accessible via a web browser

Free Access for Packt account holders

If you have an account with Packt at www.PacktPub.com, you can use this to access PacktLib today and view 9 entirely free books. Simply use your login credentials for immediate access.

Table of Contents

Preface

Salt is one of the many but unique tools available today for configuration management and orchestration. Salt not only enables us to seamlessly configure our infrastructure, but also to perform all sorts of tasks based on a variety of conditions and properties of the Salt minions. Along with super-fast module execution with the help of the ZeroMQ messaging library, Salt takes orchestration to a whole new level, which can be used for numerous day-to-day tasks starting from simple data collection to complex deployments.

This book provides a hands-on approach to the world of Salt. It provides a basic understanding of the concepts and architecture on which Salt is based, and then moves on to details about configuring it and also writing complex recipes for different tasks and scenarios.

The content of the book definitely helps professionals associated with infrastructure management to consider Salt as a potential tool for implementing their infrastructure and it also provides lot of recipes which existing Salt users can refer to. With the help of the content of the book, users can also integrate Salt with other tools and services to get the optimal results required.

The book starts off with the concepts and architecture of Salt, followed by some basic and advanced configurations and module usages. The next topics are about configuring application and database servers, cloud-based services, and event systems. It finishes off with recipes for troubleshooting Salt.

What this book covers

Chapter 1, Salt Architecture and Components, gives you a basic understanding about the concept and architecture of Salt. It explains a lot of Salt terminology, such as the Salt master, minions, states, pillars, environments, and grains, and demonstrates how to configure them.

Chapter 2, Writing Advanced Salt Configurations, goes a bit deeper into Salt configuration and gives you a detailed explanation of the various data manipulation you can perform in Salt, such as conditionals, iterations, and Python functions. It also focuses on the very important topic of targeting minions using different techniques.

Chapter 3, Modules, Orchestration, and Scaling Salt, gives you an even deeper understanding of the advanced Salt concepts of execution and state modules, using templates, requisites, and Salt runners, performing orchestration and demonstrates multi-master setups for redundancy.

Chapter 4, General Administration Tasks, provides hands-on recipes on configuring general system entities, such as users, groups, SSH configurations, scheduling with cron, volume, and disk management with network configuration. It also explains how to add custom grains to a minion.

Chapter 5, Advanced Administration Tasks, provides explanations and demonstrations about advanced system topics such as package repository configuration and package management, file and service management, managing code repositories and handling alternatives.

Chapter 6, Managing Application Servers, gives an understanding of how to configure web and application servers by handling each configuration step-by-step in the recipes. It demonstrates package and service configuration, manages the server configuration file, and deployments for application servers and security for web servers.

Chapter 7, Managing Databases, provides detailed explanations and demonstrations of database configuration for MySQL and PostgreSQL. It includes database package and service management, managing users and groups, databases, grants and queries.

Chapter 8, Configuring Salt Cloud, provides extensive knowledge about how to manage cloud infrastructures using Salt Cloud. It demonstrates the usage of Salt Cloud, providers and profiles, cloud maps, post-install scripts, and management of cloud resources such as instances and volumes using Salt Cloud.

Chapter 9, Managing Amazon Web Services, focuses specifically on how to manage the EC2 Cloud hosted by Amazon Web Services. It includes recipes to manage security groups, load balancers, DNS with Route53, Simple Queue Service, ElastiCache clusters and CloudWatch alarms.

Chapter 10, Salt Event and Reactor System, explains and demonstrates the event system of Salt and how to request and receive events using the Salt message bus. It also explains how to use the event system to configure the reactor system in Salt to perform required tasks.

Chapter 11, Troubleshooting, demonstrates several scenarios where things can go wrong with the Salt system and how you can troubleshoot and fix such problems.

What you need for this book

RedHat/CentOS/Scientific Linux, as Salt does not have support for Windows. However, the minion can be installed on a variety of systems including Solaris and Windows. The Salt system is based on Python and depends on a few Python libraries, which get automatically resolved and installed when a package manager is used to install the packages. If not automatically resolved, these dependencies need to be installed first.

Although a single system can be used to configure the master and minion, a network containing a few different systems is needed to configure and demonstrate Salt optimally by configuring a master and multiple minions, or each minion can be their own master as explained in the book.

Also, a working Internet connection is required to fetch packages for configuration.

Who this book is for

If you are a professional associated with system and infrastructure management, looking at automated infrastructure and deployments, then this book is for you. No prior experience of Salt is required.

Sections

In this book, you will find several headings that appear frequently (Getting ready, How to do it, How it works, There's more, and See also).

To give clear instructions on how to complete a recipe, we use these sections as follows:

Getting ready

This section tells you what to expect in the recipe, and describes how to set up any software or any preliminary settings required for the recipe.

How to do it...

This section contains the steps required to follow the recipe.

How it works...

This section usually consists of a detailed explanation of what happened in the previous section.

There's more...

This section consists of additional information about the recipe in order to make the reader more knowledgeable about the recipe.

See also

This section provides helpful links to other useful information for the recipe.

Conventions

In this book, you will find a number of text styles that distinguish between different kinds of information. Here are some examples of these styles and an explanation of their meaning.

Code words in text, database table names, folder names, filenames, file extensions, pathnames, dummy URLs, user input, and Twitter handles are shown as follows: "The sudo command needs to be added before the mentioned commands."

A block of code is set as follows:

```
file_roots:
  base:
    - /opt/salt-cookbook/base
  production:
    - /opt/salt-cookbook/production
  staging:
    - /opt/salt-cookbook/staging
  development:
    - /opt/salt-cookbook/development
```

Any command-line input or output is written as follows:

```
[root@salt-master ~]# service salt-master restart
```

New terms and **important words** are shown in bold, like this: "**Salt** is a systems management software created and maintained by SaltStack."

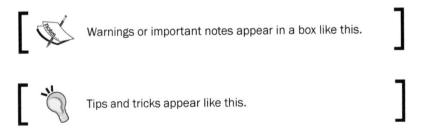

> Warnings or important notes appear in a box like this.

> Tips and tricks appear like this.

Reader feedback

Feedback from our readers is always welcome. Let us know what you think about this book—what you liked or disliked. Reader feedback is important for us as it helps us develop titles that you will really get the most out of.

To send us general feedback, simply e-mail `feedback@packtpub.com`, and mention the book's title in the subject of your message.

If there is a topic that you have expertise in and you are interested in either writing or contributing to a book, see our author guide at `www.packtpub.com/authors`.

Customer support

Now that you are the proud owner of a Packt book, we have a number of things to help you to get the most from your purchase.

Downloading the example code

You can download the example code files from your account at `http://www.packtpub.com` for all the Packt Publishing books you have purchased. If you purchased this book elsewhere, you can visit `http://www.packtpub.com/support` and register to have the files e-mailed directly to you.

Errata

Although we have taken every care to ensure the accuracy of our content, mistakes do happen. If you find a mistake in one of our books—maybe a mistake in the text or the code—we would be grateful if you could report this to us. By doing so, you can save other readers from frustration and help us improve subsequent versions of this book. If you find any errata, please report them by visiting `http://www.packtpub.com/submit-errata`, selecting your book, clicking on the **Errata Submission Form** link, and entering the details of your errata. Once your errata are verified, your submission will be accepted and the errata will be uploaded to our website or added to any list of existing errata under the Errata section of that title.

To view the previously submitted errata, go to `https://www.packtpub.com/books/content/support` and enter the name of the book in the search field. The required information will appear under the **Errata** section.

Piracy

Piracy of copyrighted material on the Internet is an ongoing problem across all media. At Packt, we take the protection of our copyright and licenses very seriously. If you come across any illegal copies of our works in any form on the Internet, please provide us with the location address or website name immediately so that we can pursue a remedy.

Please contact us at copyright@packtpub.com with a link to the suspected pirated material.

We appreciate your help in protecting our authors and our ability to bring you valuable content.

Questions

If you have a problem with any aspect of this book, you can contact us at questions@packtpub.com, and we will do our best to address the problem.

1
Salt Architecture and Components

In this chapter, you will cover:

- ▸ Installing and configuring the Salt master
- ▸ Configuring the Salt environment and pillar paths
- ▸ Understanding and configuring Salt pillars
- ▸ Understanding and writing Salt states
- ▸ Understanding and writing the top file
- ▸ Installing and configuring the Salt minion
- ▸ Configuring environment and grains on the minion
- ▸ Applying Salt states to minions

Introduction

So you have heard of this new tool called Salt, you've probably looked it up on the Internet, and now it has drawn your attention. What is Salt?

Salt is a systems management software created and maintained by SaltStack. It is used to manage infrastructure, virtualization, applications, databases, private and public clouds, software, or code. With Salt, data center automation, server provisioning, configuration management, and orchestration are a few tasks that can be done in a simple, elegant, and fast manner. Salt was first released in 2011 and has been gaining tremendous momentum ever since.

The primary advantages of Salt are as follows:

- **Simple to set up and manage**: No matter what the size of the infrastructure is, Salt is extremely easy to set up and maintain. It has a simple server/client model, which works seamlessly from a small deployment to massive data center deployments.

- **Ability for parallel execution**: Salt uses hostname, system properties called **grains** and custom configured matchers to perform remote module, state, and command execution on target nodes. These executions happen in parallel for rapid deployments.

- **Speed and security**: Salt incorporates a message broker in the Salt daemon itself by using the ZeroMQ networking library. It uses public keys for authentication between the master and the client nodes with AES encryption for faster payload communication. Salt enables light and fast network traffic using **msgpack**.

- **Scalability and flexibility**: Salt provides flexibility for systems management by providing various ways for the master and client nodes to communicate and synchronize using both the push and pull methods. The Salt master can also be scaled with multiple master configurations to support large and growing infrastructures.

- **Uses Python interface**: Salt routines can be written as Python modules, and Salt itself can be called from the command line or Python API. The Salt states even allow the use of Python style conditionals, iterators, and functions to carry out automated systems management tasks.

Apart from the few aforementioned advantages, Salt has many more features that we will explore throughout this book. Salt has a large and vibrant community, which has come up with a massive number of built-in state and execution modules to simplify the management and deployment process as much as possible.

It is to be noted that almost all of the examples mentioned in this book have been targeted to work on the CentOS operating system, unless specified otherwise. The methods for other operating systems should be similar with different package, file, and service names.

Already excited by the possibilities of Salt? Let's dive in and explore it hands on.

Installing and configuring the Salt master

In this section, we are going to configure the most important component of the Salt architecture—the Salt master. We'll install the Salt master package and configure the most important parameters needed for our infrastructure.

How to do it...

Let's see how we can install the Salt master on various types of OS.

Installing the Salt master on RedHat/CentOS/Fedora

1. Salt packages are available in the EPEL repository. First, the repository needs to be added to the system. As the system being used is CentOS 6.5 (64-bit), we are using the `epel-release` package at `http://dl.fedoraproject.org/pub/epel/6/x86_64/`. This needs to be changed as per the version and architecture of the operating system being used:

    ```
    [root@salt-master ~]# rpm -ihv \
    http://dl.fedoraproject.org/pub/epel/6/x86_64/epel-release-6-
    8.noarch.rpm
    ```

2. After the EPEL release package has been installed, we will install the `salt-master` package with the following command, and the dependencies should automatically be fetched from the repository:

    ```
    [root@salt-master ~]# yum -y install salt-master
    ```

Installing the Salt master on Ubuntu

While installing the Salt master on Ubuntu, the SaltStack PPA repository needs to be added to the system. It is to be noted that the following commands need to be executed as a privileged user, that is, either the `root` user can be used, or the `sudo` command needs to be added before the mentioned commands:

1. The following command adds the `add-apt-repository` binary to the system:

    ```
    [root@salt-master ~]# apt-get -y install python-software-
    properties
    ```

2. Now, we will add the repository with the command given here:

    ```
    [root@salt-master ~]# add-apt-repository ppa:saltstack/salt
    ```

3. The Salt master package then needs to be installed with the following command:

    ```
    [root@salt-master ~]# apt-get -y install salt-master
    ```

Configuring the Salt master

The primary configuration file for the Salt master is `/etc/salt/master`. It is also a good practice to create additional configuration files in `/etc/salt/master.d/` with the `.conf` extension, and they will get read along with all the other files when the Salt master daemon starts.

Most of the Salt configuration parameters are set by default and need not be set explicitly. However, let's look at some of the important parameters that can be altered to suit one's needs:

- To determine which network interface the service binds to:

  `interface: 0.0.0.0`

- The port on which to listen to for client node (minion) communications:

  `publish_port: 4505`

- The path that gets prepended to other files such as `log_file`, `pki_dir`, and `cache_dir` if set. It is also to be noted that this path gets prepended to all other defined configuration parameters in the master configuration files, where each of them is also explained in detail:

  `root_dir: /`

- The directory to hold the master and minion keys that have already been authenticated or rejected:

  `pki_dir: /etc/salt/pki/master`

- The file containing log entries for the master daemon:

  `log_file: /var/log/salt/master`

- The file that allows the keys of the host's that match the listed patterns to be accepted automatically (it is always a good practice to define this file). We will uncomment this line and set the filename as follows:

  `autosign_file: /etc/salt/autosign.conf`

- Edit the file `/etc/salt/autosign.conf` and set the content to be a wild card entry as follows (this is being done to facilitate easier demonstrations in the rest of the book, it is to be noted that this is a security risk otherwise):

  `*`

- The Salt service daemon then needs to be started and configured to start at boot time.

  On RedHat/CentOS/Fedora:

  ```
  [root@salt-master ~]# service salt-master start
  [root@salt-master ~]# chkconfig salt-master on
  ```

  On Ubuntu, the installation process automatically starts the daemon, hence the daemon needs to be restarted:

  ```
  [root@salt-master ~]# service salt-master restart
  [root@salt-master ~]# update-rc.d salt-master defaults
  ```

The firewall needs to be configured to allow communication on ports 4505 and 4506 from the minions:

```
[root@salt-master ~]# iptables -A INPUT -m state --state new \
-m tcp -p tcp --dport 4505 -j ACCEPT
```

```
[root@salt-master ~]# iptables -A INPUT -m state --state new \
-m tcp -p tcp --dport 4506 -j ACCEPT
```

▶ Save the firewall rules:

On RedHat/CentOS/Fedora:

```
[root@salt-master ~]# service iptables save
```

On Ubuntu:

```
[root@salt-master ~]# iptables-save
```

In the scenario that a virtualized environment is being used, such as a cloud provider, the aforementioned ports should be opened in the respective security group of the master node.

How it works...

The `salt-master` is the package for the Salt master service and it also requires a few other dependencies, such as the ZeroMQ library, msgpack, jinja, yaml, and so on, which is automatically pulled along with the package from the configured repositories.

Most of the Salt configuration parameters are set by default and need not be explicitly mentioned in the file. The options can be found commented in the file and act as the defaults. However, if they need to be changed, then they can be uncommented and necessary changes can be made.

We have explicitly uncommented the `autosign_file` parameter and set the value as `/etc/salt/autosign.conf`:

```
autosign_file: /etc/salt/autosign.conf
```

We then populated the file with a wildcard entry, that is, *, to allow all minions' certificate requests to be automatically signed and accepted by the master.

Finally, the service daemons for salt master are started/restarted, configured to start automatically at boot time, and firewalls are configured to open the ports 4505 and 4506 for communication with the minions using the system-specific commands.

See also

▶ The *Salt multi-master setup (active-active mode)* and *Salt multi-master setup (active-passive mode)* recipes in *Chapter 3, Modules, Orchestration, and Scaling Salt*, to learn more about highly available and redundant Salt master setups

▶ The *Configuring the Salt environment and pillar paths* recipe, for advanced configuration of the Salt master

Configuring the Salt environment and pillar paths

In this recipe, we are going to configure the environment and pillar paths for Salt to use when we mention environments while performing Salt operations. Ideally, any infrastructure should have environments for development, testing, QA, production, and so on, for isolation of respective code and a seamless workflow. Salt enables us to implement this in a few simple steps by providing options to define environments for states and pillars.

How to do it...

In the primary configuration /etc/salt/master file, we will configure the section called file_roots. Under this parameter option, we will name each environment we want to configure and the path of the directory that will contain the configuration files for that environment.

1. Let's create the directories we want to use as the environment paths and then configure four environments named base, production, staging, and development as follows:

   ```
   [root@salt-master ~]# mkdir -p \
   /opt/salt-cookbook/{base,production,staging,development}
   ```

2. Edit /etc/salt/master to have following content:

   ```
   file_roots:
     base:
       - /opt/salt-cookbook/base
     production:
       - /opt/salt-cookbook/production
     staging:
       - /opt/salt-cookbook/staging
     development:
       - /opt/salt-cookbook/development
   ```

3. Next, we will create the directories we want to use as pillar paths and configure them following the same environment conventions as follows:

```
[root@salt-master ~]# mkdir -p \
/opt/salt-
cookbook/pillar/{base,production,staging,development}
```

4. Edit /etc/salt/master to have following content:

```
pillar_roots:
  base:
    - /opt/salt-cookbook/pillar/base
  production:
    - /opt/salt-cookbook/pillar/production
  staging:
    - /opt/salt-cookbook/pillar/staging
  development:
    - /opt/salt-cookbook/pillar/development
```

5. We now restart the salt-master daemon for these changes to take effect:

```
[root@salt-master ~]# service salt-master restart
```

How it works...

Environments in Salt are designed to keep the configuration files for each environment isolated into respective containers for different stages of deployment such as development, QA, staging, and production. Ideally, the configurations can be written in either of the environments such as staging, and after a proper test phases, they can be migrated to the production environment.

Here, we opted for the /opt/salt-cookbook path to be the base directory of all our configurations. Next, we have chosen four environments for our infrastructure, namely, base, staging, production, and development. The base environment is the default in Salt and the path /srv/salt is taken as the base directory for all configurations if not configured explicitly as we have done earlier.

We then created the directory paths we want to use as the environment paths and mentioned them under the file_roots parameter, specifying the environment name and the path that points the configuration files for that environment:

```
file_roots:
  <environment_name>:
    - <environment_directory_path>
```

Pillars are one of the best features of Salt, which enable us to isolate data that needs to be kept secure such as keys and passwords. Next, we have chosen the /opt/salt-cookbook/pillar path to be our base directory for all pillar data and created directories for each environment that will contain pillar data, which is usable in that environment only.

We then edited the Salt master configuration file to include the environment names and their paths under the `pillar_roots` section for Salt to identify them as the pillar configuration paths:

```
pillar_roots:
  <environment_name>:
    - <pillar_directory_path>
```

Finally, we restarted the Salt master daemon for the changes to take effect.

It is also to be noted that when executing the `salt` command, the environment has to be mentioned for the minion(s). This is generally done with the `saltenv` option on the command line. However, this parameter can also be specified in the minion configuration `/etc/salt/minion` file, as follows:

```
environment: production
```

If this parameter is not set, the base environment is taken as the default environment.

See also

▶ The *Using pillar data in states* and *Writing and retrieving pillar data* recipes in *Chapter 2, Writing Advanced Salt Configurations*, to learn more about how to use pillars in states

▶ The *Understanding and configuring Salt pillars* recipe, for detailed examples of pillar configurations

Understanding and configuring Salt pillars

In this recipe, we will learn about pillars, how they fit into the Salt architecture, and how to configure them. We will create pillar data for a `user` state, which we will configure later using this pillar data.

How to do it...

We will create pillar data for the `development` environment.

1. First, we will create a directory for the name of the pillar data (usually it is named the same as the state we are configuring this pillar for, that is, if we are configuring this pillar for the `user` state, we will name this pillar directory `user`:

    ```
    [root@salt-master ~]# mkdir \
    /opt/salt-cookbook/pillar/development/user
    ```

```
[root@salt-master ~]# touch \
/opt/salt-cookbook/pillar/development/user/init.sls
```

2. Edit /opt/salt-cookbook/salt/pillar/development/user/init.sls and add the following content:

```
dev_user:
  name: thomas
  password: "$1$PG1inys0$kB2I83KzEVzVs9G7xLHjA1"
  uid: 1001
  comment: "Thomas"
```

And run the following command:

```
[root@salt-master ~]# touch \
/opt/salt-cookbook/pillar/development/top.sls
```

3. Edit /opt/salt-cookbook/pillar/development/top.sls and add the following content:

```
development:
  '*':
    - user
```

How it works...

In Salt, a pillar is a feature used to store data such as keys and passwords or any other type of data such as repetitive directory paths or usernames that are then accessed from states. All minion-specific data to be seen only by the minion is stored in pillars and is visible to the minion for which the data is meant and configured. In this recipe, we created pillar data in the development environment for a user state, which we will configure in the next recipe.

First, we created a directory similar to the name of the state that we will configure in the pillar directory path of the development environment:

```
[root@salt-master ~]# mkdir \
/opt/salt-cookbook/pillar/development/user
```

Next, we created a file called init.sls in the directory created earlier, where we will create the pillar data. The default file in a pillar directory is named init.sls, where .sls is the file extension for all Salt state, pillar, and top files. Salt manages the SLS files internally. If the user pillar is referenced, we must understand that it's the content of the init.sls file in the user directory that is being referred to. The contents of all SLS files in Salt are in the YAML format, and indentations are very important both for parsing by Salt and to keep the configurations organized.

In the `init.sls` file, we populated the pillar data that we need. Basically, we configured the first user of a user list of developers mentioning various parameters for the user, such as their username, user ID, password in hash format (note that it is enclosed in quotes to avoid problems with special characters), and the comment:

```
dev_user:
  name: thomas
  password: "$1$PG1inys0$kB2I83KzEVzVs9G7xLHjA1"
  uid: 1001
  comment: "Thomas"
```

If we are planning to add multiple users, the format can be as shown here:

```
dev_user:
  thomas:
    password: "$1$PG1inys0$kB2I83KzEVzVs9G7xLHjA1"
    uid: 1001
    comment: "Thomas"
```

The methods to parse this kind of YAML definition will be discussed later in the book.

Next, we created a file called `top.sls` in the base pillar directory of the `development` environment. The contents of the `top.sls` file determine which nodes or minions will have access to which pillar data. We created the following contents in the file:

```
development:
  '*':
    - user
```

The first line mentions the environment. Without this line, the `base` environment will be used as the default. The * operator in the second line is a wildcard, which means that all minions will have access to the `user` pillar data. This line can be manipulated to add various types of matchers to target minions that will be discussed later in the book. The third line mentions the name of the pillar directory that we created. If only the name of the directory is mentioned, we have to understand that the contents of the `init.sls` files are being referred to. If we create a file called `devs.sls` in the `user` directory, then the contents of that file can be mentioned in the `top.sls` file as `user.devs`, shown as follows:

```
development:
  '*':
    - user.devs
```

When the states are run on the minions, this file is checked and these definitions determine if that particular minion is allowed to access the contents of this pillar.

See also

▸ The *Writing and retrieving pillar data* and *Using pillar data in states* recipes in *Chapter 2, Writing Advanced Salt Configurations*, to learn more about using pillars

▸ The *Understanding and writing Salt states* recipe, to learn how to use this pillar data in states

Understanding and writing Salt states

In this recipe, we will learn one of the most important components of Salt states. We will understand what states are, how to write them, and how to use pillar data in writing states. We will configure a state called `user` to add a user to the `development` environment.

How to do it...

1. First, we will create a directory for the state and populate it with state data:

```
[root@salt-master ~]# mkdir \
/opt/salt-cookbook/development/user
[ root@salt-master ~]# touch \
/opt/salt-cookbook/development/user/init.sls
```

2. Edit `/opt/salt-cookbook/development/user/init.sls` and add the following contents:

```
generic_user:
  user.present:
    - name: {{ pillar['dev_user']['name'] }}
    - shell: /bin/bash
    - home: /home/{{ pillar['dev_user']['name'] }}
    - uid: {{ pillar['dev_user']['uid'] }}
    - password: {{ pillar['dev_user']['password'] }}
```

How it works...

In Salt, **states** are written to determine which and what kind of resources will be added to a system. States are written with the help of built-in state modules, a full list of which can be found at `http://docs.saltstack.com/en/latest/ref/states/all/`. Using these `state` modules, we can configure a massive amount of system resources, a few being users, groups, files, repositories, packages, services, code repositories, and so on. These states are then configured to be available to desired nodes or minions based on various properties.

In this recipe, we configured a user to be added to a system in the `development` environment, irrespective of the operating system.

First, we created a directory with the name of the state, that is, the `user` in the base directory of the `development` environment. Then, we created a file named `init.sls`, which is the default file in a `state` directory. **Salt State File** or **SLS** is used as the only file type of all Salt configuration files.

In the first line, we defined a custom name of this resource that can be any name, we named it `generic_user`. This name can be used in subsequent resources, when referencing this resource and have to be unique in the complete state space being used by the minion. However, this is optional as the definition could also be written as follows:

```
{{ pillar['dev_user']['name'] }}:
  user.present:
    - shell: /bin/bash
    - home: /home/{{ pillar['dev_user']['name'] }}
```

Here, we also learn about how to refer to pillar data when writing states. It is usually in the following format:

```
{{ pillar[<first_key>][<second_key>]... }}
```

However, do note that, in the reference, the directory name of the pillar, that is, `user` is never used. Instead, the reference begins from the first YAML key found in the file, that is, `dev_user`, followed by the next mentioned key. Also, note that the first keys are always unique in the environment for a minion, that is, `dev_user` can only be used once as the first key. If a second file is created, called `devs.sls`, and the first key is named `dev_user`, there will be a conflict of key names and Salt synchronization will fail.

The following method can also be used to achieve the same objective:

```
{{ pillar['pillar.get']('dev_user:name', 'defaultuser') }}:
```

This is a better method as it also gives us the option to mention a default value if the pillar is not available.

The second line mentions the built-in state module name, that is, `user` and the function is present. There can be multiple functions for a module name and this can be looked up in the URL mentioned earlier in this recipe. For the `user` module, the two functions available are present and absent, which in turn take multiple parameters such as `name`, `uid`, `gid`, `password`, and so on.

Next, we see how each of the function parameters are populated for the user using static data, as well as pillar data:

```
- name: {{ pillar['dev_user']['name'] }}
- shell: /bin/bash
- home: /home/{{ pillar['dev_user']['name'] }}
- uid: {{ pillar['dev_user']['uid'] }}
```

See also

▶ *Chapter 2, Writing Advanced Salt Configurations*, to learn more about advanced state configurations

▶ The *Understanding and writing the top file* recipe, to learn about how to make Salt states available to minions

Understanding and writing the top file

In this recipe, we will understand and learn how to write the top file, the file which determines how the states are applied to the nodes or minions in Salt. We will apply the state that we configured in the previous recipe to minions.

How to do it...

The state configured in the previous recipe will now be applied to minions in the development environment.

1. Create a file named top.sls in the base directory of the development environment:

```
[root@salt-master ~]# touch \
/opt/salt-cookbook/development/top.sls
```

2. Edit the /opt/salt-cookbook/development/top.sls file and add the following contents:

```
development:
  '*':
    - user
  'salt-minion':
    - match: list
    - hostconfig
```

How it works...

The top.sls file in Salt determines which state will be applied to which minions. It has an extension of .sls similar to all other files in Salt. It is written in the YAML format and takes minion matchers in the form of wildcards, nodegroups, lists, grains, and so on. We will look at all of the ways to match minions throughout the book when we go through each of these components.

First, we created the `top.sls` file in the base directory of the `development` environment, that is, `/opt/salt-cookbook/development`, and then we populated it with the required definitions.

The first line indicates the environment we are configuring the top file for, that is, `development`. Without this, the base environment will be used as default. The next line indicates a wildcard `*` meaning that it will match all minions and apply the listed state to all of them. Then, we listed the `user` state that we already configured:

```
development:
  '*':
    - user
```

We can also match minions when applying states in the `top.sls` file in the following manner:

```
development:
  '*':
    - user
  'salt-minion':
    - match: list
    - hostconfig
```

Here, we see a second block of node definition and state that introduces a new key called `match`. Instead of the wildcard in the preceding block, this block has the name of a minion node called `salt-minion`, which is the hostname of the minion node that will synchronize with the master and the second line in the block:

```
    - match: list
```

This line indicates that the type of minion parameter to match is a list, which is nothing but the hostname of the minion. The line that has the name of the minion can be a comma-separated line of multiple hostnames:

```
'webserver,dbserver,appserver,proxyserver'
```

The list matcher will match the line as a list of minion names. Then, we mentioned a state called `hostconfig`, which is also the name of a state not configured in the book so far. This example means that the `hostconfig` state will be applied to all the minions in the list, which in this case is the minion named `salt-minion`.

There's more...

In Salt, minions can be matched in more ways than shown in this recipe, such as nodegroups, grains, IP/subnets, and so on. We will learn how to apply them in *Chapter 3, Modules, Orchestration, and Scaling Salt*.

See also

▶ The *Installing and configuring the Salt minion* recipe, to learn how to install and configure minions

Installing and configuring the Salt minion

In this recipe, we will learn about minions, how they work, and how to install and configure them.

How to do it...

We will install the Salt minion on a second node and name the node `salt-minion`. First, we will install the `salt-minion` package.

Installing the Salt minion on RedHat/CentOS/Fedora

1. Install the `epel-release` rpm to configure the EPEL repository:

```
[root@salt-minion ~]# rpm -ihv \
http://dl.fedoraproject.org/pub/epel/6/x86_64/epel-release-6-
8.noarch.rpm
```

2. After the EPEL release package has been installed, we will install the `salt-minion` package with the following command and the dependencies should automatically be fetched from the repository:

```
[root@salt-minion ~]# yum -y install salt-minion
```

Installing the Salt minion on Ubuntu

When installing the Salt minion in Ubuntu, the SaltStack PPA repository needs to be added to the system. It is to be noted that the following commands need to be executed as a privileged user, that is, either the `root` user can be used, or the `sudo` command needs to be added before the mentioned commands.

1. The following command adds the `add-apt-repository` binary to the system:

```
[root@salt-minion ~]# apt-get -y install python-software-
properties
```

2. Now, we will add the repository with the following command:

```
[root@salt-minion ~]# add-apt-repository ppa:saltstack/salt
```

3. The Salt minion package then needs to be installed with the following command:

```
[root@salt-minion ~]# apt-get -y install salt-minion
```

Configuring the Salt minion

The configuration file for the Salt minion is /etc/salt/minion. It is also a good practice to create additional configuration files in /etc/salt/minion.d/ with the .conf extension, and they will get read along with all other files when the Salt minion daemon starts.

1. In /etc/salt/minion, uncomment and edit the following parameter:

   ```
   master: salt-master
   ```

2. Start the salt-minion service daemon and configure it to start automatically at boot time:

   On RedHat/CentOS/Fedora:

   ```
   [root@salt-minion ~]# service salt-minion start
   [root@salt-minion ~]# chkconfig salt-minion on
   ```

   On Ubuntu, the installation process automatically starts the daemon, hence the daemon needs to be restarted:

   ```
   [root@salt-minion ~]# service salt-minion restart
   [root@salt-minion ~]# update-rc.d salt-minion defaults
   ```

How it works...

In Salt, the client nodes on which the configured states are applied are known as **minions**. The minion configuration file is /etc/salt/minion, which contains the configurable parameters for the minion, and most of the parameters use the default values as mentioned in the file and are commented. Any change in the parameters can be made by uncommenting and editing the parameters.

In this recipe, we configured the repositories from which to fetch the salt-minion package. We then installed the package and the dependencies get automatically fetched from the repositories.

Next, we edited the /etc/salt/minion file, uncommented the master parameter, and edited it to have the value salt-master (as we named our salt master salt-master in the earlier recipes). Do note that, for this parameter to work on the minions, there needs to be a DNS entry or an entry in /etc/hosts of the minions for the salt-master pointing to the IP of the Salt master. This parameter enables the minion to communicate with the Salt master on the TCP ports 4505 and 4506, as we configured in the first recipe of this chapter.

The rest of the parameters can be left as defaults. Finally, we started the salt-master daemon and configured it to start automatically at boot time.

There's more...

There is one more parameter in the /etc/salt/minion file, which may be interesting for some. The id parameter enables us to set the minion ID explicitly, without which the hostname of the minion is taken up as the minion ID by default. The minion ID is the name that the Salt master is able to see when the minion requests its certificate to be signed and authenticated by the master. After the certificate signing is complete, the master knows the minion by the same minion ID and any communication which involves the minion name from the master to the minion happens using this minion ID.

For example, the minion node can have a hostname prodapp01, but we can set its minion ID in the /etc/salt/minion file, as follows:

```
id: appserver
```

This parameter will make this node known to the Salt master as appserver and not prodapp01, although the hostname is prodapp01. Without this parameter, the master will know this node as prodapp01.

The masterless minion

There is a feature in Salt that enables the minions to run in a masterless mode. In this case, the minion acts as its own master. The minion can be configured for this by changing the value of the file_client parameter in the /etc/salt/minion file from remote to local and configuring the paths to states and pillars.

Uncomment and edit the following parameters in /etc/salt/minion. The value of local for the file_client parameter enables the minion to look for states locally on it:

```
file_client:  local
```

Next, the state and pillar paths need to be set for the minion to find the state and pillar data on the system. The state and pillar files then need to be placed in these directories as discussed in earlier recipes:

```
file_roots:
  base:
    - /opt/salt-cookbook/base
  development:
    - /opt/salt-cookbook/development

pillar_roots:
  base:
    - /opt/salt-cookbook/pillar/base
  development:
    - /opt/salt-cookbook/pillar/development
```

We will learn the technique to run Salt to get the state and pillar data in the last recipe of this chapter.

See also

▶ The *Installing and configuring the Salt master* and *Configuring the Salt environment and pillar paths* recipes, to learn about the master, its port configurations, state, and pillar configurations

▶ The *Configuring environments and grains on the minion* and *Applying Salt states to minions* recipes, to learn about advanced minion configurations and synchronizing minions with masters

Configuring environments and grains on the minion

In this recipe, we will learn about some advanced minion configurations, such as environments and grains. We will understand how they work and how to configure them on the minion.

How to do it...

Uncomment and edit the `/etc/salt/minion` file to set the environment parameter:

```
environment: development
```

Setting grains in /etc/salt/minion

Uncomment and edit the `/etc/salt/minion` file to set the `grains` parameter:

```
grains:
  environment: development
  location: datacenter1
  server_type: webserver
```

Setting grains in /etc/salt/grains

Create the file `/etc/salt/grains` and populate it as follows:

```
environment: development
location: datacenter1
server_type: webserver
```

How it works...

The `environment` parameter in a Salt minion determines which environment the minion belongs to. This parameter helps Salt to determine which directory path it should look for on the master to fetch the correct configuration for the minion as per the environment specified.

As we specified in this recipe:

```
environment: development
```

When the minion calls and requests the master for its configuration, it looks for the `development` environment configured on the master and, if it finds one, it then looks for its base path, which in our case is `/opt/salt-cookbook/development`. It then looks for the relevant files in this directory.

However, do note that this `environment` parameter is useful when the minion calls the master, that is, the pull mechanism takes place. When the master pushes the configurations to minions, we can specify the environment while doing so but it only tells the master which directory path it should serve the files from. However, it does not tell the master which minions to target. To target minions from the `development` environment when pushing configurations from the master, we have to use grains, which we will discuss next.

In Salt, grains are information about system properties that helps Salt to target minions and configure pillars and states based on these properties. Salt makes a lot of grains available to us by default, a few being os, cpu, memory, hostname, domain name, IP addresses, MAC addresses, and so on. However, this feature becomes more useful when we are able to configure custom grains to suit our needs such as location, server type, application name, database name, and so on.

Grains can be configured in a couple of ways. The first option is to configure grains in the minion configuration file, that is, `/etc/salt/minion`, and the second option is to do this in a different file called `/etc/salt/grains`. In both cases, grains are configured as YAML key-value pairs.

Setting grains in /etc/salt/minion

For the first option, that is, in the `/etc/salt/minion` file, we have to configure the grains as we have done in this recipe:

```
grains:
  environment: development
  location: datacenter1
  server_type: webserver
```

Note the `grains` key in the first line. This is because the file `/etc/salt/minion` has a number of other parameters, and we have to explicitly specify that this section is for grains followed by the actual key-value pairs that determine our custom configured data.

Setting grains in /etc/salt/grains

For the second option, that is, the file /etc/salt/grains, we populated it as follows:

```
environment: development
location: datacenter1
server_type: webserver
```

Note the absence of the grains key here. The grains key is not needed in this case as this file is only for grain data. Next, we added the key-value pairs determining our custom data.

However, we have to keep in mind that grain data is static. If the grain data is modified or new grains are added, the minion has to be refreshed for the master to see the new data. This can be done with the help of execution modules, which we will learn later in the book. As of now, a restart of the salt-minion daemon should make the new data available.

See also

> ▸ The *Installing and configuring the Salt minion* recipe, to learn how to configure minions
> ▸ The *Targeting minions* recipe, in *Chapter 2, Writing Advanced Salt Configurations*, to learn about how to target minions
> ▸ The *Applying Salt states to minions* recipe, to learn how to synchronize minions with masters

Applying Salt states to minions

In this recipe, we will learn how to synchronize minions with the master and apply the states to minions that are configured on the master.

How to do it...

We will perform both the push and the pull mechanisms for applying states to minions.

1. Check if the minion has got automatically signed by the master:

   ```
   [root@salt-master ~]# salt-key -l accepted

   Accepted Keys:

   salt-minion
   ```

   If all the previous recipes were followed correctly, then the preceding output will be found and here salt-minion is the minion name whose key has been accepted.

2. The communication between the master and the minion can be checked with a couple of Salt commands:

```
[root@salt-master ~]# salt 'salt-minion' test.ping
salt-minion:
    True


[root@salt-master ~]# salt 'salt-minion' grains.items
salt-minion:
  biosreleasedate: 07/31/2013
  biosversion: 6.00

  .

  .

  zmqversion: 3.2.2
```

3. The user state that we configured can now be applied to the minion.

Applying states using the push mechanism from master to minion

States can be applied from master to minion as follows:

```
[root@salt-master ~]# salt 'salt-minion' state.sls user \
saltenv=development
salt-minion:
----------
          ID: generic_user
    Function: user.present
        Name: thomas
      Result: True
     Comment: New user thomas created
     Changes:
                 ----------
                 fullname:

                 gid:
                     1001
                 groups:
                     - thomas
                 home:
                     /home/thomas
```

```
        homephone:

        name:
            thomas
        passwd:
            x
        password:
            $1$PGlinys0$kB2I83KzEVzVs9G7xLHjA1
        roomnumber:

        shell:
            /bin/bash
        uid:
            1001
        workphone:


Summary
------------
Succeeded: 1
Failed:    0
------------
Total:     1
```

There is a second option of applying the state from master to minion, as follows:

```
[root@salt-master ~]# salt 'salt-minion' state.highstate \
saltenv=development
```

If fewer lines of output are needed, then the following command can be used:

```
[root@salt-master]# salt 'salt-minion' state.highstate \
saltenv=development --state-output=terse
salt-minion:
  Name: thomas - Function: user.present - Result: Changed


Summary
------------
Succeeded: 1
```

```
Failed:    0
------------
Total:     1
```

Applying states using the pull mechanism by minion from master

States can be fetched by minion from master, as follows:

```
root@salt-minion:~# salt-call state.highstate
[INFO    ] Loading fresh modules for state activity
[INFO    ] Fetching file from saltenv 'development', ** skipped **
latest already in cache 'salt://top.sls'
[INFO    ] Creating module dir '/var/cache/salt/minion/extmods/modules'
[INFO    ] Syncing modules for environment 'development'
[INFO    ] Loading cache from salt://_modules, for development)
[INFO    ] Caching directory '_modules/' for environment 'development'
[INFO    ] Creating module dir '/var/cache/salt/minion/extmods/states'
[INFO    ] Syncing states for environment 'development'
[INFO    ] Loading cache from salt://_states, for development)
[INFO    ] Caching directory '_states/' for environment 'development'
[INFO    ] Creating module dir '/var/cache/salt/minion/extmods/grains'
[INFO    ] Syncing grains for environment 'development'
[INFO    ] Loading cache from salt://_grains, for development)
[INFO    ] Caching directory '_grains/' for environment 'development'
[INFO    ] Creating module dir '/var/cache/salt/minion/extmods/renderers'
[INFO    ] Syncing renderers for environment 'development'
[INFO    ] Loading cache from salt://_renderers, for development)
[INFO    ] Caching directory '_renderers/' for environment 'development'
[INFO    ] Creating module dir '/var/cache/salt/minion/extmods/returners'
[INFO    ] Syncing returners for environment 'development'
[INFO    ] Loading cache from salt://_returners, for development)
[INFO    ] Caching directory '_returners/' for environment 'development'
[INFO    ] Creating module dir '/var/cache/salt/minion/extmods/
outputters'
[INFO    ] Syncing outputters for environment 'development'
[INFO    ] Loading cache from salt://_outputters, for development)
[INFO    ] Caching directory '_outputters/' for environment 'development'
[INFO    ] Loading fresh modules for state activity
```

```
[INFO    ] Fetching file from saltenv 'development', ** skipped **
latest already in cache 'salt://user/init.sls'

[INFO    ] Running state [thomas] at time 19:04:47.080222

[INFO    ] Executing state user.present for thomas

[INFO    ] Executing command 'useradd -s /bin/bash -u 1001 -m -d
/home/thomas thomas' in directory '/root'

[INFO    ] {'shell': '/bin/bash', 'workphone': '', 'uid': 1001,
'passwd': 'x', 'roomnumber': '', 'groups': ['thomas'], 'home':
'/home/thomas', 'password': '$1$PG1inys0$kB2I83KzEVzVs9G7xLHjA1',
'name': 'thomas', 'gid': 1001, 'fullname': '', 'homephone': ''}

[INFO    ] Completed state [thomas] at time 19:04:47.209616

local:
    ----------
              ID: generic_user
        Function: user.present
            Name: thomas
          Result: True
         Comment: New user thomas created
         Changes:
                  ----------
                  fullname:

                  gid:
                      1001
                  groups:
                      - thomas
                  home:
                      /home/thomas
                  homephone:

                  name:
                      thomas
                  passwd:
                      x
                  password:
                      $1$PG1inys0$kB2I83KzEVzVs9G7xLHjA1
                  roomnumber:
```

```
    shell:
        /bin/bash
    uid:
        1001
    workphone:


Summary
------------
Succeeded: 1
Failed:    0
------------
Total:     1
```

The same task can also be done by using the following command:

```
root@salt-minion:~# salt-call state.sls user saltenv=development
```

How it works...

In this recipe, we have seen how to apply Salt states to minions. Let's now look at the steps in details.

First, we tested if the certificate request for the minion had been accepted and signed by the master because we had configured it to accept all minions by defining the wildcard in the /etc/salt/autosign.conf file.

Next, we tested communication between the master and the minion with the salt binary and using what we call built-in execution modules in Salt. The test.ping module checks if the minion is available and is responding to the master and grains.items returns all the built-in and custom grains on the minion. Here, test.ping and grains.items are the execution modules and are just a couple of the numerous modules available in Salt.

Next, we look at how to actually apply the configured states to minions.

First, we see the push mechanism from the master to the minion:

```
[root@salt-master ~]# salt 'salt-minion' state.sls user \
saltenv=development
```

Here, we see the `salt` binary being used along with the name (`minion id`) of the minion, followed by another execution module `state.sls`, and then the name of the state that we had configured. Finally, the name of the environment is specified without which Salt will look for the `base` environment and fail. Any configured state can be used in this format to apply to minions, and this method is independent of the `top.sls` file that we configured in the base directory of the `development` environment.

Next, we see an alternate method to apply states to minions:

```
[root@salt-master ~]# salt 'salt-minion' state.highstate \
saltenv=development
```

Here we see the same command, without the state name and a new execution module called `state.highstate`. When `state.highstate` is mentioned, it applies all the states that have been configured for the minion in the `top.sls` file of that environment. Only the `user` state gets applied to the minion because that is the only state we have configured in `top.sls` so far.

The third command produces a slightly different output:

```
[root@salt-master]# salt 'salt-minion' state.highstate \
saltenv=development --state-output=terse
```

This command has a new option and its value is `--state-output=terse`. This option is specified if we do not want a detailed output as the first and second commands. However, it does the same task as the first and second commands

Next, we look at the method of doing the same task by fetching the states on the minion from the master by using the pull mechanism:

```
root@salt-minion:~# salt-call state.highstate
```

Here, we used the `salt-call` binary, which is available only on Salt minions along with the `state.highstate` execution module. This command will automatically take the environment from the minion configuration file, that is, `/etc/salt/minion` and look for the minion states in the `development` environment and apply all the states configured for this minion in the `top.sls` file. Note the output, we see the minion caching all required data in the system from the master before applying the states. This caching process will take place each time the data in the master changes and the `salt-call` command is run.

The other method (not used very often) to apply specific states to the minion and from the minion is shown next. These states can also be part of `highstate`, if added to the top file:

```
root@salt-minion:~# salt-call state.sls user saltenv=development
```

Here, we see the minion using the `salt-call` binary, but mentioning the `state.sls` execution module to specify a particular state instead of all the states, that is, the `user` state. However, do note that, for this to be successful, the Salt environment must be mentioned as shown, without which it will look for the base environment and fail.

There's more...

Now let's see, how to apply Salt states on masterless minions.

Applying Salt states to masterless minions

In the *Installing and configuring the Salt minion* recipe, you learned how to configure a Salt minion to be its own master. Here, we will see how to apply states to a Salt minion that acts as its own master.

The following command applies the states of a minion by fetching the state configurations from itself:

```
root@salt-minion:~# salt-call --local state.highstate
```

Here, we see that the same `salt-call` command that was used in fetching the Salt states from a separate Salt master is used to do this task, but the `--local` option has been added to let Salt know that it needs to look for the state files in itself rather than in a separate Salt master.

See also

- The *Installing and configuring the Salt master* and *Installing and configuring Salt minion* recipes, to learn how to configure the master and minions
- The *Targeting minions* recipe in *Chapter 2, Writing Advanced Salt Configurations*, to learn about how to target minions from the master

2

Writing Advanced Salt Configurations

In this chapter, you will cover:

- ▶ Writing and retrieving pillar data
- ▶ Using pillar data in states
- ▶ Using grains in states
- ▶ Using conditionals in states and pillars
- ▶ Using Python functions in conditionals
- ▶ Using iterations in states
- ▶ Setting and using variables in states
- ▶ Testing a state run before applying to minions
- ▶ Configuring nodegroups
- ▶ Targeting minions

Introduction

Now that we have gotten our hands dirty with the basics of Salt, in this chapter we are going to dive deep into the advanced configuration of Salt.

One of the notable features of Salt is flexibility, and being based on the dynamic Python language, Salt allows us to incorporate and take advantage of a large number of Python utilities into its configurations. Like most other programming languages and configuration management utilities, it's quite obvious that without the ability to manipulate our data, such as making decisions based on system properties, performing the same task quickly and efficiently for multiple entities of the same type, a tool is not of much use to users.

In this chapter, you will explore all the advanced features of Salt and how you can utilize them to automate systems efficiently and optimally.

Writing and retrieving pillar data

We already have a basic understanding of what pillars are and how to use them in Salt. In this section, we are going to learn more about writing pillars and how to retrieve them both from the master and the minion.

How to do it...

1. Create a new environment qa using the recipe *Configuring the Salt environment and pillar paths* in *Chapter 1, Salt Architecture and Components*. The state environment path should be /opt/salt-cookbook/qa, and the pillar path should be /opt/salt-cookbook/pillar/qa. Also, create the top files for the new environment in the base directory for state and the pillar, and populate them with the following entry:

    ```
    qa:
      '*':
        - user
    ```

2. Create a pillar directory user in the base pillar directory, and in it create the file init.sls. Edit /opt/salt-cookbook/pillar/qa/user/init.sls and enter the following:

    ```
    users:
      qa_user: qa-app
      qa_user_password: '$1$lhxadPoh$d5tZktsF/eI08tqiwmwBo0'
    ```

3. Configure the minion using the recipe *Configuring environments and grains on the minion* in *Chapter 1, Salt Architecture and Components*, with the environment as qa and the grains as follows:

    ```
    server_type: app
    environment: qa
    ```

4. Run the following command to view the pillar items for the minion:

    ```
    [root@salt-master ~]# salt 'salt-minion' pillar.items
    salt-minion:
        ----------
        master:
            ----------
            auth_mode:
                1
        .
        .
    ```

```
users:
    ----------
    qa_user:
        qa-app
    qa_user_password:
        $1$lhxadPoh$d5tZktsF/eI08tqiwmwBo0
```

5. Reopen /opt/salt-cookbook/pillar/qa/user/init.sls and edit the file to have the following contents:

```
users:
  qa_user: qa-app
  qa_user_password: '$1$lhxadPoh$d5tZktsF/eI08tqiwmwBo0'
  admin_user_passwd: '$1$0gH3Ry2s$sMc9yVAC9iyr/yEF/ggbr0'
```

6. Run the following command to refresh the pillar data on the minion:

```
salt 'salt-minion' saltutil.refresh_pillar
```

7. Rerun the following command:

```
[root@salt-master ~]# salt 'salt-minion' pillar.items
salt-minion:
    ----------
    master:
        .

        .

    users:
        ----------
        qa_user:
            qa-app
        qa_user_password:
            $1$lhxadPoh$d5tZktsF/eI08tqiwmwBo0
        admin_user_passwd:
            $1$0gH3Ry2s$sMc9yVAC9iyr/yEF/ggbr0
```

8. On the minion, run the following command to get the pillar data:

```
[root@salt-minion ~]# salt-call pillar.get users
local:
    ----------
    admin_user_passwd:
        $1$0gH3Ry2s$sMc9yVAC9iyr/yEF/ggbr0
```

```
qa_user:

    qa-app

qa_user_passwd:

    $1$lhxadPoh$d5tZktsF/eI08tqiwmwBo0
```

How it works...

In this recipe, we first created a new environment called `qa`. Next, we created a new pillar called `users` and the necessary files for the pillar and the top file using recipes from *Chapter 1, Salt Architecture and Components*. We also configured our minion to be in the `qa` environment.

We then wrote a pillar file with very basic information consisting of a username and password:

```
users:
  qa_user: qa-app
  qa_user_password: '$1$lhxadPoh$d5tZktsF/eI08tqiwmwBo0'
```

Next, we retrieved the pillar data for this specific minion on the master with the following command using the `pillar.items` module:

```
[root@salt-master ~]# salt 'salt-minion' pillar.items
```

We get a long output showing all the master configuration parameters available to this minion and, at the end, it shows the pillar data available to it. Next, we added a new pillar key-value pair:

```
admin_user_passwd: '$1$0gH3Ry2s$sMc9yVAC9iyr/yEF/ggbr0'
```

Next, we run the following command to refresh the pillar data on the minion and recognize the newly added pair:

```
salt 'salt-minion' saltutil.refresh_pillar
```

When we retrieve the pillar data on the master, it shows the newly added pair in the list. Do note that most of the time, refresh is not needed. The minion will automatically identify the newly added pillar data, this procedure needs to be followed if it does not do so.

In the end, we run the following command to get the same pillar data available to the minion, but it runs on the minion using the `salt-call` binary:

```
[root@salt-minion ~]# salt-call pillar.get users
```

Do note that in this command, the name of the pillar, that is, `users` is mandatory, without which an error message will be displayed.

See also

▸ The *Configuring the Salt environment and pillar paths* and *Understanding and configuring salt pillars* recipes in *Chapter 1, Salt Architecture and Components*, to understand more about configuring pillars

▸ The *Using pillar data in states* recipe to learn about the various methods to use the configured pillars in states

Using pillar data in states

How to do it...

1. Create a new state user by creating a directory called `user` in the base directory of the `qa` environment and create an `init.sls` file in the `user` directory.

2. Edit `/opt/salt-cookbook/qa/user/init.sls` and populate it with the following entries:

```
qa_deploy_user:
  user.present:
    - name: {{ pillar['users']['qa_user'] }}
    - password: {{ pillar['users']['qa_user_password'] }}
```

3. Run the following command to apply the state to the minion:

```
[root@salt-master ~]# salt 'salt-minion' state.sls user \
saltenv=qa
--state-output=terse

salt-minion:
  Name: qa-app - Function: user.present - Result: Changed


Summary
------------
Succeeded: 1
Failed:    0
------------
Total:     1
```

4. Edit the `/opt/salt-cookbook/pillar/qa/user/init.sls` file and remove the following line:

    ```
    qa_user: qa-app
    ```

5. Reopen the `/opt/salt-cookbook/qa/user/init.sls` file and edit it to have the following entries:

    ```
    qa_deploy_user:
      user.present:
        - name: {{ salt['pillar.get']('users:qa_user', 'qa-
    deploy-user') }}
        - password: {{ pillar['users']['qa_user_password'] }}
    ```

6. Run the following command to apply the modified state to the minion:

    ```
    [root@salt-master ~]# salt 'salt-minion' state.sls user \
    saltenv=qa --state-output=terse

    salt-minion:

      Name: qa-deploy-user - Function: user.present - Result:
      Changed


    Summary
    ------------
    Succeeded: 1
    Failed:    0
    ------------
    Total:     1
    ```

How it works...

In this recipe, we learn about the various methods to use the pillar data in states. First, we configured a state called `user` and configured a user with the generic name `qa_deploy_user`. We used the basic way to use the pillar data in states as seen in *Chapter 1, Salt Architecture and Components*:

```
- name: {{ pillar['users']['qa_user'] }}
- password: {{ pillar['users']['qa_user_password'] }}
```

We use the `pillar` keyword with the YAML formatted keys from the pillar files. Note that from *Chapter 1, Salt Architecture and Components* that the method to access the value of the pillar is to use the YAML keys and not the pillar directory name, for example, here although the pillar directory is named `user`, we use `users` while trying to access the values.

We then apply the state to the minion with the `-state-output=terse` parameter to shorten the output.

Next, we see a different way to use pillars. Here, we see how to specify a default value for a `pillar` key if the value of the key is not set in the pillar files. To demonstrate this, we have just modified the `name` key in the `user` state file to look like the following:

```
- name: {{ salt['pillar.get']('users:qa_user', 'qa-deploy-user')
}}
```

As seen earlier in the text, a new function called `pillar.get` has been used with the keyword `salt` instead of `pillar`. The keys are written with the delimiter as a colon, that is, `['users'][ 'qa_user']` is written as `'users:qa_user'`, and the default value is mentioned after a comma. This definition tells Salt to use the value of `qa-deploy-user` for the keys `'users:qa_user'` if the value of these keys is not set in the pillar files.

To demonstrate this, we removed the mentioned key from the pillar file and then applied the state to the minion. As a result, we see the user `qa-deploy-user` being created on the minion instead of `qa-user`, as the value for that key was not found in the pillar file.

There's more...

Including other pillars in the pillar file

Pillars can be included in other pillar files as if it was defined in the same file. If two pillars called `group` and `user` are configured, a pillar group can be included in the pillar user by inserting the following entry in to the pillar file, for example, `init.sls`:

```
include:
  - group
```

Setting pillar data at the command line

Pillar data can also be set at the command line if required. The following command can be used to achieve the same:

```
[root@salt-master ~]# salt 'salt-minion' state.sls user \
pillar='{"qa_user": "qa-deploy-user"}'
```

Here, `qa_user` is the key and `qa-deploy-user` is the value. Although this procedure is not very efficient to use in production, it can be used to perform `development` and `qa` tasks.

See also

▸ The *Writing and retrieving pillar data* recipe, to learn about how to write and retrieve pillar data

▸ *Chapter 4, General Administration Tasks*, for demonstrations about how to use pillar data in Salt states

▸ The *Using grains in states* recipe to learn about how to use grains in states

Using grains in states

Grains are one of the most important features of Salt, based on which we can perform the configuration and orchestration tasks efficiently. Salt offers the flexibility to use the default grains and also to add custom grains as and when required. In this recipe, you will learn how to use grains in state configurations.

How to do it...

Configure a new minion with the hostname or minion ID as stgdc1app01 in the staging environment. In this naming convention, stg is the environment, dc1 is the location, app is the server type, and 01 is a numeric identifier for the host.

1. Run the following command to get a full list of available grains on the minion:

   ```
   [root@salt-master ~]# salt 'stgdc1app01' grains.items
   ```

2. Next, run the following command to get information about two specific grains that we will work with:

   ```
   [root@salt-master ~]# salt 'stgdc1app01' grains.item \
   ip_interfaces fqdn
   stgdc1app01:
     fqdn: stgdc1app01
     ip_interfaces: {'lo': ['127.0.0.1'], 'eth1':
   ['192.168.0.3'], 'eth0': ['192.168.29.129']}
   ```

3. Next, create a new state called appenv by creating a directory called appenv in the base directory of the staging environment. Create a directory called files in the appenv directory and create a file named environment in the files directory. The directory structure should be as follows:

   ```
   appenv:
     - init.sls
     - files:
       - environment
   ```

4. Edit the `/opt/salt-cookbook/staging/appenv/files/environment` file to have the following entries:

```
primary_interface: {{ ipaddress }}
location: {{ location }}
```

5. Edit the `/opt/salt-cookbook/staging/appenv/init.sls` file and populate it with the following entries:

```
appenv_file:
  file.managed:
    - name: /etc/environment
    - source: salt://appenv/files/environment
    - template: jinja
    - mode: 644
    - context:
      ipaddress: {{ grains['ip_interfaces']['eth1'][0] }}
      location: {{ grains['fqdn'][3:6] }}
```

6. Apply the configured state to the minion with the following command:

```
[root@salt-master ~]# salt 'stgdc1app01' state.sls appenv \
saltenv=qa

stgdc1app01:
----------
          ID: appenv_file
    Function: file.managed
        Name: /etc/environment
      Result: True
     Comment: File /etc/environment updated
     Changes:
              ----------
              diff:
                  New file
              mode:
                  0644

Summary
------------
Succeeded: 1
Failed:    0
------------
Total:     1
```

7. Finally, view the contents of the file on the minion:

```
[root@stgdc1app01 ~]# cat /etc/environment
primary_interface: 192.168.0.3
location: dc1
```

How it works...

In this recipe, we demonstrated how to use grains in state configurations. The objective of this recipe is to create an environment file, which will be used by some random application and will contain information in key-value pairs about the system. However, the same method may be used to populate configuration files for various servers using grain data.

First, we display all the grains available on our new minion using the `grains.items` module. It gives us a long list of all the available grains in the system. Next, we display only a couple of them that we used later in our state configuration using the command:

```
[root@salt-master ~]# salt 'stgdc1app01' grains.item \ ip_interfaces
fqdn
```

The `ip_interfaces` and `fqdn` grains are only two of the many default grains available in Salt. Note that the difference in the module name, in this case, `grains.item` is used instead of `grains.items` followed by the grain names `ip_interfaces` and `fqdn`. If `grains.items` is used, then it will display the entire list of grains even though the grains are explicitly mentioned. On running the command, we get the following output:

```
stgdc1app01:
  fqdn: stgdc1app01
  ip_interfaces: {'lo': ['127.0.0.1'], 'eth1': ['192.168.0.3'],
'eth0': ['192.168.29.129']}
```

Grains can be found in various forms, two of which can be seen here, the `fqdn` grain being in a simple key-value format and the `ip_interfaces` grain being in the same key-value format, but the value being a Python dictionary. It will display as many pairs of key-value data as there are network interfaces in the minion host.

In this recipe, we configured a file definition using the `file` module and a method known as `templates` about which we will learn in *Chapter 3, Modules, Orchestration, and Scaling Salt*. The basic idea is to copy a file from the master to the minion and substitute some parts of the file with explicitly passed values. We created a template called `environment` and made a few entries in it as follows:

```
primary_interface: {{ ipaddress }}
location: {{ location }}
```

Here, the areas enclosed in double braces are the ones which will be substituted by the values passed from the state file.

In the state configuration, the area of our interest is as follows:

```
- context:
      ipaddress: {{ grains['ip_interfaces']['eth1'][0] }}
      location: {{ grains['fqdn'][3:6] }}
```

The key context tells Salt that the key-value pairs under it are variables, which need to be passed on to the template and the values need to be substituted in the areas enclosed by double braces where the variable names need to match.

Here, we see how we can access the grain values. For fqdn it's quite simple, as we use the grains keyword with the fqdn key to access its value. Here, we also get a glimpse of Salt's flexibility using [3:6], which is a Python-specific operation to extract a certain part of the string, here it is the location that is dc1. Also, for ip_interfaces, we use the method to access dictionary values, that is, grains['ip_interfaces']['eth1']. This returns a list with one value, ['192.168.0.3'], and the [0] is used to get this value from the list.

After retrieving required values from the grains, Salt passes on the values to the template and populates the file on the minion as configured.

See also

▸   The *Using conditionals in states and pillars* and *Using Python functions in conditionals* recipes, to learn about how to use grains in conditionals and other Python functions

▸   The *Setting host entries and grains* recipe in *Chapter 4, General Administration Tasks*, to learn about how to set grains via Salt states

Using conditionals in states and pillars

One of the best advantages of any programming language or configuration tool is its ability to make decisions based on various properties, and apply configurations, or perform tasks, based on these decisions. In this recipe, you will learn how to leverage the decision-making ability of Salt and use it to your advantage.

How to do it...

We will use the same minion as the previous recipe for this task:

1. Add a custom grain to the minion with the `server_type` key and value as `app`:

   ```
   server_type: app
   ```

2. In the staging environment, create two pillars named `groups` and `users`. Also, create two states named `group` and `user`. Add them to `top.sls` for both `states` and `pillars` to be available to all nodes.

3. Edit `/opt/salt-cookbook/pillar/staging/user/init.sls` to have the following content:

   ```
   users:
     {% if grains['server_type'] == 'app' %}
     stg_user: stg-app
     {% elif grains['server_type'] == 'db' %}
     stg_user: stg-db
     {% endif %}
     stg_user_passwd: '$1$lhxadPoh$d5tZktsF/eI08tqiwmwBo0'
   ```

4. Edit `/opt/salt-cookbook/staging/user/init.sls` to have the following content:

   ```
   generic_user:
     user.present:
       - name: {{ pillar['users']['stg_user'] }}
       - shell: /bin/bash
       - home: /home/{{ pillar['users']['stg_user'] }}
       - password: {{ pillar['users']['stg_user_passwd'] }}
   ```

5. Edit `/opt/salt-cookbook/pillar/staging/group/init.sls` to have the following content:

   ```
   groups:
     stg_app_group: stg-app-grp
     stg_db_group: stg-db-grp
   ```

6. Edit `/opt/salt-cookbook/staging/group/init.sls` to have the following content:

   ```
   generic_group:
     group.present:
       {% if grains['server_type'] == 'app' %}
       - name: {{ pillar['groups']['stg_app_group'] }}
       {% elif grains['server_type'] == 'db' %}
       - name: {{ pillar['groups']['stg_db_group'] }}
       {% endif %}
   ```

7. Apply the states to the minion:

```
[root@salt-master ~]# salt 'stgdc1app01' state.highstate \
saltenv=staging --state-output=terse

stgdc1app01:
  Name: stg-app-grp - Function: group.present - Result:
  Changed
  Name: stg-app - Function: user.present - Result: Changed


Summary
-----------
Succeeded: 2
Failed:    0
-----------
Total:     2
```

How it works...

In this recipe, we introduced conditionals in Salt. Being based on Python, the conditionals used in Salt are exactly the same as used in Python except for the opening and closing braces and percentage symbols used here, that is, {% and %}.

First, we added a custom grain called `server_type` with a value of `app` in the minion. We used this grain to make all decisions about our configuration in the rest of the recipe.

The condition block starts with:

```
{% if <condition> %}
```

Any other decision after that is made with:

```
{% elif <condition> %}
```

Finally, the block ends with:

```
{% endif %}
```

It is important to note that the `if` statements must be aligned with the Salt statement after it, failing this, the states will not execute.

This is correct:

```
{% if grains['server_type'] == 'app' %}
- name: {{ pillar['groups']['stg_app_group'] }}
```

However, this is incorrect:

```
{% if grains['server_type'] == 'app' %}
  - name: {{ pillar['groups']['stg_app_group'] }}
```

The purpose of this recipe is to demonstrate that conditionals can be applied to both pillars and states in Salt. For the group configuration, the pillar has normal data and the conditional is used in the state to make the decision based on the grain. In the user configuration, the pillar has the conditional and the state has normal data. Either of the combinations can be used and solely depends on the user's requirement.

For the condition being used in the example, we have taken the value of the grain and compared it with a string. However, there are numerous ways by which conditions can be used, for example, using all Python operators on various data types and using Python functions to manipulate the grain data, to name only a few.

Finally, we applied the states to the minion using the state.highstate module, which reads the states applicable to a minion from the top.sls file and applies them.

See also

▸ *Chapter 4, General Administration Tasks*, to learn more about the application of conditionals

▸ The *Using Python functions in conditionals* recipe, to learn how to use Python functions in conditionals

Using Python functions in conditionals

Being based on Python, one of the biggest advantages of Salt is to be able to use a lot of Salt-specific features such as functions. In this recipe, you will learn how to use Python functions in Salt to manipulate data and make efficient use of them to configure our infrastructure.

How to do it...

1. Configure two minions, one named stgdc1app01 and another named stgdc2app01.

2. Run the following commands to get the grains with which we will be working in this recipe:

```
[root@salt-master ~]# salt 'stgdc1app01' grains.item \
ip_interfaces hwaddr_interfaces

stgdc1app01:

  hwaddr_interfaces: {'lo': '00:00:00:00:00:00', 'eth0':
'00:0c:29:ef:d5:56', 'eth1': '00:0c:29:ef:d5:4c'}
```

```
   ip_interfaces: {'lo': ['127.0.0.1'], 'eth0':
['192.168.0.2'], 'eth1': ['192.168.29.128']}


[root@salt-master ~]# salt 'stgdc2app01' grains.item \
ip_interfaces hwaddr_interfaces
stgdc2app01:
   hwaddr_interfaces: {'lo': '00:00:00:00:00:00', 'eth0':
'00:0c:29:61:ea:08', 'eth1': '00:0c:29:61:ea:fe'}
   ip_interfaces: {'lo': ['127.0.0.1'], 'eth0': ['172.16.0.3'],
'eth1': ['172.16.29.129']}
```

3. Create a new state in the staging environment called `netconfig` and create a directory in the `netconfig` directory called `files`.

4. Create the `/opt/salt-cookbook/staging/netconfig/files/ifcfg-eth0` file and edit it to have the following contents:

```
DEVICE=eth0
HWADDR={{ hwaddr }}
TYPE=Ethernet
ONBOOT=yes
NM_CONTROLLED=no
BOOTPROTO=none
IPADDR={{ ipaddr }}
NETMASK={{ netmask }}
```

5. Next, create the `/opt/salt-cookbook/staging/netconfig/init.sls` file and edit it to have the following contents:

```
{% if grains['fqdn'].startswith('stgdc1') %}
{% set netmask = '255.255.255.0' %}
{% elif grains['fqdn'].startswith('stgdc2') %}
{% set netmask = '255.255.0.0' %}
{% endif %}


network_file:
  file.managed:
    - name: /etc/sysconfig/network-scripts/ifcfg-eth0
    - source: salt://hostconfig/files/ifcfg-eth0
    - mode: 644
    - template: jinja
    - context:
      ipaddr: {{ grains['ip_interfaces']['eth0'][0] }}
      netmask: {{ netmask }}
      hwaddr: {{ grains['hwaddr_interfaces']['eth0'].upper() }}
```

6. Run the following command to apply the state to the minions:

```
[root@salt-master ~]# salt -L 'stgdc1app01,stgdc2app01'
state.sls netconfig saltenv=staging
stgdc1app01:
----------
          ID: network_file
    Function: file.managed
        Name: /etc/sysconfig/network-scripts/ifcfg-eth0
      Result: True
     Comment: File /etc/sysconfig/network-scripts/ifcfg-eth0
updated
     Changes:
              ----------
              diff:
                  ---
                  +++
                  @@ -1,6 +1,8 @@
                   DEVICE=eth0
                   HWADDR=00:0c:29:ef:d5:56
                   TYPE=Ethernet
                   ONBOOT=yes
                   NM_CONTROLLED=no
                  -BOOTPROTO=dhcp
                  +BOOTPROTO=none
                  +IPADDR=192.168.0.3
                  +NETMASK=255.255.255.0


Summary
------------
Succeeded: 1
Failed:    0
------------
Total:     1
stgdc2app01:
----------
```

```
          ID: network_file
    Function: file.managed
        Name: /etc/sysconfig/network-scripts/ifcfg-eth0
      Result: True
     Comment: File /etc/sysconfig/network-scripts/ifcfg-eth0
updated
     Changes:
              ----------
              diff:
                  ---
                  +++
                  @@ -1,6 +1,8 @@
                   DEVICE=eth0
                   HWADDR=00:0C:29:61:EA:08
                   TYPE=Ethernet
                   ONBOOT=yes
                   NM_CONTROLLED=no
                  -BOOTPROTO=dhcp
                  +BOOTPROTO=none
                  +IPADDR=172.16.0.3
                  +NETMASK=255.255.0.0


Summary
------------
Succeeded: 1
Failed:    0
------------
Total:     1
```

How it works...

In this recipe, we demonstrated the usage of Python functions in Salt. The objective of the recipe is to make a decision based on the fqdn grain of the minion and set a variable. The variable along with some more Python function-based manipulation is then used to create a network configuration file on the minion based on a template that we created. We will learn more about templates in *Chapter 3, Modules, Orchestration, and Scaling Salt.*

First, we created two minions with different names. As subnet masks are not yet available in Salt via grains, we set the subnet masks for the minions through variables using a conditional based on the `fqdn` grain:

```
{% if grains['fqdn'].startswith('stgdc1') %}
```

Here, we can see the use of a Python function `startswith()`, which finds out if the minion name starts with `devdc1` or `devdc2`. Based on this knowledge, it sets the `netmask` variable.

Next, we used a template to create a file on the minions and passed few values to the template. The IP address is passed by a direct use of the grain value. The subnet mask is passed by use of the variable `netmask` that we had set before.

We see a second use of a Python function in the third value that is passed to the template:

```
hwaddr: {{ grains['hwaddr_interfaces']['eth1'].upper() }}
```

Here, we get the value of the MAC address of the `eth0` interface by using the grain access method. We then apply the `upper()` Python function of this value to convert all of the characters to uppercase.

Next, we applied the state to the minions by use of the list matcher:

```
[root@salt-master ~]# salt -L 'stgdc1app01,stgdc2app01'
```

When we build new hosts, most of the time the network configuration is in `dhcp` mode. In the output of the command, we see the `dhcp` mode being changed to static mode for the network configuration and the values of the IP address and subnet mask being added. The MAC address does not change because it was already present in the configuration file at the time of the build.

This recipe mentions just a couple of the Python functions that can be used to manipulate Salt data, whereas in production configurations, a lot more can be done using functions.

See also

- The *Setting host entries and grains* recipe in *Chapter 4, General Administration Tasks,* to find a demonstration of Python function in Salt conditional
- The *Targeting minions* recipe, to learn how to use matchers in Salt
- The *Using iterations in states* recipe, to learn how to implement iterations

Using iterations in states

The need to do the same task repeatedly for a number of entities of the same type is a very basic requirement of any role in an organization. To achieve this, languages and tools provide us with the feature of iterations, simply known as **loops**. In this recipe, you will learn how to apply iterations in our configuration.

How to do it...

1. We will use the same minion as the previous recipe. Modify the user pillar, that is, edit `/opt/salt-cookbook/pillar/staging/user/init.sls` to have the following contents:

    ```
    dev_user_list:
      optimus:
        uid: 7001
        passwd: '$1$Dw1TxMI7$pmeYTdmz.rlunqPd7JELR.'
      bumblebee:
        uid: 7002
        passwd: '$1$ZHUeIAfq$6sJl9rHVDX2UjBH1KrPZP1'
      ironhide:
        uid: 7003
        passwd: '$1$rcJAiq7y$bJzv3HzVTbeQlA3cIu1Gb1'
    ```

2. Edit `/opt/salt-cookbook/staging/user/init.sls` to have the following contents:

    ```
    {% for user, details in pillar['dev_user_list'].iteritems() %}
    {{ user }}:
      user.present:
        - home: /home/{{ user }}
        - uid: {{ details['uid'] }}
        - password: {{ details['passwd'] }}
        - shell: /bin/bash
    {% endfor %}
    ```

3. Apply the state to the minion:

    ```
    [root@salt-master ~]# salt 'stgdc1app01' state.sls users
    saltenv=staging --state-output=terse

    stgdc1app01:
      Name: optimus - Function: user.present - Result: Changed
      Name: bumblebee - Function: user.present - Result: Changed
      Name: ironhide - Function: user.present - Result: Changed
    ```

```
Summary
------------
Succeeded:  3
Failed:     0
------------
Total:      3
```

How it works...

In this recipe, we demonstrated the method to apply iterations to our configuration. The objective of the recipe is to create three users with similar properties available, a username, a user ID, and a password. In production scenarios, any number of entities can be configured by the same method.

First, we configured the user properties in the user pillar file, however, this time the definition is a bit different:

```
dev_user_list:
  optimus:
    uid: 7001
    passwd: '$1$Dw1TxMI7$pmeYTdmz.rlunqPd7JELR.'
  bumblebee:
    uid: 7002
    passwd: '$1$ZHUeIAfq$6sJl9rHVDX2UjBH1KrPZP1'
```

We configured the same YAML-type definition, but the usernames are the keys now instead of being a value and the other properties, such as user ID and password, are key-value pairs under them.

The `for` statement used here is again the Python iteration method. However, the opening and closing style of the statements is similar to the conditionals. The loop starts with the following code:

```
{% for <iteration logic> %}
```

It ends with:

```
{% endfor %}
```

The iteration logic that we apply here is as follows:

```
{% for user, details in pillar['dev_user_list'].iteritems() %}
```

The `pillar['dev_user_list']` parameter contains a Python dictionary with keys as the usernames and values, as another dictionary contains the user ID and the password. When the `iteritems()` Python function is applied on the dictionary, results are stored in two entities `user` and `details`. A loop is run on the dictionary, and on each turn a username is stored in the `user` entity and its properties. The dictionary containing the rest of the data is stored in `details`.

These entities can then be used to populate the user values required to apply the configuration. Any number of levels of data and entities can be used in configurations using this iteration procedure.

Finally, we applied the state to the minion, and the three configured users are created on the minion.

See also

▸ The *Adding groups and users* recipe, in *Chapter 4, General Administration Tasks*, to learn more about adding users and groups

▸ The *Setting and using variables in states* recipe, to learn how to use variables with Salt states

Setting and using variables in states

Variables are one of the most important features of any language or tool used to set user-defined data and manipulate it as and when required. In this recipe, you will learn how to set variables in Salt states and use the variables to do some advanced task.

How to do it...

1. Configure a minion in the staging environment and create a pillar and state with the name `user`. In the minion, configure the following grain:

   ```
   server_type: db
   ```

2. Edit the `/opt/salt-cookbook/pillar/staging/user/init.sls` file to have the following contents:

   ```
   app_user_list:
     optimus:
       uid: 7001
       passwd: $1$Cf1V2QaF$.qyeAQ34CLqyvEnes7/VH1
     bumblebee:
       uid: 7002
       passwd: $1$KvbpASt.$L97XRqLVc0OaspatEE/n4/
   ```

```
db_user_list:
  megatron:
    uid: 7001
    passwd: $1$8J9bAeG6$HMMV.EoMycJyLL.pb6kHj0
  cyclonus:
    uid: 7002
    passwd: $1$2HqtGifG$MF3WHFSOmKG4gksHOVvA30
```

3. Edit the `/opt/salt-cookbook/staging/user/init.sls` file to have the following contents:

```
{% if grains['server_type'] == 'app' %}
{% set user_list = 'app_user_list' %}
{% elif grains['server_type'] == 'db' %}
{% set user_list = 'db_user_list' %}
{% endif %}

{% for user, details in pillar[user_list].iteritems() %}
{{ user }}:
  user.present:
    - home: /home/{{ user }}
    - uid: {{ details['uid'] }}
    - password: {{ details['passwd'] }}
    - shell: /bin/bash
{% endfor %}
```

4. Apply the state to the minion:

```
[root@salt-master ~]# salt 'stgdc1app02' state.sls user \
saltenv=staging --state-output=terse

stgdc1app02:
    Name: cyclonus - Function: user.present - Result: Changed
    Name: megatron - Function: user.present - Result: Changed


Summary
------------
Succeeded: 2
Failed:    0
------------
Total:     2
```

How it works...

In this recipe, we introduced the concept of **variables** in Salt. The objective of the recipe is to have two different lists of users in the pillar definition, one for application users and one for database users. In the state, depending on the type of the server, a variable is set with the name of the user list and the variable is used to run iteration in the state to add the users in the list.

First, we configured the minion to have a grain called `server_type` with the value of `db`, which tells Salt that this is a database server.

Next, we populated the pillar file with a list of users similar to the recipe *Using iterations in states*. However, there are two such lists here, one with the name `app_user_list` for application servers and the other is `db_user_list` for database servers.

Next, we configured the state with an initial block of conditionals:

```
{% if grains['server_type'] == 'app' %}
{% set user_list = 'app_user_list' %}
{% elif grains['server_type'] == 'db' %}
{% set user_list = 'db_user_list' %}
{% endif %}
```

Here, we set a variable with the statement:

```
{% set user_list = 'app_user_list' %}
```

The `set` keyword is used to set the variable with `user_list` as the variable name and the value is `app_user_list` or `db_user_list` depending on the type of the server.

Next, we use this variable in iterating through the user list from the pillar data:

```
{% for user, details in pillar[user_list].iteritems() %}
```

Since the server is a database host, the value of `db_user_list` is stored in the variable `user_list`. So, instead of using `pillar['db_user_list'].iteritems()`, we are using `pillar[user_list].iteritems()`. Do note that there are no quotes when the variable name is mentioned instead of the generic name of the list. This is a much cleaner approach to doing similar tasks than to use conditionals with iterations. Variables can be used for numerous other tasks in Salt.

Finally, we applied the state to the minion, and the database users from the list have been created on the host.

See also

▸ The *Using iterations in states* and *Using conditionals in states and pillars* recipes, to learn about conditionals and iterations

▸ The *Testing a state run before applying to minions* recipe, to learn about how to test state run before applying to minions

Testing a state run before applying to minions

Sometimes, even the smallest of typos or mistakes in configurations can create the biggest problems in infrastructure if not tested and checked before applying them. In this recipe, you will learn how to test state configurations before applying them to minions.

How to do it...

We will make use of the minion and states configured in the previous recipe *Setting and using variables in states*. We will also assume that the minion is a fresh install with no previous configurations applied to it:

1. Run the following command:

```
[root@salt-master ~]# salt 'stgdc1app02' state.sls user \
saltenv=staging test=True

stgdc1app02:
----------
          ID: cyclonus
    Function: user.present
      Result: None
     Comment: User cyclonus set to be added
     Changes:
----------
          ID: megatron
    Function: user.present
      Result: None
     Comment: User megatron set to be added
     Changes:

Summary
```

```
------------
Succeeded: 0
Failed:    0
Not Run:   2
------------
Total:     2
```

2. On the minion, edit the `/etc/salt/minion` file, uncomment the following line, and restart the minion daemon:

   ```
   test: True
   ```

3. On the master, run the following command:

   ```
   [root@salt-master ~]# salt 'stgdc1app02' state.sls user \
   saltenv=staging
   stgdc1app02:
   ----------
             ID: cyclonus
       Function: user.present
         Result: None
        Comment: User cyclonus set to be added
        Changes:
   ----------
             ID: megatron
       Function: user.present
         Result: None
        Comment: User megatron set to be added
        Changes:

   Summary
   ------------
   Succeeded: 0
   Failed:    0
   Not Run:   2
   ------------
   Total:     2
   ```

4. On the master, run the following command:

```
[root@salt-master ~]# salt 'stgdc1app02' state.sls user \
saltenv=staging --state-output=terse test=False
stgdc1app02:
    Name: cyclonus - Function: user.present - Result: Changed
    Name: megatron - Function: user.present - Result: Changed


Summary
------------
Succeeded: 2
Failed:    0
------------
Total:     2
```

How it works...

In this recipe, we demonstrated how to test our configuration before applying them to minions.

First, we run the command to apply the `user` state to the minion, but with the following parameter:

```
test=True
```

The output of the command shows us the changes that will be applied to the minion on running the states but does not actually apply them. This is clear by the following lines:

```
stgdc1app02:
----------
        Result: None
        Comment: User cyclonus set to be added
----------
        Result: None
        Comment: User megatron set to be added


Summary
------------
Succeeded: 0
Failed:    0
Not Run:   2
------------
Total:     2
```

It clearly tells us that the users are set to be added, but has not been added yet. The `Results` key has the value of `None` showing that there was no result because nothing was actually done. Also, the following two lines show that the states were not applied:

```
Succeeded: 0
Not Run:   2
```

Next, we see how to set the `test` parameter on the minion. We edited the main minion configuration file `/etc/salt/minion` and uncommented the line:

```
test: True
```

This tells the minion that all states applied on it from the master will be in test mode, that is, no configuration will be actually applied. We then run the command to apply the state to the minion without the `test` parameter and see that the state runs in test mode because the minion is set to test mode.

Next, we see how to override the minion's `test` parameter by setting the `test` parameter with the salt command. We set the `test` parameter to be `False`, and when the state is applied to the minion, the salt command's `test` parameter overrides the `test` parameter of the minion and the state gets applied successfully.

See also

▶ The *Applying Salt states to minions* recipe, in *Chapter 1, Salt Architecture and Components*, to learn more about applying states to minions

▶ The *Configuring nodegroups* recipe, to learn how to configure nodegroups to group similar nodes for targeting minions

Configuring nodegroups

A feature that makes Salt very efficient is its ability to configure nodegroups. They are groups of hosts that we can configure based on various system properties and use the group name to target minions. In this recipe, you will learn how to configure nodegroups.

How to do it...

1. Edit the `/etc/salt/master` file on the Salt master and uncomment the key `nodegroups`. Edit the lines following the `nodegroups` key so that the entire nodegroups configuration looks as follows:

```
nodegroups:
  stgdb: 'G@environment:staging and G@server_type:db'
```

```
      dc1devapp: 'G@location:dc1 and G@environment:development
and G@server_type:app'
      prodmon: 'L@prddc1mon01,prddc2mon03,prddc3mon10'
```

2. Restart the `salt-master` daemon for the changes to take place.

How it works...

In this recipe, we demonstrated how to configure nodegroups in various ways.

The `nodegroups` key in the master configuration file needs to be uncommented and all entries under it are identified as configured nodegroups.

The first line is configured as follows:

```
stgdb: 'G@environment:staging and G@server_type:db'
```

This states that the group name is `stgdb`, and it includes all nodes having the value of the environment grain as staging and the value of the `server_type` grain as db. The `G@` parameter is used to specify grains and their values.

The second line defines a nodegroup called `dc1devapp` that has a similar configuration to the first line with an extra grain called `location`.

The third line defines a nodegroup called `prodmon` and includes a list of hosts as mentioned in the configuration. The `L@` parameter is used to specify a comma-separated list of minions.

These nodegroups can now be used to target minions.

See also

▶ The *Configuring the Salt environment and pillar paths* recipe, in *Chapter 1, Salt Architecture and Components*, to learn more about environments

▶ The *Using grains in states* recipe, to know more about configuring grains

▶ The *Targeting minions* recipe, to learn how to target minions using nodegroups

Targeting minions

One of the biggest advantages of Salt is the ability to target minions based on various parameters. This gives us the flexibility to apply states, run commands, and gather information from any combination of minions that we need. In this recipe, you will learn how to target minions using different methods.

How to do it...

Since there are quite a lot of ways to target minions, we will not run the command and view the output for each of them. We will look at the possible ways of targeting minions and the methods to implement them. Each of the following examples show the procedure to target minions from the Salt command and also in the `top.sls` file. However, examples for `top.sls` are provided only for matchers that have this feature.

The procedure to target minions on the `salt` command line is as follows:

▶ Name-based matching with shell style globbing:

```
[root@salt-master ~]# salt 'devdc1app01' state.sls group
[root@salt-master ~]# salt '*.salt-cookbook.com' state.sls \
user
```

```
'*.salt-cookbook.com':
  - group
  - user
```

▶ List-based matching:

```
[root@salt-master ~]# salt -L 'prddc1mon01,prddc2mon05' \
state.highstate
```

```
'prddc1mon01,prddc2mon05':
  - match: list
  - hostconfig
```

▶ Regular expression-based matching:

```
[root@salt-master ~]# salt 'dev-(dc1|dc2|dc3)-db' state.sls \
mysql
```

```
'dev-(dc1|dc2|dc3)-db':
  - match: pcre
  - mysql
```

▶ Grain-based matching:

```
[root@salt-master ~]# salt -G 'server_type:app' state.sls \
tomcat
```

```
'server_type:app':
  - match: grain
  - tomcat
```

▶ Subnet/IP-based matching:

```
[root@salt-master ~]# salt -S 10.0.0.0/24 state.sls hostconfig
[root@salt-master ~]# salt -S 192.168.0.1 state.sls dns


'10.0.0.0/24':
  - match: ipcidr
  - dns
```

▶ Pillar-based matching:

```
[root@salt-master ~]# salt -I 'app_user:stg-app' \
state.highstate


'app_user:stg-app':
  - match: pillar
  - postgres
```

▶ Matching on grain-based regular expressions:

```
[root@salt-master ~]# salt -grain-pcre 'os:(RedHat|CentOS)' \
pillar.items


'os:(RedHat|CentOS) ':
  - match: grain_pcre
  - hostconfig
```

▶ Compound matching:

```
[root@salt-master ~]# salt -C 'G@os:Ubuntu and \
S@172.32.0.0/24' pillar.item fqdn


'G@os:Ubuntu and S@172.32.0.0/24':
  - match: compound
  - hostconfig
```

▶ Nodegroup matching:

```
[root@salt-master ~]# salt -N prodmon state.sls monitoring


'prodmon':
  - match: nodegroup
  - monitoring
```

How it works...

The various methods of targeting minions demonstrated earlier are described here:

1. **Name-based matching with shell style globbing**: Name-based matching is nothing but the Building Web Applications with Python and Neo4j name of the minion ID, which in most cases is the FQDN of the minion node. We can also apply matches with * to match all hosts of a domain name as shown. This format can be used for numerous other use cases.

2. **List-based matching**: List-based matching is simply a comma separated list of minion IDs and specified by the -L parameter in the command line and the list matcher in the top file.

3. **Regular expression-based matching**: Regular expression patterns enable us to match minions based on regular expressions applied on the minion ID such as dev-(dc1|dc2|dc3)-db. It is specified by pcre in the top file and in quotes in the command line.

4. **Grain-based matching**: Grain-based matches enable us to target minions based on their grains and values of the grains. One or multiple grains can be matched at a time. This is specified with the -G parameter on the command line and grain in the top file.

5. **Subnet/IP-based matching:** This type of matching allows us to target minions based on their IP addresses. The matcher can be a single IP address or an entire subnet with a CIDR notation such as 10.0.0.0/24. This matcher is specified with -S on the command line and ipcidr in the top file.

6. **Pillar-based matching**: Pillar-based matching can be used to target minions by specifying the pillar key and value available to the minion. It may seem similar to grains, but the difference between them is that grains data is obtained from the minions and pillar data is obtained from the master. It is specified by -I on the command line and pillar in the top file.

7. **Matching on grain-based regular expressions**: Similar to regular expressions in minion IDs, grain values can also be matched using regular expressions similar to os:(RedHat|CentOS). This is specified on the command line with -grain-pcre and with grain_pcre in the top file.

8. **Compound matching**: Compound matchers are probably the most important matchers available in Salt. It helps us combine the power of all other types of matchers and use them in combination to target minions. Each and every matcher in this list can be used in the compound matcher. In this example, we demonstrated a combination of grain-based and CIDR-based matching to target minions.

   It is specified by -C on the command line and compound in the top file.

9. **Nodegroup matching**: In the previous recipe, you learned how to configure nodegroups. Here, we used the nodegroups to target minions. This is just another way to implement the compound matcher, that is, we define nodegroups in the main configuration file using compound matcher and then use the nodegroup here to target minions.

   This keeps the complex combinations in the master configuration file and gives us a clean way to target minions by just supplying the nodegroup name. It is specified by `-N` on the command line and `nodegroup` in the top file.

See also

▸ The *Understanding and configuring Salt pillars* recipe, in *Chapter 1, Salt Architecture and Components*, to learn more about pillars

▸ The *Writing and retrieving pillar data* recipe, to learn more about pillars

▸ The *Using grains in states* and *Configuring nodegroups* recipes, to know more about grains and nodegroups

▸ *Chapter 3, Modules, Orchestration, and Scaling Salt*, to learn about more advanced configurations in Salt

3

Modules, Orchestration, and Scaling Salt

In this chapter, you will cover:

- ▶ Using execution modules
- ▶ Using state modules
- ▶ Configuring templates
- ▶ Using requisites
- ▶ Using Salt runners
- ▶ Orchestration with Salt orchestrate
- ▶ Salt multi-master setup (active-active mode)
- ▶ Salt multi-master setup (active-passive mode)

Introduction

In the previous chapter, you learned about how you can leverage the power of data manipulation techniques in Salt. In this chapter, we are going to look at more Salt-specific features. First, you will learn all about modules, which contribute the most toward the configuration management feature of Salt. You will then move on to more advanced configuration techniques using templates, use of requisites, and Salt runners. You will also learn about these features in detail, which will act as the foundation for the advanced configurations we will be carrying out in the rest of the book.

You will then move on to some of the unique features of Salt, such as orchestration, and learn how you can use them to configure infrastructure stacks. Finally, you will look at a couple of ways to scale the Salt infrastructure by introducing methods to add more Salt masters for load balancing and redundancy.

Without further delay, let's dive into some more advanced Salt configurations.

Using execution modules

Modules are the basic foundations of configuration management in Salt. Using Salt modules, we can configure systems from Salt state files, as well as from the command line. In this chapter, you will learn about how to use Salt modules from the command line.

How to do it...

Configure a minion in the staging environment. We will call it stgdc1log01.

1. Run the following command to list all the cron entries for the root user on the minion:

    ```
    [root@salt-master ~]# salt 'stgdc1log01' cron.list_tab root
    stgdc1log01:
        ----------
        crons:
        env:
        pre:
        special:
    ```

2. Run the following command to add a new cron entry for the root user:

    ```
    [root@salt-master ~]# salt 'stgdc1log01' cron.set_job root
    '00' '12' '*' \ '*' '*' 'find /var/log/ -mtime +30 -exec rm -
    rf {} \;'
    stgdc1log01:
        new
    ```

3. Run the following command to verify that the new cron was added properly:

    ```
    [root@salt-master ~]# salt 'stgdc1log01' cron.list_tab root
    stgdc1log01:
        ----------
        crons:
            |_
    ```

```
          ----------
          cmd:
              find /var/log/ -mtime +30 -exec rm -rf {} \;
          comment:
              None
          daymonth:
              *
          dayweek:
              *
          hour:
              12
          identifier:
              None
          minute:
              0
          month:
              *
      env:
      pre:
      special:
```

4. Run the following command to remove the cron entry:

```
[root@salt-master  ~]# salt 'stgdc1log01' cron.rm_job root
'find /var/log/ -mtime +30 -exec rm -rf {} \;'
stgdc1log01:
    removed
```

5. Run the following command to verify that it was removed:

```
[root@salt-master  ~]# salt 'stgdc1log01' cron.list_tab root
stgdc1log01:
    ----------
    crons:
    env:
    pre:
    special:
```

How it works...

Salt modules are the entity that contains the parameters and information required to perform necessary configurations on minions. In Salt, modules are of two types: **state** and **execution** modules. In this recipe, you will learn about the details of execution modules and methods by which to use them.

Execution modules are the ones that can be used from the command line of the Salt master using the `salt-binary` command. A complete list of all the available Salt execution modules can be found at `http://docs.saltstack.com/en/latest/ref/modules/all`. The number of execution modules available in Salt is generally more than the number of state modules. Both the types of modules are extremely helpful in configuring minions.

The general structure of running an execution module consists of the `salt` command, the target minion using the various targeting methods, the module name along with the function, and the data being passed to the minion.

In this recipe, we made use of the `cron` execution module to perform some configuration related to `crontab` scheduling on the minion.

First, we listed the available `crontab` configurations for the `root` user:

```
[root@salt-master ~]# salt 'stgdc1log01' cron.list_tab root
```

The first word in the command is `salt`, which is the `salt` command. Next, we specified the minion to target for this action; this targeting can be performed by using the various methods demonstrated in *Chapter 2, Writing Advanced Salt Configurations*. The next entity in the command is what we are interested in, that is, `cron.list_tab`, which is our execution module implementation. Here, `cron` is the name of the module and `list_tab` is a function under the module. There are multiple functions available for all modules that can be looked up from the list of modules in the preceding link. We have then mentioned the user for which we want to retrieve the `crontab` list.

In the next few commands, we added a new `cron` entry for the root user, verified that it got added, and then removed the entry and again verified it. To carry out these tasks, we used a few more functions of the `cron` module, such as `set_job` and `rm_job`, with the proper number of data fields, which need to be passed for each of them. The number of fields of data that needed to be passed differ as per the function being used and are very well documented in the preceding link.

The list of execution modules in Salt is quite large and supports a wide range of tasks that can be performed on the minions. We will look at some of the most important of them in later chapters.

See also

▶ The *Targeting minions* recipe in *Chapter 2, Writing Advanced Salt Configurations*, to learn about how to target minions

▶ The *Using state modules* recipe, to learn how to use state modules

Using state modules

In the previous recipe, you learned about how you can use execution modules to perform configuration tasks in Salt. In this recipe, you are going to learn about of what state modules are and how to use them.

How to do it...

We will use the same minion and the same example as the previous recipe, but we will do the same task using state modules.

1. Create a new state in the staging environment called `cron` by creating a new directory called `cron` and create a file in it called `init.sls`.

2. Edit the `init.sls` file to have the following contents:

```
find /var/log/ -mtime +30 -exec rm -rf {] \;:
  cron.present:
    - user: root
    - minute: 00
    - hour: 12
    - daymonth: '*'
    - month: '*'
    - dayweek: '*'
```

3. Run the following command to apply the state to the minion:

```
[root@salt-master  ~]# salt 'stgdc1log01' state.sls cron
saltenv=staging

stgdc1log01:
----------
          ID: find /var/log/ -mtime +30 -exec rm -rf {] \;
    Function: cron.present
      Result: True
     Comment: Cron find /var/log/ -mtime +30 -exec rm -rf {]
\; added to root's crontab
     Started: 05:19:18.830011
```

```
        Duration: 75.282 ms
          Changes:
                    ----------
                root:
                    find /var/log/ -mtime +30 -exec rm -rf {] \;


        Summary
        ------------
        Succeeded: 1 (changed=1)
        Failed:    0
        ------------
        Total states run:      1
```

How it works...

In this recipe, you learned how to perform configurations tasks on minions using state modules.

State modules in Salt are configured by creating proper directory structures for the module and populating the necessary files in the directory. The directory of the module is created in the base directory of the environment, in which we are configuring the module and use the name of the directory as the module name to perform configuration tasks. A complete list of the available state modules can be found at `http://docs.saltstack.com/en/latest/ref/states/all`.

In this recipe, we made the same configuration task as the previous recipe, that is, to configure a `cron` entry for the `root` user, which looks for files older than 30 days in the `/var/log` directory and deletes them. However, we used the state module instead of the execution module to do this.

First, we created the directory called `cron` in the base directory of the staging environment, and our state will be called `cron`, based on the name of this directory. Next, we created a file called `init.sls` in the directory. The contents of this file are referenced when the state is called `cron`. If there is a second file called `app.sls`, then it will be called `cron.app`. All configuration files should have the `.sls` extension.

We then populated the file with the following entries:

```
find /var/log/ -mtime +30 -exec rm -rf {] \;:
  cron.present:
    - user: root
    - minute: 00
    - hour: 12
```

```
- daymonth: '*'
- month: '*'
- dayweek: '*'
```

The first line indicates the `cron` command that will be updated in the `crontab` file. The second line is the one that indicates the module and the function being used. Here, the state module `cron` is being used along with the present function. This indicates that the `cron` entry should be added if absent and should have the correct configuration if already present. We then define the user, day, and time configurations for the `cron` entry in YAML format. All the available data fields for all the state modules are defined in the preceding link.

Often a generic name for the particular configuration can be defined in the state files. Let's assume that we are configuring a file, for which there are two ways to define it.

▸ The first method is as follows:

```
/etc/hosts:
  file.managed:
    - source: salt://hostconfig/files/hosts
```

▸ The second method is as follows:

```
host_config_file:
  file.managed:
    - name: /etc/hosts
    - source: salt://hostconfig/files/hosts
```

In the first method, we defined the name of the file, that is, its path in the first line and then the configurations were done. However, in the second method, we defined a generic name called `host_config_file` to reference this configuration and then defined the actual name of the file with the `- name` field. In all subsequent configurations, the name mentioned in the first line is used to reference this configuration, which can be the real name and path of the file or the generic name.

Finally, we applied the state to the minion with the following command:

```
[root@salt-master ~]# salt 'stgdc1log01' state.sls cron
saltenv=staging
```

In this command, we tell `salt` that the module that we are going to apply to the minion is a state module by mentioning `state.sls`. We then mention the name of the state, that is, `cron` and the environment of the minion. If the configured file was `app.sls` instead of `init.sls`, we would mention `cron.app` in the command. Do note that `state.sls` is actually an execution module which is used to apply state modules to minions.

There's more...

There is an alternate method of applying state modules to a minion, which is known as **highstate**. After a state is configured, the `top.sls` file of the relevant environment is edited to have an entry similar to the following:

```
staging:
  '*':
    - cron
```

There can be a list of states similar to `cron`, which can be entered one after the other. The minions can also be targeted by using the methods demonstrated in *Chapter 2, Writing Advanced Salt Configurations*.

Next, the state can be applied to the minion using the following command:

```
[root@salt-master ~]# salt 'stgdc1log01' state.highstate
```

This command will apply all the matching states from the `top.sls` file to the minion. This method is usually used when there are multiple states to be applied to a minion, and applying them one by one using the first method can be tedious.

See also

▸ *Chapter 4, General Administration Tasks*, to demonstrate the use of state modules

▸ The *Configuring templates* recipe, to learn about how to leverage the power of Salt in configuring custom templates for services and system configurations

Configuring templates

In infrastructure management, we often face situations when we have to push files to multiple hosts but the information in the files is host-specific such as the hostname, IP address, and so on. In Salt, we can achieve the same objectives using templates, and in this recipe, we are going to learn about how to use templates.

How to do it...

We will use the minion `stgdc1log01` that we configured in the last recipe, *Using state modules*.

1. Create a new state in the staging environment named `hostconfig` by creating a directory called `hostconfig` in the base directory of the staging environment. Create a directory called `files` in the `hostconfig` directory and also a file named `init.sls`.

2. Edit the `init.sls` file to have the following contents:

```
hosts_file:
  file.managed:
    - name: /etc/hosts
    - source: salt://hostconfig/files/hosts
    - user: root
    - hroup: root
    - mode: 644
    - template: jinja
    - context:
      local_ip_address: {{ grains['ip4_interfaces']['eth1'][0] }}
      local_host_name: {{ grains['fqdn'] }}
```

3. Create a file named `hosts` in the `/opt/salt-cookbook/staging/hostconfig/files` directory and populate it with the following entries:

```
127.0.0.1    localhost localhost.localdomain localhost4
::1          localhost localhost.localdomain localhost6
{{ local_ip_address }} {{ local_host_name }} salt-master
```

4. Now, run the following command to apply the state to the minion:

```
[root@salt-master ~]# salt 'stgdc1log01' state.sls
hostconfig.hosts saltenv=staging

stgdc1log01:
----------
          ID: hosts_file
    Function: file.managed
        Name: /etc/hosts
      Result: True
     Comment: File /etc/hosts updated
     Started: 03:39:33.815985
    Duration: 403.902 ms
     Changes:
              ----------
              diff:
                  ---
                  +++
                  @@ -1,6 +1,3 @@
                     127.0.0.1    localhost localhost.localdomain
localhost4 localhost4.localdomain4
```

```
                         ::1           localhost localhost.localdomain
         localhost6 localhost6.localdomain6
                   +192.168.0.3 stgdc1log01 salt-master



         Summary
         -----------
         Succeeded: 1 (changed=1)
         Failed:    0
         -----------
         Total states run:     1
```

How it works...

Template is an excellent feature of Salt, which provides us with lot of flexibilities with regards to configuration management. Often, administrators prefer to implement a masterless infrastructure for configuration management by keeping the entire Salt repository on each minion and configuring the minion to be its own master. In this recipe, you learned how to configure the `/etc/hosts` file to enable the minion to point to itself as the Salt master.

First, we created a new state called `hostconfig`. In the `init.sls` file of the state, we configured a file definition to manage the `/etc/hosts` file of the minion. We entered a generic name for the definition called `hosts_file`, and then specified the state module to use, which was `file.managed`. We then specified the actual file to manage, which was `/etc/hosts` and then specified all other parameters such as the user, group, and mode. The source of the file has been mentioned as follows:

```
- source: salt://hostconfig/files/hosts
```

In the preceding line, `salt` means that we are looking for the file in the Salt `file_roots` environment path, `hostconfig` is the state directory, and the rest is the path to the `template` file that we configured. The context section refers to variables that we are going to pass to the `template` file. Here, we defined two variables to pass to the template, that is, the hostname and the IP address of the minion. The `template` parameter is extremely important when defining a template. It specifies the `template` format that we are using and in the case of Salt, it is **jinja**.

Next, we created the template file `/opt/salt-cookbook/staging/hostconfig/files/hosts` and entered the following content into it:

```
127.0.0.1    localhost localhost.localdomain localhost4
::1          localhost localhost.localdomain localhost6
{{ local_ip_address }} {{ local_host_name }} salt-master
```

Here, we can see that the values of the variables that we had passed to the template from the state file are being mentioned in the {{ variable_name }} format, where the actual values of the variables will be substituted when the states are applied to the minions.

Finally, we applied the state to the minion, and from the output, it is visible how the configured values are being substituted in the target file.

See also

- The *Managing files* recipe in *Chapter 5, Advanced Administration Tasks,* to find out more about handling files with Salt

- The *Using requisites* recipe, to learn how to create dependencies between Salt definitions

Using requisites

In infrastructure management, almost all the time, we have situations where we need a task to happen only if another condition is true. This is achieved by creating dependencies between definitions. In Salt, these dependencies are known as requisites, and in this recipe, you will learn about how to use them.

How to do it...

We will use the same minion as the previous recipe.

1. Create a new state called ntp by creating a directory called ntp in the base directory of the staging environment, and then create a directory called files in the ntp state directory.

2. Create a file called init.sls in the ntp state directory and edit it to have the following entries:

```
ntp_package:
  pkg.installed:
    - name: ntp

ntp_conf_file:
  file.managed:patch antenna circular polarization
    - name: /etc/ntp.conf
    - source: salt://ntp/files/ntp.conf
    - user: root
    - group: root
    - mode: 644
```

```
      - require:
        - pkg: ntp_package

  ntp_service:
    service:
      - name: ntpd
      - running
      - enable: True
      - require:
        - file: ntp_conf_file
      - watch:
        - file: ntp_conf_file
```

3. Create a file called `ntp.conf` in the `files` directory of the `ntp` state and populate it with the following entries:

```
driftfile /var/lib/ntp/drift

restrict default kod nomodify notrap nopeer noquery
restrict -6 default kod nomodify notrap nopeer noquery

restrict 127.0.0.1
restrict -6 ::1

server 0.centos.pool.ntp.org iburst
server 1.centos.pool.ntp.org iburst

includefile /etc/ntp/crypto/pw

keys /etc/ntp/keys
```

4. Apply the state to the minion by using the following command:

```
[root@salt-master  ~]# salt 'stgdc1log01' state.sls ntp
saltenv=staging -state-output=terse
stgdc1log01:
  Name: ntp - Function: pkg.installed - Result: Changed
  Name: /etc/ntp.conf - Function: file.managed - Result:
Changed
  Name: ntpd - Function: service.running - Result: Changed

Summary
------------
Succeeded: 3 (changed=3)
Failed:    0
------------
Total states run:     3
```

How it works...

In this recipe, we configured a very basic `ntp` service for the minion to synchronize with global `ntp` servers. We used three state modules: `pkg`, `file`, and `service` for the definitions. We made them interdependent using requisites.

Requisites are certain conditions that need to be defined in Salt configurations, which make definitions dependent on each other, that is, one definition executes only if the dependent definition holds true.

In this recipe, we have first made use of the `pkg` state module to define the `ntp` package to be installed on the minion. Next, we made a `file` definition and defined the `ntp.conf` file from the Salt repository to be copied over to the minion. In the file definition, we have a new attribute called `require` with the value as another key-value pair that mentions the `pkg` definition and the name of the `pkg` definition:

```
require:
  - pkg: ntp_package
```

This tells Salt to copy over the file to the minion only if the `ntp package` definition holds true or has succeeded in installing the package. Next, we defined the `ntp` service to be enabled at startup and to be in the running state. However, here we have again mentioned the `require` requisite to make sure that the `ntp.conf` file has been successfully copied over and exists in the minion. This creates a chain of dependencies; the file depends on the package and the service depends on the file. Therefore, the service will fail if the package has not been installed.

However, we used a second requisite here called `watch`:

```
- watch:
  - file: ntp_conf_file
```

We asked the service definition to keep an eye on the file, look for changes, and restart/reload itself if there was a change in the file. The `watch` attribute makes sure that these functions are carried out.

There is an alternate way to achieve the same objectives. Each of the requisites have a corresponding `_in` versions; `require` has a second version called `require_in` and `watch` has `watch_in`. For example, the definitions used in this recipe can be rewritten as follows:

```
ntp_package:
  pkg.installed:
    - name: ntp
  Require_in:
    - file: ntp_conf_file
```

```
ntp_conf_file:
    file.managed:
        - name: /etc/ntp.conf
        - source: salt://ntp/files/ntp.conf
        - user: root
        - group: root
        - mode: 644
```

As we can see from the preceding snippet, the objective remains the same, but the requisite is used in the other definition. That is, instead of the file definition, the requisite is used in the package definition, and we tell the package definition to be aware that it is needed for the file to be copied over to the minion. Either of the two ways can be used, it just depends on the user as to which version is used.

There's more...

Apart from `require` and `watch`, there are a few more requisites that can be very useful in configuring states. The `use` requisite is one of the requisites that has been there for some time. It is used to make use of attributes of one definition in another. For example:

```
/etc/hosts:
    file.managed:
        - source: salt://hostconfig/files/hosts
        - user: root
        - group: root
        - mode: 644

/etc/nsswitch.conf:
    file.managed:
        - source: salt://hostconfig/files/nsswitch.conf
        - use:
            - file: /etc/hosts
```

The preceding configuration tells Salt to use all the attributes such as `user`, `group`, and `mode` of the `/etc/hosts` file definition in the `/etc/nsswitch.conf` file definition.

In the latest Salt release `2014.7.0`, a few more requisites have been introduced:

- ▶ `onfail`: This requisite, when used in a definition, looks for a failure in the target definition and executes only if the failure occurs

- ▶ `onchanges`: This requisite looks for changes in the target definition and only if the watched definition's result is `True`

- `unless`: This requisite has commands as its values and holds true only if their result is `False`
- `onlyif`: This requisite also has commands as its values and holds true only if the result of the commands is `True`

See also

- *Chapter 4*, *General Administration Tasks*, to demonstrate the use of requisites
- The *Using state modules* recipe, to learn how to configure state modules
- The *Using Salt runners* recipe, to learn how to use Salt runners

Using Salt runners

We have been learning about how to perform all sorts of functions on the minion. However, there are methods to run utility functions on the Salt master itself, to perform various tasks such as looking up the job history, finding out minion details, and so on. In this recipe, we will look at how we can do these tasks using Salt runners.

How to do it...

1. Configure two minions in the staging environment called `stgdc1log01` and `stgdc1app01`. Start the minions, let them authenticate with the Salt master, and then shut down the minion service daemon on `stgdc1app01`.

2. Run the following command to see the overall minion data:

```
[root@salt-master  ~]# salt-run manage.status
down:
    - stgdc1app01
up:
    - stgdc1log01
```

3. Run the following command to get a grain detail from one of the minions:

```
[root@salt-master  ~]# salt -vv 'stgdc1log01' grains.item
server_type
Executing job with jid 20141123180047497261
-------------------------------------------

stgdc1log01:
    ----------
    server_type:
        log
```

4. Run the following command to revisit the output of the previous job:

```
[root@salt-master ~]# salt-run jobs.lookup_jid \
20141123180047497261

stgdc1log01:
    ----------
    server_type:
        log
```

5. Run the following command to get a detailed output of the job:

```
[root@salt-master ~]# salt-run jobs.print_job \
20141123180047497261

20141123180047497261:
    ----------
    Arguments:
        - server_type
    Function:
        grains.item
    Minions:
        - stgdc1log01
    Result:
        ----------
        stgdc1log01:
            ----------
            out:
                grains
            return:
                ----------
                server_type:
                    log
    StartTime:
        2014, Nov 23 18:00:47.497261
    Target:
        stgdc1log01
    Target-type:
        glob
    User:
        root
```

6. Run the following command to get a history of all detectable past jobs and their details:

```
[root@salt-master  ~]# salt-run jobs.list_jobs
```

How it works...

Salt **runners** are utilities that can be run on the Salt master to get detailed information about the environment, minions, jobs, status, and lot of other information. The `salt-run` command is used to execute the Salt runners and a full list of available runners is available at `http://docs.saltstack.com/en/latest/ref/runners/all/index.html#all-salt-runners`.

Runners are basically Python scripts and functions defined in the scripts. Custom runners can be added to the Salt infrastructure by modifying few parameters. For example, if we wanted to add a new runner called `environment` and display details about the Salt master environment, we would ideally perform the following steps:

1. Choose a location in which to store the runner script. Let's say we store the script in `/opt/salt-cookbook/runners`.

2. Create a Python script called `environment.py` in the preceding location and create a function in the script called `master` and put our environment logic for the Salt master in it.

3. Open the Salt master configuration file, `/etc/salt/master`. Uncomment the `runner_dirs: []` line and enter the path of our runner script in this definition as `runner_dirs: ['/opt/salt-cookbook/runners']`. Restart the Salt master service daemon.

4. Run the runner with the following command:

```
# salt-run environment.master
```

In this recipe, we demonstrate the use of a couple of the default Salt runners, such as `manage` and `jobs`. In the first command, we find out the overall status of our minions by using the `manage.status` runner, which gives us the minions that Salt thinks are up and responding along with the minions that Salt thinks are down and not responding. To only find out minions that are up, we can use `manage.up`, and to find out minions that are down, we can use `manage.down`.

In the next few examples, we used the `jobs` runner to find out a lot of details about the Salt commands that we have run till now.

First, we run the following command to get the `server_type` grain value from the `stgdc1log01` minion:

```
[root@salt-master  ~]# salt -vv 'stgdc1log01' grains.item server_type
```

Each Salt command that we run has a job ID. In this command, we use the −vv option to get the job ID of this Salt command.

Next, using the job ID, we looked up the job from the job history with the following command:

```
[root@salt-master ~]# salt-run jobs.lookup_jid \
20141123180047497261
```

This command gives us the exact same output that we had received when we initially ran the command. Next, we found out a lot more details about the job with the jobs.print_job runner.

Finally, we listed a history of all the jobs that were run in the past using the runner jobs. list_jobs. This command produces a long output listing all the jobs with their job IDs and other details about the jobs.

Thus, we see the importance and advantages of using runners in Salt in this recipe. There are lots of other default runners available in Salt, which can be used to search for information or perform tasks. The feature to add custom runners can also be leveraged to do advanced tasks on the Salt master.

See also

- ▶ The *Orchestration with Salt orchestrate* recipe, to learn about the very important feature of orchestration in Salt and to see a demonstration of Salt runners
- ▶ *Chapter 8, Configuring Salt Cloud*, for a demonstration of Salt runner in the Salt cloud

Orchestration with Salt orchestrate

Orchestration, as we know, is an extremely important feature that should be available in any configuration management system. In Salt, this objective has been achieved till date by overstate. However, a new runner, called orchestrate, has been introduced in Salt to achieve the same objective in a much more efficient manner, and it replaces overstate. In this recipe, you will learn about how to use the orchestrate runner.

How to do it...

1. Configure two minions, stgdc1web01 and stgdc1dbs01. Configure the server_type grain in stgdc1web01 with the value web and in stgdc1dbs01 as db.
2. Create two new states called nginx and mysql by creating directories for both in the base directory of the staging environment.

3. Create the `/opt/salt-cookbook/staging/nginx/init.sls` file and edit it to have the following entries:

```
nginx_package:
  pkg.installed:
    - name: nginx

nginx_service:
  service:
    - name: nginx
    - running
    - enable: True
    - require:
      - pkg: nginx_package
```

4. Similarly, create `/opt/salt-cookbook/staging/mysql/init.sls` and populate it with the following entries:

```
mysql_package:
  pkg.installed:
    - name: mysql-server

mysql_service:
  service:
    - name: mysqld
    - running
    - enable: True
    - require:
      - pkg: mysql_package
```

5. Now that the two states are configured, create a directory called `orchestration` in the base directory of the staging environment and create a file in it called `stack.sls`. Edit `stack.sls` to have the following entries:

```
webserver_deploy:
  salt.state:
    - tgt: 'server_type:web'
    - tgt_type: grain
    - sls: nginx
    - require:
      - salt: dbserver_deploy

dbserver_deploy:
  salt.state:
    - tgt: 'server_type:db'
    - tgt_type: grain
    - sls: mysql
```

6. Run the following command to apply the configuration to the configured minions:

```
[root@salt-master  ~]# salt-run state.orchestrate
orchestration.stack saltenv=staging

salt-master_master:

----------

          ID: dbserver_deploy
    Function: salt.state
      Result: True
     Comment: States ran successfully. Updating stgdc1dbs01.
     Started: 20:04:14.864462
    Duration: 121276.62 ms
     Changes:
                  stgdc1dbs01:

                  ----------

                            ID: mysql_package
                      Function: pkg.installed
                          Name: mysql-server
                        Result: True
                       Comment: The following packages were
installed/updated: mysql-server.
                       Started: 20:04:16.655747
                      Duration: 115597.375 ms
                       Changes:
                                  ----------
                                  mysql:
                                      ----------
                                      new:
                                          5.1.73-3.el6_5
                                      old:

     .

     .

     .


                                  ----------
                            ID: mysql_service
                      Function: service.running
```

```
                  Name: mysqld
                Result: True
               Comment: Service mysqld has been enabled,
and is running
               Started: 20:06:12.253749
              Duration: 3754.955 ms
               Changes:
                         ----------
                         mysqld:
                             True


        Summary
        ------------
        Succeeded: 2 (changed=2)
        Failed:    0
        ------------
        Total states run:     2
----------
          ID: webserver_deploy
    Function: salt.state
      Result: True
     Comment: States ran successfully. Updating stgdc1web01.
     Started: 20:06:16.142043
    Duration: 247332.219 ms
     Changes:
              stgdc1web01:
              ----------
                        ID: nginx_package
                  Function: pkg.installed
                      Name: nginx
                    Result: True
                   Comment: The following packages were
installed/updated: nginx.
                   Started: 20:06:16.136173
                  Duration: 244164.046 ms
                   Changes:
```

```
                                   ----------
                                   GeoIP:
                                      ----------
                                      new:
                                           1.5.1-5.el6
                                      old:

              .

              .

              .


                     ----------
                             ID: nginx_service
                       Function: service.running
                           Name: nginx
                         Result: True
                        Comment: Service nginx has been enabled,
and is running
                        Started: 20:10:20.301435
                       Duration: 783.461 ms
                        Changes:
                                 ----------
                                 nginx:
                                      True


                  Summary
                  ------------
                  Succeeded: 2 (changed=2)
                  Failed:    0
                  ------------
                  Total states run:     2


           Summary
           ------------
           Succeeded: 2 (changed=2)
           Failed:    0
           ------------
           Total states run:     2
```

How it works...

Orchestration is a feature of Salt, the power of which can be harnessed to produce amazing results. Using orchestration, we can launch entire application stacks by making each tier of the stack dependent on each other, thus making sure that each component is ready before the next component is launched. Following this workflow, application stacks of any design and architecture can be seamlessly launched.

In this recipe, we have seen how to use orchestration. The objective of the recipe is to launch two tiers of an application stack, the web tier and the database tier, and to make sure that the database tier launches before the web tier so that the database servers are ready before the web servers can access them.

First, we created one state each for the web and the database servers, namely, `nginx` and `mysql`. The `nginx` state makes sure that the `nginx` web server is installed and the `nginx` service is running. Similarly, the `mysql` state makes sure that the `mysql-server` package is installed and the `mysqld` service is running. Both of the states have been configured using state modules.

The next step is an interesting one with which we are more concerned in this recipe. Orchestration files are also the `.sls` files. They are similar to normal states and can be created under the base directory of the environment. We created a directory called `orchestration` (this can be any name), and then we created a file called `stack.sls` (again, this can be any name). Next, we configured it as follows:

```
webserver_deploy:
  salt.state:
    - tgt: 'server_type:web'
    - tgt_type: grain
    - sls: nginx
    - require:
      - salt: dbserver_deploy

dbserver_deploy:
  salt.state:
    - tgt: 'server_type:db'
    - tgt_type: grain
    - sls: mysql
```

In this configuration, we created two blocks, one for the web server, `webserver_deploy` and one for the database server `dbserver_deploy`. In each of the blocks, we mentioned `salt.state`, which makes sure that we are going to run salt states in the orchestration configuration. Next, we targeted minions as per their `server_type` grain and mentioned the target type as `grain`. The targeting can be done based on multiple properties as discussed in the *Targeting minions* recipe in *Chapter 2, Writing Advanced Salt Configurations*.

Next, we mentioned the states to be applied to the minions with the `sls` attribute. Finally, we made sure that the database tier gets created before the web tier by applying the `require` attribute:

```
- require:
  - salt: dbserver_deploy
```

There is an alternate way to achieve the same objective. Often, there are configurations which involve a lot of states for the minions and listing all of them in the orchestration SLS file might not be optimal. In these cases, we can list the states in the `top.sls` file of the environment with proper minion targeting. Then, in the orchestration SLS file, we can mention something like the following:

```
dbserver_deploy:
  salt.state:
    - tgt: 'server_type:db'
    - tgt_type: grain
    - highstate: True
```

As we can see, the only new attribute in this snippet is the `highstate` attribute. When we set this attribute as `True`, the list of states for the targeted minions is fetched from the `top.sls` file of the environment, thus avoiding the use of multiple state names in the orchestration file.

Finally, we run the following command to apply the configuration to the stack:

```
[root@salt-master  ~]# salt-run state.orchestrate orchestration.stack
saltenv=staging
```

Here, we used the `state` runner with the orchestrate function and run the command by using the `salt-run` command. The third parameter is the name of the directory that we had created, orchestration, along with the name of the state file in the directory, that is, `stack.sls`. The output from the command gives us two sets of outputs that can be also called a nested output.

The first output block is produced under the name `salt-master_master`. Usually, the outputs are under the names of the minions, however, as there are no minions being targeted from the command itself, Salt categorizes them under the Salt master and the name is mentioned as the hostname of the Salt master joined with `_master`.

Under the master, we see a second block of output that involves the changes taking place for each of the minions and are placed under the respective minion IDs. In larger configurations, there will be a block of output for each minion that gets configured. Finally, we see two changes under each of the minions and two changes under `salt-master_master`, indicating that the two definitions that we had made in the orchestration file, that is, `webserver_deploy` and `dbserver_deploy` have executed successfully. Also, do note that because of the dependency that we created, the database server gets configured first and then the web server, although `webserver_deploy` is configured first in the orchestration file.

See also

▸ The *Salt multi-master setup (active-active mode)* recipe, to learn how to scale the Salt infrastructure by creating redundant Salt masters

Salt multi-master setup (active-active mode)

In very large infrastructures, high availability and redundancy are important requirements. Fortunately, Salt has support for redundant Salt masters that provide a level of redundancy and also a means to scale the infrastructure to support large deployments.

How to do it...

We will use our existing Salt master, but rename it to `salt-master-1` from `salt-master`. Also, configure a second Salt master called `salt-master-2` by following the *Installing and configuring the Salt master* and *Configuring the Salt environment and pillar paths* recipes from *Chapter 1, Salt Architecture and Components*.

The second node will be configured in the exact same way as the first one. After installing the `salt-master` package, copy over the following files and directories from `salt-master-1` to the exact same locations in `salt-master-2`.

1. Create the directories if they do not exist:
   - `/etc/salt/master`
   - `/etc/salt/autosign.conf`
   - `/etc/salt/pki/master/master.pem`
   - `/etc/salt/pki/master/master.pub`
   - `/opt/salt-cookbook`

2. Start the `salt-master` service daemon on `salt-master-2` or restart it if it is already running.

3. Configure a minion called `stgdc1app01` and edit the `/etc/salt/minion` file on `stgdc1app01` to have both the salt masters listed as `master`, as follows:

```
master:
  - salt-master-1
  - salt-master-2
```

4. Start the `salt-minion` service daemon on `stgdc1app01`. Run the following commands on both the Salt masters:

```
[root@salt-master-1 ~]# salt-key -L
Accepted Keys:
stgdc1app01
Unaccepted Keys:
Rejected Keys:


[root@salt-master-1 ~]# salt 'stgdc1app01' test.ping
stgdc1app01:
    True


[root@salt-master-2 ~]# salt-key -L
Accepted Keys:
stgdc1app01
Unaccepted Keys:
Rejected Keys:


[root@salt-master-2 ~]# salt 'stgdc1app01' test.ping
stgdc1app01:
    True
```

How it works...

Redundant masters are an excellent feature of Salt to support scaling and redundancy. In this recipe, you learned how to implement an active-active Salt master pair to scale our infrastructure.

Our objective in this recipe is to create a second Salt master, which will act as the redundant master node in our infrastructure. We renamed our existing Salt master to `salt-master-1` and created a new node called `salt-master-2`. We installed the `salt-master` package in `salt-master-2` and copied over the required files and directories to create an exact replica of our first master node.

The environment and pillar paths should be at the same location in both nodes and should be synchronized to keep content on both nodes the same. A preferable way to do that will be to push configurations to a repository, such as Git, and then pull the configurations periodically.

Both nodes should have the same master configuration file and autosign file. The master keys, `master.pem` and `master.pub`, should also be copied over to the redundant master node because the minions should see both nodes as the same. Once the files and directories are in place, the `salt-master` service daemon can be started on `salt-master-2`.

Now, to configure the minion to see both the master nodes as valid Salt masters, we created a new minion and made the following configuration:

```
master:
  - salt-master-1
  - salt-master-2
```

This tells the minion that both the nodes are valid Salt masters, and either of them can be reached to get configurations. Finally, we check if the key for the new minion has been accepted on both the master nodes and if the minion is responding to both the masters.

It must be noted that there can be any number of Salt masters in an infrastructure that is configurable in the same manner as we just learned from this recipe. Salt commands can be run from either of the master nodes. However, key deletions, rejections, and acceptance will not be managed by default on both nodes, and it has to be done manually. Another way to achieve this is to share the `/etc/salt/pki/master` directory on both nodes. However, this is not a good practice and can lead too serious security concerns. Hence, it should be avoided.

See also

▸ The *Installing and configuring the Salt master* and *Configuring the Salt environment and pillar paths* recipes from *Chapter 1*, *Salt Architecture and Components*, to learn how to configure Salt masters

▸ The *Salt multi-master setup (active-passive mode)* recipe, to learn how to configure an active-passive Salt multi-master setup

Salt multi-master setup (active-passive mode)

In the previous recipe, we talked about configuring a multi-master setup with a couple of Salt masters in active-active mode, where we could run salt commands from either of them. While this method is good for the push mechanism, as the minions are connected to both the masters at all times, there should be a method to achieve the same objective when using the pull method of getting configurations from the Salt master, while being aware of master-server issues and failing over to a redundant node. This can be achieved with the active-passive setup. In this recipe, you will learn how to achieve this objective.

How to do it...

1. Configure two nodes, `salt-master-1` and `salt-master-2`, and install the salt-master package on both. On `salt-master-1`, edit the configuration file `/etc/salt/master` to have the following entries:

```
master_sign_pubkey: True
```

2. Start the `salt-master` service daemon on `salt-master-1`. Run the following command:

```
[root@salt-master-1 ~]# ls -l /etc/salt/pki/master/
-r--------. 1 root root 3243 Nov 25 02:55 master.pem
-rw-r--r--. 1 root root  800 Nov 25 02:55 master.pub
-r--------. 1 root root 3247 Nov 25 02:55 master_sign.pem
-rw-r--r--. 1 root root  800 Nov 25 02:55 master_sign.pub
```

3. Copy over the following files and directories to `salt-master-2`:

   ❑ `/etc/salt/master`

   ❑ `/etc/salt/pki/master`

4. Start the `salt-master` service on `salt-master-2`.

5. Configure a minion `salt-minion` and edit the file `/etc/salt/minion` to have the following entries:

```
master:
  - salt-master-1
  - salt-master-2

master_type: failover
verify_master_pubkey_sign: True
master_alive_interval: 30
```

6. Copy over the file `/etc/salt/pki/master/master_sign.pub` from `salt-master-1` to the location `/etc/salt/pki/minion/master_sign.pub` on the minion.

7. Run the following command on the minion:

```
[root@salt-minion ~]# salt-minion -l debug
[DEBUG   ] Reading configuration from /etc/salt/minion
[DEBUG   ] Using cached minion ID from /etc/salt/minion_id:
salt-minion
[DEBUG   ] Configuration file path: /etc/salt/minion
[INFO    ] Setting up the Salt Minion "salt-minion"
[DEBUG   ] Created pidfile: /var/run/salt-minion.pid
```

```
[DEBUG    ] Reading configuration from /etc/salt/minion

[INFO     ] Got list of available master addresses: ['salt-
master-1', 'salt-master-2']

[DEBUG    ] Attempting to authenticate with the Salt Master at
192.168.0.2

[INFO     ] Generating keys: /etc/salt/pki/minion

[DEBUG    ] Loaded minion key: /etc/salt/pki/minion/minion.pem

[DEBUG    ] salt.crypt.verify_signature: Loading public key

[DEBUG    ] salt.crypt.verify_signature: Verifying signature

[DEBUG    ] Successfully verified signature of master public
key with verification public key master_sign.pub

[INFO     ] Received signed and verified master pubkey from
master salt-master-1

[DEBUG    ] Decrypting the current master AES key

[DEBUG    ] Loaded minion key: /etc/salt/pki/minion/minion.pem

[INFO     ] Authentication with master at 192.168.0.2
successful!
```

8. Now, stop the `salt-master` service on `salt-master-1`. The output on `salt-minion` should continue as follows:

```
[INFO     ] Connection to master salt-master-1 lost

[INFO     ] Trying to tune in to next master from master-list

[INFO     ] Removing possibly failed master salt-master-1 from
list of masters

[WARNING ] Master ip address changed from 192.168.0.2 to
192.168.0.3

[DEBUG    ] Attempting to authenticate with the Salt Master at
192.168.0.3

[DEBUG    ] Loaded minion key: /etc/salt/pki/minion/minion.pem

[DEBUG    ] Decrypting the current master AES key

[DEBUG    ] Loaded minion key: /etc/salt/pki/minion/minion.pem

[INFO     ] Authentication with master at 192.168.0.3
successful!

[INFO     ] Re-initialising subsystems for new master salt-
master-2

[DEBUG    ] Generated random reconnect delay between '1000ms'
and '11000ms' (1870)

[DEBUG    ] Setting zmq_reconnect_ivl to '1870ms'

[DEBUG    ] Setting zmq_reconnect_ivl_max to '11000ms'
```

```
[DEBUG    ] Decrypting the current master AES key

[DEBUG    ] Loaded minion key: /etc/salt/pki/minion/minion.pem

[DEBUG    ] Removed obsolete sreq-object from sreq_cach e for
master tcp://192.168.0.2:4506

[DEBUG    ] Decrypting the current master AES key

[DEBUG    ] Loaded minion key: /etc/salt/pki/minion/minion.pem

[INFO     ] Minion is ready to receive requests!
```

9. Terminate the `salt-minion` command and start the `salt-minion` service daemon.

How it works...

The active-passive method of Salt multi-master with failover capability is aimed primarily at the pull method of getting configuration from the master by the minion. It holds true for the push mechanism. However, this process makes extensive use of the capability of both the master and minion to sign and verify public keys, which are used for authentication between the master and the minion.

First, we configured two Salt masters and mentioned the following parameter in the configuration file of `salt-master-1`:

```
master_sign_pubkey: True
```

This parameter makes sure that the Salt master signs the public key that will be verified by the minion when authenticating with the master. When the master is started on `salt-master-1`, two new files are generated at the location `/etc/salt/pki/master` called `master_sign.pem` and `master_sign.pub`. These two files are the signed master key and the public key that the master will henceforth use for authentication.

Next, we copy over the master configuration file and the generated keys to the second Salt master, `salt-master-2`, and then start the `salt-master` service on it.

A minion is then configured. The `/etc/salt/pki/master/master_sign.pub` file from the master is copied over to the location `/etc/salt/pki/minion/master_sign.pub` on the minion, and the minion configuration file is edited to have the following options:

```
master:
  - salt-master-1
  - salt-master-2

master_type: failover
verify_master_pubkey_sign: True
master_alive_interval: 30
```

The first parameter mentions the two Salt master nodes being used. The second parameter, `master_type`, indicates the type of the multi-master setup. That is, it tells the minion to failover to a different node if the first authenticated master is down. The next parameter, `verify_master_pubkey_sign`, makes sure that the minion verifies the master's key with the `master_sign.pub` key, which we had copied over from the master to the minion. The last option `master_alive_interval` indicates the time for which the minion waits for communication from a master node before failing over to the next available master.

Finally, we run the `salt-minion` binary in debug mode and see that the minion authenticates successfully with `salt-master-1` using the public key made available to it. We then stop the `salt-master` service on `salt-master-1` and watch the output on the minion as it successfully fails over to `salt-master-2` after determining `salt-master-1` as down and successfully authenticates with it.

See also

- The *Salt multi-master setup (active-active mode)* recipe, to learn how to configure an active-active multi-master setup
- *Chapter 4*, *General Administration Tasks*, to start implementing infrastructure components using Salt

4

General Administration Tasks

In this chapter, you will cover:

- ▸ Running commands
- ▸ Setting host entries and grains
- ▸ Setting time zone, locale, and kernel configuration
- ▸ Handling archive files
- ▸ Adding groups and users
- ▸ Performing SSH authentication tasks
- ▸ Scheduling jobs with cron
- ▸ Managing volumes
- ▸ Working with disks and mounts
- ▸ Managing network configurations

Introduction

In the earlier chapters, we have seen various methods on how to install, configure, scale, and manage Salt as an infrastructure tool. We have also looked at a lot of Salt-specific terminologies, how and where they fit in the tool, and how to use them to achieve our objectives when managing infrastructure.

Starting from this chapter and for the next few chapters, we will learn about some of the most common built-in modules of Salt that can be used to configure our infrastructure, details about how to use them, and various options available and the methods in which to use them to achieve optimum results.

In this chapter, we will look at how to perform the most general system administration tasks and then move on to advanced tasks in the next chapters. Without further delay, let's jump in and get hands on with Salt modules and configuration.

Running commands

In this recipe, you will learn how to run simple shell commands on minions at the same time as fulfilling various conditions, making sure that the requirements are met, and creating dependencies between definitions based on the output of commands.

How to do it...

1. Configure a Salt minion in the staging environment, and call it `salt-minion`. Create a new state in the staging environment called **ruby** by creating a directory called `ruby` in the base directory of the staging environment. Create the `/opt/salt-cookbook/staging/ruby/init.sls` file and edit it to have the following contents:

```
install_rvm_key:

  cmd.run:

    - name: "gpg2 --keyserver hkp://keys.gnupg.net --recv-
keys D39DC0E3"

      - shell: /bin/bash

      - unless: "stat /root/.gnupg/trustdb.gpg || gpg2 --list-
keys D39DC0E3"


ruby-1.9.3:

  rvm.installed:

    - default: True

  require:

    - cmd: install_rvm_key


set_ruby:

  cmd.wait:

    - name: 'source /etc/profile.d/rvm.sh; rvm use 1.9.3 --
default'
```

```
    - shell: /bin/bash
    - stateful: False
    - require:
      - rvm: ruby-1.9.3
    - watch:
      - rvm: ruby-1.9.3
```

2. Apply the state to the minion by running the following command:

```
[root@salt-master ~]# salt 'salt-minion' state.sls ruby
saltenv=staging

salt-minion:
----------
          ID: install_rvm_key
    Function: cmd.run
        Name: gpg2 --keyserver hkp://keys.gnupg.net --recv-
keys D39DC0E3
      Result: True
     Comment: gpg: keyring `/root/.gnupg/secring.gpg' created
              gpg: requesting key D39DC0E3 from hkp server
keys.gnupg.net
              gpg: /root/.gnupg/trustdb.gpg: trustdb created
              gpg: key D39DC0E3: public key "Michal Papis (RVM
signing) <mpapis@gmail.com>" imported
              gpg: no ultimately trusted keys found
              gpg: Total number processed: 1
              gpg:               imported: 1  (RSA: 1)
     Started: 21:33:38.481924
    Duration: 1343.254 ms
     Changes:
----------
          ID: ruby-1.9.3
    Function: rvm.installed
      Result: True
     Comment: Successfully installed ruby.
     Started: 20:08:26.575100
    Duration: 679442.523 ms
```

```
        Changes:
                ----------
                ruby-1.9.3:
                        Installed
        ----------
               ID: set_ruby
         Function: cmd.run
             Name: source /etc/profile.d/rvm.sh; rvm use 1.9.3 --
default
           Result: True
          Comment: Command "source /etc/profile.d/rvm.sh; rvm use
1.9.3 --default" run
          Started: 21:09:11.709420
         Duration: 865.603 ms
          Changes:
                ----------
                pid:
                    57408
                retcode:
                    0
                stderr:
                stdout:
                        Using /usr/local/rvm/gems/ruby-1.9.3-p551
```

How it works...

In this recipe, we demonstrated the use of the cmd state, which is used to run commands on the minions. Usually in CentOS, the version of Ruby is older than the recent version; however, the repositories do not have the recent versions from where we can install them. The objective of this recipe is to install a more recent version of Ruby using rvm (Ruby Version Manager), and make sure that the system uses this version of Ruby as the default one.

To execute commands on minions, the state module called `cmd` is used. First, we used the module function `cmd.run` to download and install a public key if it is not present. The `rvm` install process requires this key, and without it the installation fails.

```
install_rvm_key:
  cmd.run:
    - name: "gpg2 --keyserver hkp://keys.gnupg.net --recv-keys D39DC0E3"
    - shell: /bin/bash
    - unless: "stat /root/.gnupg/trustdb.gpg || gpg2 --list-keys D39DC0E3"
```

Here we have mentioned the command to run with the `name` attribute, by giving a generic name to the definition called `install_rvm_key`, and made sure that it uses the bash shell while executing with the `shell` attribute. Also, note that in Ubuntu the default command to do this task is `gpg` and not `gpg2`. We mentioned the `unless` attribute, which makes sure that the definition only runs if the command given in the `unless` attribute returns as `False`, that is, if the `/root/.gnupg/trustdb.gpg` file is not present or if the key is already installed. There is a second `onlyif` attribute, which acts in the same way as `unless`, but it makes sure that the definition runs only when the command mentioned returns `True`.

Next we made a definition for the `ruby-1.9.3` package to be installed, but instead of the system-specific package manager, such as `yum` or `apt-get`, we use the `rvm` package manager. Salt has excellent support for all the well-known package managers available. We will look at package management in more details in *Chapter 5, Advanced Administration Tasks*.

In the end, we made the following definition to make sure that the system uses the newly installed Ruby version:

```
set_ruby:
  cmd.wait:
    - name: 'source /etc/profile.d/rvm.sh; rvm use 1.9.3 -- default'
    - shell: /bin/bash
    - stateful: False
    - require:
      - rvm: ruby-1.9.3
    - watch:
      - rvm: ruby-1.9.3
```

Here we used `cmd.wait` instead of `cmd.run`, which means that the command only runs when there is a change in the definition on which it depends; that is, here it will run only if the `ruby-1.9.3` package is installed, or is upgraded and notifies this definition of a change. The `cmd.run` function generally runs the command, irrespective of the previous definitions. In this command, we tell the system to use the newly installed Ruby version as the default for the system.

Finally, we applied the state to the minion and watch as the definitions are applied sequentially to the minion.

There's more...

The `cmd` state has a few more notable attributes that come in handy when configuring states.

- ▶ `cwd`: This attribute takes a directory path as a value and makes sure that the working directory is changed to this directory before the command is run.

- ▶ `user`: This attribute takes a valid username as the value and makes sure that the command runs as this user.

- ▶ `group`: This attribute takes a valid group name as the value and makes sure that the group context of the running user is changed to this group.

- ▶ `env`: This attribute sets custom environment variables when running the command, and is used as follows:

  ```
  - env :
    - HOME: /usr/local/apache
  ```

- ▶ `creates`: This attribute takes the name or path of a file and makes sure that this file is created when the command runs. The command does not run if this file is already present.

See also

- ▶ `http://docs.saltstack.com/en/latest/ref/states/all/salt.states.cmd.html#module-salt.states.cmd`, for a full list of available `cmd` module options

- ▶ The *Setting host entries and grains* recipe, to learn about setting host entries and grains in the minion

Setting host entries and grains

In this recipe, we will continue with the general administration tasks and look at some more tasks that can be done efficiently with Salt. We will look at how to populate the system hosts file with entries for host lookup and how to populate minions with custom grains.

How to do it...

1. Configure a minion in the staging environment called `stgdc2dbs01`. Do not configure any custom grains on the minion.

2. Create a new state in the staging environment called `hostconfig`.

3. Create and edit `/opt/salt-cookbook/staging/hostconfig/hosts.sls` to have the following entries:

```
ntp-server:
  host.present:
    - ip: 192.168.0.10
```

4. Create and edit `/opt/salt-cookbook/staging/hostconfig/grains.sls` to have the following entries:

```
location:
  grains.present:
    {% if grains['fqdn'][3:6] == "dc1" %}
    - value: dc1
    {% elif grains['fqdn'][3:6] == "dc2" %}
    - value: dc2
    {% endif %}


server_type:
  grains.present:
    {% if grains['fqdn'][6:9] == "app" %}
    - value: app
    {% elif grains['fqdn'][6:9] == "dbs" %}
    - value: db
    {% endif %}
```

5. Create and edit `/opt/salt-cookbook/staging/hostconfig/init.sls` to have the following entries:

```
include:
  - hostconfig.hosts
  - hostconfig.grains
```

6. Apply the states to the minion by running the following command:

```
[root@salt-master ~]#  salt 'stgdc2dbs01' state.sls hostconfig
saltenv=staging

stgdc2dbs01:
----------
          ID: ntp-server
    Function: host.present
      Result: True
     Comment: Added host ntp-server (192.168.0.10)
     Started: 02:10:14.345720
    Duration: 1.566 ms
```

```
            Changes:
                    ----------
                    host:
                        ntp-server
    ----------
            ID: location
      Function: grains.present
        Result: True
       Comment: Set grain location to dc2
       Started: 02:10:14.347494
      Duration: 9048.129 ms
       Changes:
                    ----------
                    location:
                        dc2
    ----------
            ID: server_type
      Function: grains.present
        Result: True
       Comment: Set grain server_type to db
       Started: 02:10:23.395788
      Duration: 74.828 ms
       Changes:
                    ----------
                    server_type:
                        db


Summary
------------
Succeeded: 3 (changed=3)
Failed:    0
------------
Total states run:     3
```

How it works...

In this recipe, we demonstrated the methods to populate host entries in the /etc/hosts file of the minions, and also to populate custom grains in the minions based on certain conditions.

First, we looked at the state configuration for host entries. The host state module is quite simple to use and takes the IP address and the hostname to populate in the /etc/hosts file. In this demonstration, we mentioned one IP address and one corresponding hostname to be added. However, multiple hostnames can be easily added for an IP address in the following manner:

```
ntp-server:
  host.present:
    - ip: 192.168.0.10
    - names:
      - ntp-server
      - stgdc1adm01
```

If a host entry is changed, the existing one does not get removed automatically and has to be removed using the host.absent state function.

Next we configured a couple of grain definitions. We made use of Salt conditionals, and configured the states to check certain substrings of the hostname and create custom grains based on the substring.

```
location:
  grains.present:
    {% if grains['fqdn'][3:6] == "dc1" %}
    - value: dc1
    {% elif grains['fqdn'][3:6] == "dc2" %}
    - value: dc2
    {% endif %}
```

As we can see, even this state is quite simple to use as we just have to mention the grain name and the value it will contain. For this task, we make use of the grains.present state function. If there are multiple values that need to be added for a grain, the grains.append function can be used where an additional value is added to an already existing grain. In the case of adding multiple values to a grain or if the grain has a single initial value, though it may be the case that multiple values need to be added at a later time, the grains.list_present needs to be used instead of grains.present. This stores the multiple values in the form of a Python list. To remove grains, grains.absent and grains.list_absent can be used as required.

In this recipe, we introduced a method to run multiple state files at the same time through including them in the init.sls file of the state. We include each of the state files in the init.sls file, and when we call the state when applying to the minion, all the state files listed in the init.sls file get applied to the minion.

Corresponding execution modules can also be used to perform these tasks on the minion from the command line. To configure host entries, the `hosts` execution modules can be used; while to configure grains, the `grains` execution module can be used with respective parameters. The functions used for the tasks in the execution modules are almost the same in all cases as in the state modules.

See also

▸ `http://docs.saltstack.com/en/latest/ref/states/all/salt.states.host.html#module-salt.states.host`, to learn more about the host module

▸ The *Setting time zone, locale, and kernel configuration*, recipe, to learn how to configure time zones, locale, and manipulate kernel configuration parameters in the minions

Setting time zone, locale, and kernel configurations

In this recipe, we will see some simple yet important system configurations, with the help of respective Salt modules. We will learn how to set time zones, locales, and manage kernel parameter configurations.

How to do it...

We will use the same minion as the previous recipe. We will also use the same state `hostconfig`, and new configurations will be added in new files.

1. Create and edit `/opt/salt-cookbook/staging/hostconfig/timezone.sls` to have the following entries:

```
{% if grains['location'] == "dc1" %}
Asia/Singapore:
{% elif grains['location'] == "dc2" %}
Europe/Amsterdam:
{% endif %}
  timezone.system
```

2. Create and edit `/opt/salt-cookbook/staging/hostconfig/locale.sls` to have the following entries:

```
en_US.UTF-8:
  locale.system
```

3. Create and edit `/opt/salt-cookbook/staging/hostconfig/sysctl.sls` to have the following entries:

```
net.ipv4.conf.default.rp_filter:
  sysctl.present:
    - value: 1

net.ipv4.tcp_syncookies:
  sysctl.present:
    - value: 1
```

4. Edit `/opt/salt-cookbook/staging/hostconfig/init.sls` to have the following entries:

```
include:
  - hostconfig.timezone
  - hostconfig.locale
  - hostconfig.sysctl
```

5. Run the following command to apply the states to the minion:

```
[root@salt-master ~]#  salt 'stgdc2dbs01' state.sls hostconfig
saltenv=staging

Stgdc2dbs01:
----------
            ID: Europe/Amsterdam
      Function: timezone.system
        Result: True
       Comment: Set timezone Europe/Amsterdam
       Started: 20:35:57.815599
      Duration: 25200058.248 ms
       Changes:
                ----------
                timezone:
                    Europe/Amsterdam
----------
            ID: en_US.UTF-8
      Function: locale.system
        Result: True
       Comment: System locale en_US.UTF-8 already set
       Started: 03:35:57.874268
      Duration: 10.126 ms
```

```
        Changes:
   ----------
            ID: net.ipv4.conf.default.rp_filter
      Function: sysctl.present
        Result: True
       Comment: Updated sysctl value
  net.ipv4.conf.default.rp_filter = 1
       Started: 03:35:57.884810
      Duration: 89.463 ms
        Changes:
                  ----------
                  net.ipv4.conf.default.rp_filter:
                      1
   ----------
            ID: net.ipv4.tcp_syncookies
      Function: sysctl.present
        Result: True
       Comment: Updated sysctl value net.ipv4.tcp_syncookies = 1
       Started: 03:35:57.974604
      Duration: 90.242 ms
        Changes:
                  ----------
                  net.ipv4.tcp_syncookies:
                      1


Summary
------------
Succeeded: 4 (changed=3)
Failed:    0
------------
Total states run:     4
```

How it works...

In this recipe, we demonstrated the procedure to configure a few more general system properties, such as the time zone, locale, and the kernel parameters in the sysctl.conf file. All the module uses are fairly simple and easily customizable.

First, we configured the time zone in the file called `timezone.sls` under the `hostconfig` state directory. We used conditionals to decide the location of the minion based on the custom location grain, and assign the appropriate time zone from the list of time zones found under `/usr/share/zoneinfo`. The `timezone.system` module function has been used to set the time zone. However, there is no function to remove the time zone, if it needs to be changed. Changing the zone in the SLS file will update the minion when the state is applied.

Next we configured the locale of the minion, using the `locale.system` module. It takes the name of the locale as the parameter, makes sure the system locale is the same as the parameter, and updates it if the value is something else.

Finally, we configured the state file to update the values of a few kernel parameters in the minion. There are lots of performance tuning and optimization parameters available in a Linux system and they reside in the file `/etc/sysctl.conf`. The appropriate values of the parameters need to be updated alongside these parameters in the file for the system to identify and use them. The `sysctl.present` module function is used to update the values of these parameters. It takes the name of the parameter and its value as the arguments, and makes sure that they are updated in the `/etc/sysctl.conf` file. Here, we demonstrated a couple of these parameters that are required for some network-related functions, such as route verification and protection against a certain type of network attack. We see that Salt successfully updates the values of the parameters on the minion.

See also

▸ The *Handling archive files* recipe, to learn how to handle and extract archived files

Handling archive files

In infrastructure management, we often face situations when a certain package or tool is not available as a system package, but needs to be fetched and extracted to a certain location in the system to be made available for use. To complete these kinds of tasks, often remote commands are used. However, Salt has a solution to this problem, and you will learn how to handle archive files in this recipe.

How to do it...

1. We will use a new minion called `salt-minion` in the staging environment. Create a new state directory in the staging environment called `tomcat`.

2. Create and edit `/opt/salt-cookbook/staging/tomcat/package.sls` to have the following entries:

```
tomcat-server:
  archive:
```

```
    - extracted
    - name: /opt/
    - source: http://mirror.nus.edu.sg/apache/tomcat/tomcat-
6/v6.0.43/bin/apache-tomcat-6.0.43.tar.gz
      - source_hash: md5=0abbb1852a608c8b4ccb7003c700337b
      - archive_format: tar
      - if_missing: /opt/apache-tomcat-6.0.43/
```

3. Apply this state to the minion by running the following command:

```
[root@salt-master ~]# salt 'salt-minion' state.sls
tomcat.package saltenv=staging

salt-minion:
----------
          ID: tomcat-server
    Function: archive.extracted
        Name: /opt/
      Result: True
     Comment: http://mirror.nus.edu.sg/apache/tomcat/tomcat-
6/v6.0.43/bin/apache-tomcat-6.0.43.tar.gz extracted in /opt/
     Started: 04:46:34.347868
    Duration: 8377.282 ms
     Changes:
              ----------
              directories_created:
                  - /opt/
                  - /opt/apache-tomcat-6.0.43/
              extracted_files:
                  - apache-tomcat-6.0.43/bin/catalina.sh
                  - apache-tomcat-6.0.43/bin/daemon.sh

                  .
                  .
                  .

                  - apache-tomcat-
6.0.43/webapps/manager/status.xsd
                  - apache-tomcat-
6.0.43/webapps/manager/xform.xsl
```

```
Summary
------------
Succeeded: 1 (changed=1)
Failed:     0
------------
Total states run:      1
```

4. Apply the state to the minion again:

```
[root@salt-master ~]# salt 'salt-minion' state.sls
tomcat.package saltenv=staging
salt-minion:
----------
          ID: tomcat-server
    Function: archive.extracted
        Name: /opt/
      Result: True
     Comment: /opt/apache-tomcat-6.0.43/ already exists
     Started: 04:47:34.807034
    Duration: 0.854 ms
     Changes:

Summary
------------
Succeeded: 1
Failed:     0
------------
Total states run:      1
```

How it works...

In this recipe, we demonstrated the `archive` state module that has been added to Salt very recently. Usually, it appears that administrators and engineers prefer to use the archived package for the Apache Tomcat application server instead of the one which comes with the package manager repository. This is because the archived package gives them greater flexibility to configure and customize it, and also to resolve dependencies which the application might have on a specific version of the application server. There were various ways to achieve this, that is, by writing a script to fetch the archive file and extract it to the desired location, by creating the `rpm` or `deb` packages from the archive file contents, and others. We can use the archive module in Salt to achieve this objective in a very simplistic manner.

First, we gave a generic name for the definition, that is, `tomcat-server`. Next we mentioned the function name of the module to be used to perform the extraction function:

```
- extracted
```

We then mentioned the path of the location where the file needs to be extracted to, that is, `/opt/`, with the `name` attribute:

```
- name: /opt/
```

Next we mentioned the source URL of the file that needs to be downloaded with the `source` attribute:

```
- source: http://mirror.nus.edu.sg/apache/tomcat/tomcat-
6/v6.0.43/bin/apache-tomcat-6.0.43.tar.gz
```

The next parameter, `source_hash`, allows us to define the md5 hash value that is used to compare against the downloaded package to verify if the file has been downloaded correctly. The hash value is usually available at the location from where the file is being downloaded:

```
- source_hash: md5=0abbb1852a608c8b4ccb7003c700337b
```

Next we mentioned the format of the archive that is being extracted with the `archive_format` attribute. Here the format is TAR. The other available formats are ZIP and RAR.

```
- archive_format: tar
```

Finally, we have put in a condition to verify if the extracted directory already exists on the minion and in the same location, or not. If the directory exists, the extract operation will not execute. We do this with the `if_missing` attribute:

```
- if_missing: /opt/apache-tomcat-6.0.43/
```

The `archive_user` attribute is used to mention the file that needs to be extracted, if any, to the user. Also, the `tar_options` attribute is used to mention any additional options preferred if the archive format is TAR.

See also

▶   `http://docs.saltstack.com/en/latest/ref/states/all/salt.states.archive.html#module-salt.states.archive`, to learn more about the archive model
▶   The *Adding groups and users* recipe, to learn how to configure groups and users

Adding groups and users

Users and groups constitute some of the fundamental components of any infrastructure, starting from users logging in to systems, to running applications and databases as a particular user. In this recipe, you will learn how to configure users and groups with Salt.

How to do it...

Configure a minion called `salt-minion` in the staging environment, and create two states called `groups` and `users` by creating respective directories for them. In the base pillar directory of the staging environment, create two directories called `groups` and `users`.

1. Create and edit `/opt/salt-cookbook/pillar/staging/groups/init.sls` to have the following entries:

   ```
   app_group:
     group_name: stg-app
     group_id: 2001
   ```

2. Create and edit `/opt/salt-cookbook/pillar/staging/users/init.sls` to have the following entries:

   ```
   app_user:
     user_name: stg-app
     user_id: 5001
     user_passwd: '$1$NNTmEkPc$accotn129NokBn/d9C224/'
   ```

3. Edit `/opt/salt-cookbook/pillar/staging/top.sls` to have the following entries:

   ```
   staging:
     '*':
       - groups
       - users
   ```

4. Create and edit `/opt/salt-cookbook/staging/groups/init.sls` to have the following entries:

   ```
   {{ pillar['app_group']['group_name'] }}:
     group.present:
       - gid: {{ pillar['app_group']['group_id'] }}
   ```

5. Create and edit `/opt/salt-cookbook/staging/users/init.sls` to have the following entries:

    ```
    include:
      - groups

    generic_app_user:
      user.present:
        - name: {{ pillar['app_user']['user_name'] }}
        - fullname: Staging App User
        - shell: /bin/sh
        - home: /home/{{ pillar['app_user']['user_name'] }}
        - uid: {{ pillar['app_user']['user_id'] }}
        - gid: {{ pillar['app_group']['group_id'] }}
        - password: {{ pillar['app_user']['user_passwd'] }}
        - require:
          - group: {{ pillar['app_group']['group_name'] }}
    ```

6. Edit `/opt/salt-cookbook/staging/top.sls` to have the following entries:

    ```
    staging:
      '*':
        - groups
        - users
    ```

7. Apply the states to the minion with the following command:

    ```
    [root@salt-master ~]# salt 'salt-minion' state.highstate
    saltenv=staging

    salt-minion:
    ----------
              ID: stg-app
        Function: group.present
          Result: True
         Comment: The following group attributes are set to be
    changed:
                  gid: 2001
         Started: 01:19:23.457135
        Duration: 305.786 ms
         Changes:
                  ----------
                  Final:
                      All Changed applied successfully
    ----------
    ```

```
            ID: generic_app_user
      Function: user.present
          Name: stg-app
        Result: True
       Comment: Updated user stg-app
       Started: 01:19:23.763305
      Duration: 654.397 ms
       Changes:
                ----------
                fullname:
                    Staging App User
                lstchg:
                    16408
                passwd:
                    $1$NNTmEkPc$accotn129NokBn/d9C224/
                shell:
                    /bin/sh
                uid:
                    5001


Summary
------------
Succeeded: 2 (changed=2)
Failed:    0
------------
Total states run:     2
```

How it works...

In this recipe, we demonstrated how to configure groups and users on minions with Salt. We made use of pillars as discussed in the *Understanding and configuring Salt pillars* recipe in *Chapter 1, Salt Architecture and Components*. The objective of this recipe is to add a generic application group using the group name and group ID from the pillar data. This is followed by adding a generic application user, using the group ID of the group that we added earlier as the group for the user, while using most of the user information from the pillar data.

First, we created two pillar directories called `groups` and `users` for the group and user information to be stored, respectively. We added the key-value pairs of the group and the user in the `init.sls` files of each of these directories and made sure that they were available to the minion by editing the `top.sls` file of the pillar directory of the staging environment and adding the following entries:

```
staging:
  '*':
    - groups
    - users
```

To limit these pillars to application servers, the grain matcher can be used as follows:

```
'server_type:app':
  - match: grain
```

Now that the pillar data has been configured, we added the group definition using the `group.present` function:

```
{{ pillar['app_group']['group_name'] }}:
  group.present:
    - gid: {{ pillar['app_group']['group_id'] }}
```

There is a `group.absent` function to make sure that mentioned groups are removed from minions. The `group.present` definition has a useful attribute called `system` which, if set to `True`, sets the group as a system group. A list of users can also be added to and removed from the group using the following method:

```
- addusers:
  - tom
  - harry
- delusers:
  - ben
```

If the `members` attribute is used instead of `addusers` with a list of users, it tells Salt to remove the existing users and replace them with the new list of users.

Next we defined the user along with the required options, fetching some data from pillars and providing the rest in the definition. In this file, we included the `groups` state as follows:

```
include:
  - groups
```

This was done so that the user definition could be made dependent on the group definition with the `require` attribute. Without the `include` statement, the `require` attribute will not work.

The user module has numerous options to provide granular control over the user addition process and all of the options can be found at `http://docs.saltstack.com/en/latest/ref/states/all/salt.states.user.html#module-salt.states.user`.

Finally, we added both the `groups` and the `users` states to the `top.sls` file of the staging environment and applied the states to the minion by running the `salt` command with the `state.highstate` module function.

See also

▶ `http://docs.saltstack.com/en/latest/ref/states/all/salt.states.group.html#module-salt.states.group` and `http://docs.saltstack.com/en/latest/ref/states/all/salt.states.user.html#module-salt.states.user`, to learn more about the `group` and `user` modules

▶ The *Performing SSH authentication tasks* recipe, to learn how to configure SSH keys and files

Performing SSH authentication tasks

Managing SSH keys and the associated files is a key task that needs to be performed in most infrastructure at present to facilitate a number of functions with remote access between servers. Although this task can be achieved by propagating files to the minions using the file module, Salt has a better way to do it using SSH-specific modules. In this recipe, you will learn how to use these modules.

How to do it...

1. Configure two minions called `salt-minion` and `backup-server`. Configure the `server_type` grain of `salt-minion` to have the value `app` and the backup server's value to be `backup`.

2. Create a new state called `sshauth`, and create two files inside this directory called `pubkey.sls` and `known_hosts.sls`. Also create a directory called `sshkeys` inside the `sshauth` directory.

    We will assume that the `groups` and `users` modules, configured in the last recipe, have been applied on both the minions.

3. On the `salt-minion` minion, change to the `stg-app` user, and run the following command to generate a SSH key pair and display the contents of the public key file:

    ```
    [stg-app@salt-minion ~]$ ssh-keygen
    Generating public/private rsa key pair.
    ```

```
Enter file in which to save the key (/home/stg-
app/.ssh/id_rsa):

Created directory '/home/stg-app/.ssh'.

Enter passphrase (empty for no passphrase):

Enter same passphrase again:

Your identification has been saved in /home/stg-
app/.ssh/id_rsa.

Your public key has been saved in /home/stg-
app/.ssh/id_rsa.pub.

The key fingerprint is:

a6:e7:7a:dc:f0:8b:ea:1e:b3:59:fa:6a:e2:0e:b9:06 stg-app@salt-
minion

The key's randomart image is:

+--[ RSA 2048]----+
|                 |
|                 |
|                 |
|                 |
|        S        |
|E   o.           |
| .o   +.o+       |
| .o. .Xo.o       |
| ..oo=X*+ ..     |
+-----------------+
```

```
[stg-app@salt-minion ~]$ cat .ssh/id_rsa.pub
```

```
ssh-rsa
AAAAB3NzaC1yc2EAAAABIwAAAQEAzn3+9ltpiTfA/I3LNhPmOy52WRw+EElhx6
/fc5gQImSCD7/FWMOzc05gfLfCIXIm17hUyJ5zeYa5xavZu8IYtFzK7CTHnS+i
JYvnVJf1aidjCeKz9q1CRk/RvrSCykZM04nuwTTzf1/KgNnwuuMhDqpoXU7DW0
hHrCpxkEPgixowlvVxr81Go/Tlpf9kSCA8yPvbetb6obf8AS9IYHz8q/HFTvfD
XaAkrautaWu+6PBxiLgO0Qu4kXXKynQe2LcjhSYDeQ/jF1f5UR0WXvIZAwIOQ6
K5efiBITSM2uI9Cj5ibKBtowUtHJ6LVsBkm5XbZOfSVZzY98SsKwV5ZYfIUw==
stg-app@salt-minion
```

4. Copy over the /home/stg-app/.ssh/id_rsa.pub file to the /opt/salt-cookbook/staging/sshauth/sshkeys directory as stg-app.id_rsa.pub.

5. Now from `salt-minion`, try to access the backup server via SSH. Answer `no` when asked for confirmation to connect:

    [stg-app@salt-minion ~]$ ssh backup-server

    The authenticity of host 'backup-server (192.168.0.20)' can't be established.

    RSA key fingerprint is 21:28:71:ad:65:92:90:a6:28:6a:37:08:eb:e1:a 6:7a.

    Are you sure you want to continue connecting (yes/no)? no

    Host key verification failed.

6. Edit the `/opt/salt-cookbook/staging/sshauth/pubkey.sls` file to have the following contents:

    ```
    stg_app_ssh_pubkey:
      ssh_auth:
        - present
        - user: {{ pillar['app_user']['user_name'] }}
        - enc: ssh-rsa
        - source: salt://sshauth/sshkeys/{{
    pillar['app_user']['user_name'] }}.id_rsa.pub
    ```

7. Edit the `/opt/salt-cookbook/staging/sshauth/known_hosts.sls` file to have the following contents:

    ```
    backup-server:
      ssh_known_hosts:
        - present
        - user: {{ pillar['app_user']['user_name'] }}
        - fingerprint:
    21:28:71:ad:65:92:90:a6:28:6a:37:08:eb:e1:a6:7a
    ```

8. Now edit the `top.sls` file of the staging environment to have the following entries:

    ```
    staging:
      '*':
        - groups
        - users

      'server_type:app':
        - match: grain
        - sshauth.known_hosts

      'server_type:backup':
        - match: grain
        - sshauth.pubkey
    ```

9. Apply the states to the minions with the following command:

```
[root@salt-master ~]# salt 'salt-minion,backup-server'
state.highstate saltenv=staging
salt-minion:
----------
          ID: backup-server
    Function: ssh_known_hosts.present
      Result: True
     Comment: backup-server's key saved to .ssh/known_hosts
(fingerprint: 21:28:71:ad:65:92:90:a6:28:6a:37:08:eb:e1:a6:7a)
     Started: 03:35:59.197138
    Duration: 91.285 ms
     Changes:
              ----------
              new:
                  ----------
                  enc:
                      ssh-rsa
                  fingerprint:
                      21:28:71:ad:65:92:90:a6:28:6a:37:08:eb:e1:a6
:7a
                  hostname:
                      |1|7eZ59Y6ZydJI1+dhNdnnq31zffw=|ulGEOz7RexT/
fYKBtU181CGeT/Y=
                  key:

AAAAB3NzaC1yc2EAAAABIwAAAQEAkcbBayw81UWDqNALQY+gmqt9BnGxnM3U+T
FR3wCimu8POBtHbdPHqq47WtaVQzmpCOeUmGGrgwToGddr1f2U/CjbNO4TdwKw
26TZmT1K8GTHtd1PVBFRv9mZBonBB3TfRaGfmxyq6jq4/Rz1tTmnNqe0Civ/AZ
zy01u41pPgUvrTx7xebCBq4zD75iuQ5I+50jW3k9YwE+vcNIHXBWYRwaPM57XP
GhGiL4p+5OLzWNBLkCwXDrWc5toPjO7Yfk8TiESoaH0zjhnn1hqydAsXwGd9AB
FkQjv7StwoU1zacBe4E3nm3+xTWS5QKDeWiWs3uwS6+XSoMJe3rkC1NVOa7w==
              old:
                  None


backup-server:
----------
          ID: stg_app_ssh_pubkey
    Function: ssh_auth.present
```

```
        Result: True
        Comment: The authorized host key stg_app_ssh_pubkey for
user stg-app was added
        Started: 02:30:10.080032
       Duration: 851.585 ms
        Changes:
                ----------
                stg_app_ssh_pubkey:
                    New

Summary
------------
Succeeded: 2 (changed=2)
Failed:    0
------------
Total states run:      2
```

How it works...

In this recipe, we demonstrated the usage of modules for SSH-specific activities. The objective of this recipe is that two minions, called `salt-minion` (with grain `server_type` and value of `app`) and backup-server (with `server_type` grain and value of `backup`) are configured. Both the minions have the same user configured. On `salt-minion`, we generate a user SSH key pair and configure the Salt state to add the public key of this pair to the backup-server's user `authorized_keys` file so that when the key-based authentication takes place the backup server identifies the private key coming from `salt-minion`, and the authentication takes place successfully.

When the SSH connection takes place, and even when the keys are in place, the system asks for a confirmation to the connecting system's user asking if the connection can be completed. In automated processes, like scripts, this confirmation step does not let the connection complete. Hence, we have taken the fingerprint of the destination server and configured a state to add the backup-server's authentication data to the `known_hosts` file of `salt-minion`. When this whole procedure is done, the SSH connection can take place from `salt-minion` to the backup server without any problems. To find out in detail about the SSH authentication procedure, please refer to the appropriate documentation mentioned in the *See also* section later in the text. Let's now analyze our recipe.

First, we generated an SSH key pair in `salt-minion` and found out the contents of the public key file. Next we tried to connect to the backup server from `salt-minion` and got the fingerprint of the backup server while doing so.

```
RSA key fingerprint is
21:28:71:ad:65:92:90:a6:28:6a:37:08:eb:e1:a6:7a
```

We then copied over the public key file to the Salt path for the `sshauth` state that we created in the staging environment.

Next we created a new file called `pubkey.sls` with the following contents:

```
stg_app_ssh_pubkey:
  ssh_auth:
    - present
    - user: {{ pillar['app_user']['user_name'] }}
    - enc: ssh-rsa
    - source: salt://sshauth/sshkeys/{{
pillar['app_user']['user_name'] }}.id_rsa.pub
```

We used the `ssh_auth` module to add the public key of the SSH key pair that we had generated on backup server. The source of the file is mentioned as the file that we had copied over to the Salt path. An alternate way to do this will be to save the contents of the file in a pillar definition:

```
stg_app_ssh_pubkey:
  key:
'AAAAB3NzaC1yc2EAAAABIwAAAQEAzn3+9ltpiTfA/I3LNhPmOy52WRw+EElhx6/fc5gQ
ImSCD7/FWMOzc05gfLfCIXIm17hUyJ5zeYa5xavZu8IYtFzK7CTHnS+iJYvnVJflaidjC
eKz9q1CRk/RvrSCykZM04nuwTTzf1/KgNnwuuMhDqpoXU7DW0hHrCpxkEPgixowlvVxr8
1Go/T1pf9kSCA8yPvbetb6obf8AS9IYHz8q/HFTvfDXaAkrautaWu+6PBxiLgO0Qu4kXX
KynQe2LcjhSYDeQ/jFlf5UR0WXvIZAwIOQ6K5efiBITSM2uI9Cj5ibKBtowUtHJ6LVsBk
m5XbZOfSVZzY98SsKwV5ZYfIUw=='
```

Then, write the `ssh_auth` definition as follows:

```
{{ pillar['stg_app_ssh_pubkey']['key'] }}:
  ssh_auth:
    - present
    - user: {{ pillar['app_user']['user_name'] }}
    - enc: ssh-rsa
```

Next we configured the definition to populate the `known_hosts` file on `salt-minion` as follows:

```
backup-server:
  ssh_known_hosts:
    - present
    - user: {{ pillar['app_user']['user_name'] }}
    - fingerprint: 21:28:71:ad:65:92:90:a6:28:6a:37:08:eb:e1:a6:7a
```

We used the `ssh_known_hosts` module and the fingerprint that we received while trying to connect from `salt-minion` to the backup server manually. The fingerprint can also be saved as pillar data and accessed accordingly.

Finally, we updated the `top.sls` file of the staging environment to apply the appropriate state files to the minions based on the grain data:

```
'server_type:app':
  - match: grain
  - sshauth.known_hosts

'server_type:backup':
  - match: grain
  - sshauth.pubkey
```

After the states are applied successfully, a manual attempt to connect from `salt-minion` to backup server will succeed without any problem.

See also

▶ Links `http://docs.saltstack.com/en/latest/ref/states/all/salt.states.ssh_auth.html#module-salt.states.ssh_auth` and `http://docs.saltstack.com/en/latest/ref/states/all/salt.states.ssh_known_hosts.html#module-salt.states.ssh_known_hosts`, to learn more about the modules for SSH tasks

▶ The *Scheduling jobs with cron* recipe, to learn how to configure scheduled jobs with cron

Scheduling jobs with cron

There are numerous occasions, no matter which infrastructure tier we work in, that we need to run automated tasks at some point of the day, week, month, and so on. In Linux systems, this functionality is achieved with cron. In this module, you will learn how to configure cron jobs using Salt modules.

How to do it...

We will use the `salt-minion` minion that we configured in the previous recipe.

1. Create a new state called `cron` in the staging environment.

2. Create and edit the `/opt/salt-cookbook/staging/cron/init.sls` file to have the following entries:

```
clean_tomcat_logs:
  cron.present:
    - name: find /opt/apache-tomcat-6.0.43/logs/ -mtime +30
-exec rm -rf {} \;
    - user: root
    - minute: 00
    - hour: 01
    - daymonth: '*'
    - month: '*'
    - dayweek: '*'
```

3. Apply the state to the minion:

```
[root@salt-master ~]# salt 'salt-minion' state.sls cron
saltenv=staging

salt-minion:
----------
          ID: clean_tomcat_logs
    Function: cron.present
        Name: find /opt/apache-tomcat-6.0.43/logs/ -mtime +30
-exec rm -rf {} \;
      Result: True
     Comment: Cron find /opt/apache-tomcat-6.0.43/logs/ -mtime
+30 -exec rm -rf {} \; added to root's crontab
     Started: 03:54:17.521898
    Duration: 97.139 ms
     Changes:
              ----------
              root:
                  find /opt/apache-tomcat-6.0.43/logs/ -mtime
+30 -exec rm -rf {} \;
```

```
Summary
------------
Succeeded: 1 (changed=1)
Failed:    0
------------
Total states run:    1
```

How it works...

In this recipe, we demonstrated the use of the `cron` module to add cron jobs to minions. The objective of the recipe is to add a cron job to the root user's account, which will look for log files older than 30 days in the Tomcat server's log directory and delete them, and it will run at 1:00 am every day.

First, we gave a generic name to the definition called `clean_tomcat_logs` for identification purpose. We then used the `cron.present` module function to make sure that the following cron entry is present.

Next, the command to be executed is mentioned with the `name` attribute:

```
- name: find /opt/apache-tomcat-6.0.43/logs/ -mtime +30 -exec rm -rf
{} \;
```

An alternate way to do this will be to get rid of the `name` attribute and specify the command in the place of the generic name given. If there are multiple commands to be executed, a script can be written and the path of the script can be specified with the name attribute.

We then specified the user that will have this cron entry, that is, `root` in our case.

Next we mentioned the time of the job execution with the `minute`, `hour`, `daymonth`, `month`, and `dayweek` attributes. If any of the attributes are not mentioned, the default value is *.

There are other module functions, such as `cron.absent`, to remove cron entries.

See also

- ▶ `http://docs.saltstack.com/en/latest/ref/states/all/salt.states.cron.html#module-salt.states.cron`, for a full list of available functions
- ▶ The *Managing volumes* recipe, to learn how to configure efficient disk layouts with logical volume management

Managing volumes

Running out of disk space and having to provision new storage is something that cannot be overlooked in infrastructure management. To make this process simpler, volume management was introduced. Although there are a lot of proprietary products out there to do this job, the default Linux volume management tool or LVM, is an excellent choice to get started, and lot of critical production infrastructure relies on this tool. Salt makes configuring LVM much easier with its `lvm` module.

How to do it...

We will use the minion backup server from the recipe SSH authentication tasks earlier in this chapter. Make sure that the minion has two new identical disks called `/dev/sdb` and `/dev/sdc` (these can be different based on host architecture and platform).

1. Create a new state directory in the staging environment called `lvm`.

2. Create and edit `/opt/salt-cookbook/staging/lvm/init.sls` to have the following entries:

```
/dev/sdb:
  lvm.pv_present

/dev/sdc:
  lvm.pv_present

backup_vg:
  lvm.vg_present:
    - devices: /dev/sdb,/dev/sdc
    - require:
      - lvm: /dev/sdb
      - lvm: /dev/sdc

backup_lv:
  lvm.lv_present:
    - vgname: backup_vg
    - size: 4G
    - require:
      - lvm: backup_vg
```

3. Apply the state to the minion with the following command:

```
[root@salt-master ~]# salt 'backup-server' state.sls lvm
saltenv=staging

backup-server:
```

```
----------
            ID: /dev/sdb
      Function: lvm.pv_present
        Result: True
       Comment: Created Physical Volume /dev/sdb
       Started: 01:28:27.726869
      Duration: 861.501 ms
       Changes:    Invalid Changes data:    Physical volume
"/dev/sdb" successfully created
----------
            ID: /dev/sdc
      Function: lvm.pv_present
        Result: True
       Comment: Created Physical Volume /dev/sdc
       Started: 01:28:28.588727
      Duration: 579.202 ms
       Changes:    Invalid Changes data:    Physical volume
"/dev/sdc" successfully created
----------
            ID: backup_vg
      Function: lvm.vg_present
        Result: True
       Comment: Created Volume Group backup_vg
       Started: 01:39:10.230161
      Duration: 698.282 ms
       Changes:
                  ----------
                  Output from vgcreate:
                      Volume group "backup_vg" successfully
created
                  backup_vg:
                  ----------
    .
    .
    .

                      Volume Group Name:
                          backup_vg
```

```
                    Volume Group Size (kB):
                        10477568
                    Volume Group Status:
                        772

    - - - - - - - - - -
                ID: backup_lv
          Function: lvm.lv_present
            Result: True
           Comment: Created Logical Volume backup_lv
           Started: 01:39:10.929286
          Duration: 868.571 ms
           Changes:
                    - - - - - - - - - -
                    /dev/backup_vg/backup_lv:
                        - - - - - - - - - -

    .

    .

    .

                    Volume Group Name:
                        backup_vg
                    Output from lvcreate:
                        Logical volume "backup_lv" created


Summary
- - - - - - - - - - - -
Succeeded: 4 (changed=4)
Failed:    0
- - - - - - - - - - - -
Total states run:    4
```

How it works...

In this recipe, we demonstrated the ability of Salt to perform logical volume management using the lvm module. In LVM, a volume group is created using multiple physical disks configured as physical volumes. Logical volumes are created on these volume groups, which are formatted to have a filesystem and then mounted.

First, we created and configured the physical disks to be physical volumes so that they are identified in the correct format while creating volume groups. This is done using the `lvm.pv_present` module function.

```
/dev/sdb:
  lvm.pv_present
```

Next, the volume group is created by providing a name for the volume, that is, `backup_vg`. The list of disks in comma-separated format will be used to create the volume group.

```
backup_vg:
  lvm.vg_present:
    - devices: /dev/sdb,/dev/sdc
```

A dependency has also been created with the physical volume definitions.

Finally, the logical volume definition is created by providing a name for the logical volume, the volume group to be used to create it, and the size of the volume.

```
backup_lv:
  lvm.lv_present:
    - vgname: backup_vg
    - size: 4G
```

A few other options are also available such as `extent`, `snapshot`, `stripes`, and `stripesize`.

For each of the LVM components, a corresponding `absent` function is also available to remove them if necessary.

See also

- `http://docs.saltstack.com/en/latest/ref/states/all/salt.states.lvm.html#module-salt.states.lvm`, to learn more about volume management
- The *Working with disks and mounts* recipe, to learn how to configure and get details about disks and mounts

Working with disks and mounts

Working with disks, configuring their mount points, and gathering useful data about them at times of emergency are some of the most critical tasks in system management. In this recipe, you will learn how Salt helps us perform all of these tasks efficiently.

How to do it...

We will use the same minion and logical volume configured in the previous recipe.

1. Create a new state directory called `disk`.

2. Create and edit `/opt/salt-cookbook/staging/disk/format.sls` to have the following entries:

```
include:
  - lvm

backup_volume:
  blockdev.formatted:
    - name: /dev/backup_vg/backup_lv
    - fs_type: ext4
    - require:
      - lvm: backup_lv
```

3. Create and edit `/opt/salt-cookbook/staging/disk/mount.sls` to have the following entries:

```
include:
  - disk.format

backup_mount:
  mount.mounted:
    - name: /backup
    - device: /dev/backup_vg/backup_lv
    - fstype: ext4
    - mkmnt: True
    - opts: defaults
    - persist: True
    - mount: True
    - dump: 0
    - pass_num: 0
    - require:
      - blockdev: backup_volume
```

4. Create and edit `/opt/salt-cookbook/staging/disk/init.sls` to have the following entries:

```
include:
  - disk.format
  - disk.mount
```

5. Apply the states to the minion with the following command:

```
[root@salt-master ~]# salt 'backup-server' state.sls disk
saltenv=staging
backup-server:
----------
  .
  .
  .
----------
          ID: backup_volume
    Function: blockdev.formatted
        Name: /dev/backup_vg/backup_lv
      Result: True
     Comment: /dev/backup_vg/backup_lv has been formatted with
ext4
     Started: 01:59:16.660068
    Duration: 1150.85 ms
     Changes:
              ----------
              new:
                    ext4
              old:
                    ext4
----------
          ID: backup_mount
    Function: mount.mounted
        Name: /backup
      Result: True
     Comment: Target was successfully mounted. Added new entry
to the fstab.
     Started: 02:05:04.451058
    Duration: 121.623 ms
     Changes:
              ----------
              mount:
                    True
```

```
                    persist:

                        new


        Summary
        - - - - - - - - - - - -
        Succeeded: 6  (changed=2)

        Failed:    0
        - - - - - - - - - - - -
        Total states run:      6
```

How it works...

In this recipe, we demonstrated Salt's ability to work with disks, filesystems, and mount points. The objective of the recipe is to create a filesystem on the logical volume created in the previous recipe, and mount it on a specified mount point, all the while maintaining the dependency between the definitions.

First, we created a separate file for defining the format operation called `format.sls`. We then defined the format operation as follows:

```
include:
  - lvm

backup_volume:
  blockdev.formatted:
    - name: /dev/backup_vg/backup_lv
    - fs_type: ext4
    - require:
      - lvm: backup_lv
```

We first included the `lvm` state so that we could create a dependency of the format definition with the LVM definition. We then provided a generic name for the format operation and mentioned the module to use, that is, `blockdev.formatted`.

We then mentioned the name of the device to format and the filesystem which should be created on it:

```
fs_type: ext4
```

At the end, we made this definition depend on the definition for the logical volume, as the format operation takes place on the logical volume.

We then created a separate file for the mount operation called `mount.sls` and defined the mount operation as follows:

```
include:
  - disk.format

backup_mount:
  mount.mounted:
    - name: /backup
    - device: /dev/backup_vg/backup_lv
    - fstype: ext4
    - mkmnt: True
    - opts: defaults
    - persist: True
    - mount: True
    - dump: 0
    - pass_num: 0
    - require:
      - blockdev: backup_volume
```

First, we included the format state file to create the dependency of the mount operation on the format definition. Next we gave the definition a generic name and mentioned the module to be used, that is, `mount.mounted`.

The name of the mount point is specified with the `name` attribute:

```
- name: /backup
```

The device to mount on the mount point is specified with the `device` attribute:

```
- device: /dev/backup_vg/backup_lv
```

The `fstype` attribute specifies the filesystem of the device, and the `mkmnt` attribute with the `True` value make, sure that the mount point is created if it is not present already.

The `opts` attribute specifies the filesystem mounting options, and `dump` specifies the value to perform backup on the mount point automatically. The `pass_num` attribute specifies the order of the `fsck` program check at boot time.

The `persist` attribute makes sure that an entry for this mount is added to `/etc/fstab` to persist across system reboot. The `mount` attribute makes sure that the filesystem is immediately mounted.

There's more...

There is an extremely useful execution module called `disk`, which provides a lot of useful information about disks on the minion, shown as follows:

```
[root@salt-master ~]# salt 'backup-server' disk.blkid
/dev/backup_vg/backup_lv
[root@salt-master ~]# salt 'backup-server' disk.inodeusage
[root@salt-master ~]# salt 'backup-server' disk.percent
[root@salt-master ~]# salt 'backup-server' disk.usage
```

See also

▶   The *Managing network configurations* recipe, to learn how to perform network configurations with Salt

Managing network configurations

Network configuration can be termed as one of the most critical steps in infrastructure management. Without this, or with the slightest mistake in the configuration, one can easily mess up the infrastructure. However, with a little bit of care, this task can be efficiently managed with Salt using the network module. In this recipe, you will learn how to do the same.

How to do it...

We will use the same minion as the previous recipe. Make sure the minion has a new interface added, and we will use it as `eth2` interface.

1. Create a new state directory called `network` in the staging environment.

2. Create and edit `/opt/salt-cookbook/staging/network/init.sls` to have the following entries (the network data will differ):

```
eth2:
  network.managed:
    - enabled: True
    - type: eth
    - proto: none
    - ipaddr: 192.168.0.15
    - netmask: 255.255.255.0
    - dns:
      - 8.8.8.8
```

```
routes:
  network.routes:
    - name: eth2
    - routes:
      - name: dmz_network
        ipaddr: 192.168.2.0
        netmask: 255.255.255.0
        gateway: 192.168.0.1
```

3. The state is then applied to the minion with the following command:

```
[root@salt-master ~]# salt 'backup-server' state.sls network
saltenv=staging
[root@backup-server network-scripts]# cat ifcfg-eth2
DEVICE="eth2"
HWADDR="00:0c:29:61:ea:1c"
USERCTL="no"
BOOTPROTO="none"
ONBOOT="yes"
IPADDR="192.168.0.15"
NETMASK="255.255.255.0"
PEERDNS="yes"
DNS1="8.8.8.8"

[root@backup-server network-scripts]# cat route-eth2
# dmz_network
ADDRESS0="192.168.2.0"
NETMASK0="255.255.255.0"
GATEWAY0="192.168.0.1"
```

Do note that the network module does not provide an output, so the verification is done from the minion. However, outputs may be received for platforms such as Ubuntu.

How it works...

In this recipe, we demonstrated the capability of Salt to handle network configurations. We configured a new interface for the minion with some common options.

First, we configured the interface itself using the `network.managed` module function:

```
eth2:
  network.managed:
    - enabled: True
    - type: eth
    - proto: none
    - ipaddr: 192.168.0.15
    - netmask: 255.255.255.0
    - dns:
      - 8.8.8.8
```

Some of the attributes are common to the system-specific configuration files; however, some are different. The `enabled` attribute corresponds to the `ONBOOT` option in the system, and the value of the attribute `type` is `eth`, which corresponds to the value `Ethernet` on the system. Apart from these options, the other attributes are the same as the ones in the system configuration file for the interface.

Next we configured the route for the interface as follows:

```
routes:
  network.routes:
    - name: eth2
    - routes:
      - name: dmz_network
        ipaddr: 192.168.2.0
        netmask: 255.255.255.0
        gateway: 192.168.0.1
```

Here, we used the `network.routes` module function and provided all the other necessary information for the route to be set up, including the destination `subnet`, `netmask`, and the `gateway` to use.

Salt does not provide an output for this module, so we verified the files on the minion after applying the states, and they look good.

The network module has support for operating systems, such as RHEL, CentOS, Scientific Linux, and so on. There is experimental support for Debian/Ubuntu.

See also

- ▶ http://docs.saltstack.com/en/latest/ref/states/all/salt.states.network.html#module-salt.states.network, to learn more about the network module

- ▶ *Chapter 5*, *Advanced Administration Tasks*, to learn about some other general tasks such as managing packages, package repositories, and code repositories

5
Advanced Administration Tasks

In this chapter, you will cover:

- ▸ Managing package repositories
- ▸ Managing packages using the default package manager
- ▸ Managing packages using rvm, gem, and pip
- ▸ Managing files
- ▸ Managing services
- ▸ Managing code repositories with Git
- ▸ Managing code repositories with svn
- ▸ Configuring alternatives

Introduction

After going through an exciting chapter on actual Salt implementations, it's now time for us to move on to more advanced tasks on infrastructure management. However, at the present time, we have to keep in mind that using configuration management and orchestration tools are no longer limited to just infrastructure management, it has moved deeper into other departments, such as development.

At the present time, using code repositories are a must for any dynamic organization, and they come with challenges and complexities of their own. To some extent, Salt tries to address the management process of code repositories and provides methods to implement and use them efficiently in an infrastructure.

In this chapter, you will move on to learn advanced topics such as managing package repositories, package management with most of the well-known package managers available, managing files and services, and various methods about how to manage and use code repositories. Let's dive in and explore these amazing features of Salt.

Managing package repositories

Managing packages is an extremely important and base requirement of infrastructure management. However, to manage packages, we need proper package repositories configured. In this chapter, you will learn about how to efficiently manage package repositories with Salt.

How to do it...

Configure two new minions called `salt-minion-centos` (with OS as CentOS) and `salt-minion-ubuntu` (with OS as Ubuntu). Configure the `environment` grain with the value of staging environment in both the minions:

1. Create a new state directory called `pkg_repo` in the staging environment.

2. Create and edit `/opt/salt-cookbook/staging/pkg_repo/init.sls` to have the following entries:

```
salt-repo:
  pkgrepo.managed:
    {% if grains['lsb_distrib_id'] == "CentOS" %}
    - humanname: CentOS-$releasever - Epel Repo
    - mirrorlist:
https://mirrors.fedoraproject.org/metalink?repo=epel-
6&arch=$basearch
    - comments:
        - "#baseurl=http://download.fedoraproject.org/pub/
epel/6/$bas
earch"
    - gpgcheck: 1
    - gpgkey: file:///etc/pki/rpm-gpg/RPM-GPG-KEY-EPEL-6
    {% elif grains['lsb_distrib_id'] == "Ubuntu" %}
    - humanname: Ubuntu Salt Repo
    - name: "deb http://ppa.launchpad.net/saltstack/salt/ubuntu {{
grains['oscodename'] }} main"
    - dist: {{ grains['oscodename'] }}
    - file: /etc/apt/sources.list.d/saltstack-{{
grains['oscodename'] }}.list
    - keyid: 0E27C0A6
    - keyserver: keyserver.ubuntu.com
    {% endif %}
```

3. Apply the state to both the minions with the following command:

```
[root@salt-master ~]# salt -G 'environment:staging' state.sls
pkg_repo saltenv=staging
salt-minion-centos:
----------
          ID: salt-repo
    Function: pkgrepo.managed
      Result: True
     Comment: Configured package repo 'salt-repo'
     Started: 04:08:35.948162
    Duration: 30.657 ms
     Changes:
              ----------
              repo:
                  salt-repo
salt-minion-ubuntu:
----------
          ID: salt-repo
    Function: pkgrepo.managed
        Name: deb
http://ppa.launchpad.net/saltstack/salt/ubuntu precise main
      Result: True
     Comment: Configured package repo 'deb
http://ppa.launchpad.net/saltstack/salt/ubuntu precise main'
     Started: 05:05:39.286080
    Duration: 9102.918 ms
     Changes:
              ----------
              file:
                  ----------
                  new:
                      /etc/apt/sources.list.d/saltstack-
precise.list
```

```
Summary
------------
Succeeded: 2  (changed=2)
Failed:    0
------------
Total states run:     2
```

How it works...

In this recipe, we demonstrated the ability of Salt to configure package repositories. However, package repositories are not the same for different platforms. For RedHat/CentOS/Fedora-based systems it is YUM and for Ubuntu it's called apt-get. Salt manages this difference quite well by providing attributes for both types of repository management. The objective of this recipe is to configure repositories on two minions with different OS platforms for the Salt packages.

First, we have given a generic name to the repository and mentioned the module and the function to use, that is, pkgrepo.managed:

```
salt-repo:
  pkgrepo.managed:
```

Next, we used conditionals to apply the configured definitions based on the grain lsb_distrib_id. This grain tells us if the OS is CentOS or Ubuntu. Based on this conditional, the respective definitions have been configured.

For CentOS, we have the following definition:

```
    - humanname: CentOS-$releasever - Epel Repo
    - mirrorlist: https://mirrors.fedoraproject.org/
metalink?repo=epel-
6&arch=$basearch
    - comments:
        - "#baseurl=http://download.fedoraproject.org/pub/
epel/6/$basearch"
    - gpgcheck: 1
    - gpgkey: file:///etc/pki/rpm-gpg/RPM-GPG-KEY-EPEL-6
```

Here we see similar attributes that we see in the files with .repo extensions located in the /etc/yum.repos.d directory in a CentOS system except for the humanname attribute, which corresponds to the name attribute on the system files.

For Ubuntu, we have the following definition:

```
- humanname: Ubuntu Salt Repo
- name: "deb http://ppa.launchpad.net/saltstack/salt/ubuntu {{
grains['oscodename'] }} main"
- dist: {{ grains['oscodename'] }}
- file: /etc/apt/sources.list.d/saltstack-{{
grains['oscodename'] }}.list
- keyid: 0E27C0A6
- keyserver: keyserver.ubuntu.com
```

Here, we mentioned the contents of the files with the `.list` extensions located in the `/etc/apt/sources.list.d` directory or the `/etc/apt/sources.list` file. The file attribute mentions the filename where these contents are going to be saved. The `keyserver` attribute mentions the key server from where the key with an explicit ID for the Salt repository needs to be downloaded for the repository to authenticate properly, and the `keyid` attribute mentions the key to look for.

There is another way to configure **Personal Package Archives** (**PPA**) repositories using the `pkgrepo` module in the following manner:

```
saltstack-ppa:
  pkgrepo.managed:
    - ppa: saltstack/salt
```

See also

▸ `http://docs.saltstack.com/en/latest/ref/states/all/salt.states.`
   `pkgrepo.html#module-salt.states.pkgrepo`, to know more about the
   pkgrepo module

▸ The *Managing packages using the default package manager* recipe, to learn how to
   manage packages on different platforms

Managing packages using the default package manager

After learning about package repositories, it is now time that you move on to learn about how to use Salt to manage packages. There are various types of operating system platforms being used, and Salt does an excellent job of providing a common interface to all of them. In this recipe, you will learn about how to manage packages with Salt.

How to do it...

We will use the same minions as the previous recipe. Create a new state directory called
`base` in the staging environment and create a directory called `rpm` in the base directory.
We downloaded the `collectd-5.4.0-1.el6.x86_64.rpm` file and stored it in the
`rpm` directory:

1. Create and edit the `/opt/salt-cookbook/staging/base/ssh_packages.sls`
   file to have the following entries:

   ```
   {% if grains['lsb_distrib_id'] == 'CentOS' %}
   openssh-clients:
   {% elif grains['lsb_distrib_id'] == 'Ubuntu' %}
   openssh-client:
   {% endif %}
     pkg.installed
   ```

2. Create and edit the `/opt/salt-cookbook/staging/base/ruby_packages.sls`
   file to have the following entries:

   ```
   ruby_packages:
     pkg.installed:
       - pkgs:
         - ruby
         - rubygems
   ```

3. Create and edit the `/opt/salt-cookbook/staging/base/collectd_packages.sls`
   file to have the following entries:

   ```
   collectd_package:
     pkg.installed:
       - sources:
         - collectd: salt://base/rpm/collectd-5.4.0-
   1.el6.x86_64.rpm
   ```

4. Apply the states to the minions with the following commands:

   ```
   [root@salt-master ~]# salt -G 'environment:staging' state.sls
   base.ssh_packages --state-output=terse saltenv=staging
   salt-minion-centos:
     Name: openssh-clients - Function: pkg.installed - Result:
   Clean

   Summary
   ------------
   Succeeded: 1
   Failed:    0
   ```

```
-----------
Total states run:     1
salt-minion-ubuntu:

  Name: openssh-client - Function: pkg.installed - Result:
Clean


Summary
-----------
Succeeded: 1
Failed:    0
-----------
Total states run:     1


[root@salt-master ~]# salt -G 'environment:staging' state.sls
base.ruby_packages --state-output=terse saltenv=staging
salt-minion-ubuntu:

  Name: ruby_packages - Function: pkg.installed - Result:
Changed


Summary
-----------
Succeeded: 1 (changed=1)
Failed:    0
-----------
Total states run:     1
salt-minion-centos:

  Name: ruby_packages - Function: pkg.installed - Result:
Changed


Summary
-----------
Succeeded: 1 (changed=1)
Failed:    0
-----------
Total states run:     1
```

```
[root@salt-master ~]# salt -G 'environment:staging' state.sls
base.collectd_packages --state-output=terse saltenv=staging
salt-minion-ubuntu:


Summary
-----------
Succeeded: 0
Failed:    0
-----------
Total states run:      0
salt-minion-centos:
  Name: collectd_package - Function: pkg.installed - Result:
Changed


Summary
------------
Succeeded: 1 (changed=1)
Failed:      0
-----------
Total states run:      1
```

How it works...

In this recipe, we demonstrated the ability of Salt to efficiently manage packages. The objective of the recipe is to demonstrate package management in three different ways.

In the first file ssh_packages.sls, we used conditionals to decide which OpenSSH client package to install, based on the OS distribution. We used the pkg.installed module function to implement the package install. Salt takes the same definition for all platforms and uses the respective package manager to perform the task depending on the OS platform.

In the second file, ruby_packages.sls, we demonstrated how to install multiple packages using the pkgs attribute in the following manner:

```
- pkgs:
  - ruby
  - rubygems
```

In the third file, we demonstrated the method to fetch the file from a specific location and then install it on the minion:

```
collectd_package:
  pkg.installed:
    - sources:
      - collectd: salt://base/rpm/collectd-5.4.0-1.el6.x86_64.rpm
```

In this example, we fetched the file to be installed from the Salt repository, however, the file can be fetched from a URL, such as an HTTP or FTP file location or a local file path, on the minion.

There are a few more important attributes that can be used with this module function:

- ▸ `fromrepo`: This is used to mention the repo name from which to install the package
- ▸ `version`: This mentions the version number of the package to install
- ▸ `refresh`: This updates the repository database before installing the package
- ▸ `hold`: This is used to force the package to be in its present installed version

The `pkg` module also has a function called `latest` that makes sure that the installed packages are in the latest versions.

See also

- ▸ `http://docs.saltstack.com/en/latest/ref/states/all/salt.states.pkg.html#module-salt.states.pkg`, to learn more about the `pkg` module and its options
- ▸ The *Managing packages using rvm, gem, and pip* recipe, to learn about how to use other package managers apart from the default system package managers

Managing packages using rvm, gem, and pip

At the present time, like all other aspects of the operating system, package management is no longer limited to the default system package managers such as `yum` and `apt-get`. With the widespread uses of Ruby and Python-based frameworks, the need to manage packages and supporting libraries for them have become an absolute necessity. This is where package managers like rvm, gem, and pip come in. In this recipe, you will learn how to manage packages with these package managers using Salt.

How to do it...

Create two minions called `stgdc1app01` and `stgdc1app02`. Configure a grain called `app_type` in both the minions and set the value of the grain as `rails` in `stgdc1app01` and as `django` in `stgdc1app02`:

1. Create a new state directory called `app` in the staging environment.

2. Create and edit the `/opt/salt-cookbook/staging/app/rails.sls` file to have the following entries:

```
ruby-2.1.5:
  rvm.installed:
    - default: True

set_ruby:
  cmd.run:
    - name: 'source /etc/profile.d/rvm.sh; rvm use 2.1.5 --
default'
    - shell: /bin/bash
    - stateful: False
    - require:
      - rvm: ruby-2.1.5
    - unless: 'rvm current | grep 2.1.5'

rails:
  gem.installed:
    - require:
      - rvm: ruby-2.1.5
```

3. Create and edit the `/opt/salt-cookbook/staging/app/django.sls` file to have the following entries:

```
python_packages:
  pkg.installed:
    - pkgs:
      - python
      - python-pip

django:
  pip.installed:
    - name: django >= 1.6
    - require:
      - pkg: python_packages
```

4. Apply the states to the minions with the following commands:

```
[root@salt-master ~]# salt -G 'app_type:rails' state.sls
app.rails saltenv=staging
stgdclapp01:
----------
          ID: ruby-2.1.5
    Function: rvm.installed
      Result: True
     Comment: Successfully installed ruby.
     Started: 03:54:54.507659
    Duration: 487224.834 ms
     Changes:
              ----------
              ruby-2.1.5:
                  Installed
----------
          ID: set_ruby
    Function: cmd.run
        Name: source /etc/profile.d/rvm.sh; rvm use 2.1.5 --
default
      Result: True
     Comment: Command "source /etc/profile.d/rvm.sh; rvm use
2.1.5 --default" run
     Started: 04:03:01.746856
    Duration: 973.718 ms
     Changes:
              ----------
              pid:
                  20326
              retcode:
                  0
              stderr:

              stdout:
                  Using /usr/local/rvm/gems/ruby-2.1.5
----------
          ID: rails
```

```
         Function: gem.installed

           Result: True

          Comment: Gem was successfully installed

          Started: 04:03:02.721188

         Duration: 45206.713 ms

          Changes:
                        ----------

                        rails:

                             Installed


Summary
------------

Succeeded: 3 (changed=3)

Failed:      0
------------

Total states run:      3


[root@salt-master ~]# salt -G 'app_type:django' state.sls
app.rails saltenv=staging

stgdc1app02:
----------

               ID: python_packages

         Function: pkg.installed

           Result: True

          Comment: The following packages were installed/updated:
python-pip. The following packages were already installed:
python.

          Started: 04:06:33.441650

         Duration: 27585.314 ms

          Changes:
                        ----------

                        python-pip:
                             ----------

                             new:

                                  1.3.1-4.el6

                             old:
```

```
        python-setuptools:
            ----------
            new:
                0.6.10-3.el6
            old:

    ----------
          ID: django
    Function: pip.installed
        Name: django >= 1.6
      Result: True
     Comment: Package was successfully installed
     Started: 04:07:01.027655
    Duration: 37654.449 ms
     Changes:
            ----------
            Django==1.7.1:
                Installed

Summary
------------
Succeeded: 2 (changed=2)
Failed:    0
------------
Total states run:    2
```

How it works...

In this recipe, we demonstrated the ability of Salt to configure packages using some package managers other than the default system package managers such as rvm, gem, and pip. The objective of the recipe is to configure two application servers, one containing a Ruby on Rails application and the other containing a Django application.

In the first example, we created a file called `rails.sls` and mentioned the latest Ruby version (v2.1.5) to be installed with the `rvm.installed` module function. As the default Ruby available with most distributions is quite old, RVM (Ruby Version Manager) comes in quite handy when managing the latest Ruby versions and `gemsets`.

Next, we configured a command to run where it sets the recently installed Ruby version as the default Ruby for the system. We have also put in a condition to only run the command if the present Ruby being used is not of the mentioned version.

Finally, we configured the `rails` framework to be installed using the latest Ruby version with the `gem.installed` module function:

```
rails:
  gem.installed:
    - require:
      - rvm: ruby-2.1.5
```

We also created a dependency on the Ruby package being installed previously.

The `ruby` attribute can also be used in the gem definitions to set the Ruby version to use while installing the gem. Also, the `version` attribute can be used to set the version of the gem being installed.

In the second example, we created a file called `django.sls`. We made sure that the prerequisites, that is, the `python` and the `python-pip` packages are installed before Django can be installed using `pip`.

Next, we configured the definition for Django to be installed with the `pip.installed` module function:

```
django:
  pip.installed:
    - name: django >= 1.6
    - require:
      - pkg: python_packages
```

The `name` attribute contains the name of the package to be installed and, optionally, the version number can be mentioned along with the >=, <=, and == operators to make sure a desired version of the package is installed.

See also

- ▶ `http://docs.saltstack.com/en/latest/ref/states/all/salt.states.pip_state.html#module-salt.states.pip_state`, to learn more about the pip module and its numerous other attributes

- ▶ `http://docs.saltstack.com/en/latest/ref/states/all/salt.states.gem.html#module-salt.states.gem`

- ▶ `http://docs.saltstack.com/en/ latest/ref/states/all/salt.states.pip_state.html#module-salt. states.pip_state`

- ▶ `http://docs.saltstack.com/en/latest/ref/ states/all/salt.states.rvm.html#module-salt.states.rvm`

- ▶ The *Managing files* recipe, to learn how to manage files using Salt

Managing files

One of the very basic and important tasks in infrastructure management is to manage files. In this recipe, you will learn how to manage files and its variants such as directories and symlinks using Salt.

How to do it...

1. Configure a minion called `salt-minion`. Create a new state directory called `apache`.

2. In the `apache` directory, create the following directory structure:

    ```
    [root@salt-master ~]# mkdir -p /opt/salt-
    cookbook/staging/apache/files/apache_root/{produxts,services,b
    log,about}
    ```

    Also create an `/opt/salt-cookbook/staging/apache/files/index.html` file with some test HTML content in it.

3. Create and edit `/opt/salt-cookbook/staging/apache/init.sls` to have the following contents:

    ```
    httpd_source:
      file.managed:
        - name: /opt/httpd-2.4.10.tar.gz
        - source: http://mirror.nus.edu.sg/apache//httpd/httpd-
    2.4.10.tar.gz
        - source_hash: http://www.apache.org/dist/httpd/httpd-
    2.4.10.tar.gz.md5

    extract_httpd_source:
      archive:
        - extracted
        - name: /opt/
        - source: /opt/httpd-2.4.10.tar.gz
        - source_hash: http://www.apache.org/dist/httpd/httpd-
    2.4.10.tar.gz.md5
        - archive_format: tar
        - if_missing: /opt/httpd-2.4.10
        - require:
          - file: httpd_source

    /opt/apache:
      file.symlink:
    ```

```
      - target: httpd-2.4.10
      - require:
        - archive: extract_httpd_source

/opt/apache_root:
  file.recurse:
    - source: salt://apache/files/apache_root
    - include_empty: True
    - dir_mode: 0755

/opt/apache_root/careers:
  file.directory:
    - user: root
    - group: root
    - mode: 0755
    - makedirs: True

/opt/apache_root/index.html:
  file.managed:
    - source: salt://apache/files/index.html
    - user: root
    - group: root
    - mode: 0644
```

4. Apply the state to the minion with the following command:

```
[root@salt-master ~]# salt 'salt-minion' state.sls apache
saltenv=staging --state-output=terse

salt-minion:
  Name: /opt/httpd-2.4.10.tar.gz - Function: file.managed -
Result: Changed
  Name: /opt/ - Function: archive.extracted - Result: Changed
  Name: /opt/apache - Function: file.symlink - Result: Changed
  Name: /opt/apache_root - Function: file.recurse - Result:
Changed
  Name: /opt/apache_root/careers - Function: file.directory -
Result: Changed
  Name: /opt/apache_root/index.html - Function: file.managed -
Result: Changed


Summary
------------
Succeeded: 6 (changed=6)
```

```
Failed:     0
------------
Total states run:     6
```

How it works...

In this recipe, we demonstrated the ability of Salt to manage files with the versatile `file` module, which can perform quite a number of file-related functions. The objective of the recipe is to download the source package for the Apache web server, extract it to get the source directory, create a symbolic link to this directory, fetch a bunch of multilevel directories from the Salt master to act as `DocumentRoot` of the web server, create a directory, and also create a file by fetching it from the Salt master `salt/states/mount.py`.

Although this entire operation can be performed by more efficient modules, such as `archive` and `git/svn`, we performed this task in this manner to demonstrate the various capabilities of the file module.

Before we configured the state file, we created a directory called `apache_root` in the files directory of the state and created few other directories in it so that we can copy over this entire directory to the minion later.

First, we fetched the web server file from its official HTTP location:

```
httpd_source:
  file.managed:
    - name: /opt/httpd-2.4.10.tar.gz
    - source: http://mirror.nus.edu.sg/apache//httpd/httpd-
2.4.10.tar.gz
    - source_hash: http://www.apache.org/dist/httpd/httpd-
2.4.10.tar.gz.md5
```

The `file.managed` function has been used here to make sure the file is present and the source can be any HTTP, HTTPS, FTP, or Salt repo location. If the source is an HTTP or HTTPS location, the `source_hash` attribute is important to check the integrity of the downloaded file.

Next, we extracted the file using the `archive` module, about which we had learned in the *Handling archive files* recipe of *Chapter 4, General Administration Tasks*.

We then created a symbolic link pointing to the extracted directory using the `file.symlink` function:

```
/opt/apache:
  file.symlink:
    - target: httpd-2.4.10
    - require:
      - archive: extract_httpd_source
```

Next, we demonstrated the `file` module's ability to fetch multilevel directory structures recursively from the Salt repo using the `file.recurse` function:

```
/opt/apache_root:
  file.recurse:
    - source: salt://apache/files/apache_root
    - include_empty: True
    - dir_mode: 0755
```

The `include_empty` attribute makes sure that empty directories are also fetched. The permissions of the files or directories can be set with three different attributes:

- `mode`: This sets permissions for both directories and files

- `file_mode`: This sets permissions for the files only

- `dir_mode`: This sets permissions for the directories only

Next, we learned how to create a directory using the `file.directory` function:

```
/opt/apache_root/careers:
  file.directory:
    - user: root
    - group: root
    - mode: 0755
    - makedirs: True
```

The `makedirs` attribute makes sure that if any of the directories in the path are missing, it creates them.

Finally, we learned how to manage a basic file by fetching it from the Salt repo using the `file.managed` function.

The `file.mknod` function helps to create special files such as character, pipe, and block devices.

See also

- http://docs.saltstack.com/en/latest/ref/states/all/salt.states.file.html#module-salt.states.file

- The *Managing services* recipe, to learn how to manage services

Managing services

After packages and files, services are the entities to look out for in infrastructure management. For any system or application software, after the package is installed and the configuration files are modified, the next task is to make sure that the service is running and serves its purpose. In this recipe, you will learn how to manage services using Salt.

How to do it...

We will use the same minion and state directory as the previous recipe:

1. Create and edit the `/opt/salt-cookbook/staging/apache/service.sls` file to have the following entries:

    ```
    {% if grains['lsb_distrib_id'] == "CentOS" %}
    httpd:
    {% elif grains['lsb_distrib_id'] == "Ubuntu" %}
    apache2:
    {% endif %}
      pkg:
        - installed
      service:
        - running
        - enable: True
        - reload: True
    ```

2. Apply the state to the minion with the following command:

    ```
    [root@salt-master ~]# salt 'salt-minion' state.sls
    apache.service saltenv=staging --state-output=terse
    salt-minion:
      Name: apache2 - Function: pkg.installed - Result: Changed
      Name: apache2 - Function: service.running - Result: Clean

    Summary
    ------------
    Succeeded: 2 (changed=1)
    Failed:    0
    ------------
    Total states run:    2
    ```

How it works...

In this recipe, we demonstrated the ability of Salt to manage services. The objective of the recipe is to install the Apache web server package and make sure that the service is configured to be running.

First, we created a file called `service.sls` and used conditionals to determine the name of the web server package, that is, in CentOS the package name is `httpd` and in Ubuntu the package name is `apache2`. In both the platforms, the service names are also same as the package names. Hence, we defined both the package definition and the service definition under the same name.

```
{% if grains['lsb_distrib_id'] == "CentOS" %}
httpd:
{% elif grains['lsb_distrib_id'] == "Ubuntu" %}
apache2:
{% endif %}
  pkg:
    - installed
  service:
    - running
    - enable: True
    - reload: True
```

The module to use for service management is `service`. The `running` function makes sure that the service is running. The `enabled` attribute makes sure that the service is configured to start at boot time. If the service is watching a file and the file changes, a restart of the service is performed. However, if the objective is to reload the service instead of restarting it, the `reload` attribute needs to be set as `True`.

To make sure that the service is stopped, the `pkg.dead` function can be used, and to disable it at boot time, the `disabled` attribute can be used.

See also

▶ `http://docs.saltstack.com/en/latest/ref/states/all/salt.states.service.html#module-salt.states.service`, to know more about the service module

▶ The *Managing code repositories with Git* recipe, to learn how to configure code repositories using Git

Managing code repositories with Git

In modern dynamic environments, usage of code repositories is considered vital for efficient code management, collaboration, and practices such as **Continuous Integration**. Fortunately, Salt makes it easy enough to manage code repositories using its modules. In this recipe, you will learn how to manage code repositories using Git.

How to do it...

We will use the same minion and state directory as the previous recipe:

1. Create and edit the `/opt/salt-cookbook/staging/apache/git_repo.sls` file to have the following entries:

```
git:
  pkg:
    - installed
  user:
    - present
    - home: /home/git

/opt/apache-repo:
  file.directory:
    - user: git
    - group: git
    - dir_mode: 0755
    - require:
      - user: git

/home/git/.ssh:
  file.directory:
    - user: git
    - group: git
    - dir_mode: 775
    - require:
      - user: git

git-key:
  file.managed:
    - name: /home/git/.ssh/id_rsa
    - source: salt://apache/keys/id_rsa
    - user: git
    - group: git
    - mode: 400
    - require:
      - file: /home/git/.ssh
```

```
    github.com:
      ssh_known_hosts:
        - present
        - user: git
        - fingerprint: ac:23:34:10:83:24:79:3b:61:26:e9:bf:4e:f0:78:fa
        - require:
          - user: git

    git-repo:
      git.latest:
        - name: git@github.com:GITHUBUSER/apache-repo.git
        - rev: master
        - user: git
        - target: /opt/apache-repo
        - require:
            - pkg: git
            - file: /opt/apache-repo
            - ssh_known_hosts: github.com
```

2. Apply the state to the minion with the following command:

```
[root@salt-master ~]# salt 'salt-minion' state.sls
apache.git_repo saltenv=staging --state-output=terse
salt-minion:
  Name: git - Function: pkg.installed - Result: Changed
  Name: git - Function: user.present - Result: Changed
  Name: /opt/apache-repo - Function: file.directory - Result:
Changed
  Name: /home/git/.ssh - Function: file.directory - Result:
Changed
  Name: /home/git/.ssh/id_rsa - Function: file.managed -
Result: Changed
  Name: github.com - Function: ssh_known_hosts.present -
Result: Changed
  Name: git@github.com:GITHUBUSER/apache-repo.git - Function:
git.latest - Result: Changed


Summary
------------
Succeeded: 7 (changed=7)
Failed:    0
------------
Total states run:      7
```

How it works...

In this recipe, we demonstrated the ability of Salt to manage code repositories with Git. The objective of the recipe is to configure a user, the private key for the user, and the known hosts for the `github.com` repository, and create the target directory where the repository is to be fetched.

We used a lot of the modules in the recipe that you learned before, such as `user`, `ssh_known_hosts`, `file`, `pkg`, and so on.

First, we made sure that the `git` package is installed and a `git` user is created:

```
git:
  pkg:
    - installed
  user:
    - present
    - home: /home/git
```

The `git` package is required to install the Git binaries and libraries required to interact with Git repositories.

Next, we created the target directory on the minion, where the repository will be fetched and made sure that the private key required to make a password-less connection with the `github.com` server is present in the `git` user's home directory.

We then configured the fingerprint of the `github.com` server to be added to the `known_hosts` file of the `git` user on the minion. The fingerprint can be found by running the following command manually on the minion:

```
# git clone REPOSITORY-URL
```

The fingerprint can also be found in the `github.com` dashboard.

Finally, we configured the definition for the repository to be fetched on the minion:

```
git-repo:
  git.latest:
    - name: git@github.com:GITHUBUSER/apache-repo.git
    - rev: master
    - user: git
    - target: /opt/apache-repo
    - require:
        - pkg: git
        - file: /opt/apache-repo
        - ssh_known_hosts: github.com
```

The module being used is `git.latest`, and the URL of the Git repository is provided with the `name` attribute. The branch of the repository to be fetched is mentioned with the `rev` attribute. The `user` attribute specifies the user to fetch the repository. The `target` attribute mentions the path where the repository is to be fetched.

The `git` module has numerous other attributes and options. If the HTTPS URL of the repository is used instead of the SSH URL, then the username and password of the `github.com` account can be provided with the `https_user` and `https_pass` attributes respectively, for authentication.

The Git configuration on the minion can also be performed with the `git.config` module, which helps to add the name and the email address to the Git configuration.

See also

> ▸ `http://docs.saltstack.com/en/latest/ref/states/all/salt.states.git.html#module-salt.states.git`, to know more about the available attributes and functions of the Git module

> ▸ The *Managing code repositories with svn* recipe, to learn how to manage code repositories with svn

Managing code repositories with svn

Subversion was used widely before Git surfaced and became the ultimate standard for code repositories. However, even now, a lot of organizations use Subversion widely and require efficient management methods for deployments. In this recipe, you will learn about how to manage Subversion code repositories using Salt.

How to do it...

We will use the same minion and the state directory as the previous recipe. We will assume that a Subversion repository server has been set up and a user called `deploy` is allowed to authenticate at the repository with the password `C00kbook`. We will also assume that a repository called `apache-repo` has been created and is available to check out at `http://svnserver/svn/apache-repo`:

1. Create and edit the `/opt/salt-cookbook/pillar/staging/apache/init.sls` file to have the following entries:

```
svn:
  user: deploy
  passwd: C00kbook
```

2. Edit the `/opt/salt-cookbook/pillar/staging/top.sls` file to have the following entries:

```
staging:
  '*':
    - apache
```

3. Create and edit the `/opt/salt-cookbook/staging/apache/svn_repo.sls` file to have the following entries:

```
subversion:
  pkg.installed

deploy:
  user:
    - present
    - home: /home/deploy

/opt/apache-repo:
  file.directory:
    - user: deploy
    - group: deploy
    - dir_mode: 0755
    - require:
      - user: deploy

svn-repo:
  svn.latest:
    - name: http://svnserver/svn/apache-repo
    - target: /opt/apache-repo
    - user: deploy
    - username: {{ pillar['svn']['user'] }}
    - password: {{ pillar['svn']['passwd'] }}
    - require:
        - pkg: subversion
        - file: /opt/apache-repo
```

4. Edit the `/opt/salt-cookbook/staging/top.sls` file to have the following entries:

```
staging:
  'salt-minion':
    - apache.svn_repo
```

5. Apply the state to the minion with the following command:

```
[root@salt-master ~]# salt 'salt-minion' state.highstate
saltenv=staging --state-output=terse

salt-minion:
   Name: subversion - Function: pkg.installed - Result: Changed
   Name: deploy - Function: user.present - Result: Changed
   Name: /opt/apache-repo - Function: file.directory - Result:
Changed
   Name: http://svnserver/svn/apache-repo - Function:
svn.latest - Result: Changed


Summary
-----------
Succeeded: 4 (changed=4)
Failed:    0
-----------
Total states run:     4
```

How it works...

In this recipe, we demonstrated the ability of Salt to manage and fetch Subversion repositories. The objective of this recipe is to fetch the latest version of a preconfigured Subversion repository to a desired location on the minion. We assumed that a repository called `apache-repo` has already been configured on a local Subversion server.

We created a pillar file for this recipe and added the username and password definitions for the Subversion server.

First, we created a user called `deploy`, which will be used to fetch the repository and is allowed to authenticate with the Subversion server using the password `C00kbook`. We also installed the `subversion` package to make the required binaries available:

```
subversion:
  pkg.installed

deploy:
  user:
    - present
    - home: /home/deploy
```

Next, we created the local directory, where the repository will be fetched using the `file.directory` module.

Finally, we configured the repository to be fetched using the `svn.latest` module function:

```
svn-repo:
  svn.latest:
    - name: http://svnserver/svn/apache-repo
    - target: /opt/apache-repo
    - user: deploy
    - username: {{ pillar['svn']['user'] }}
    - password: {{ pillar['svn']['passwd'] }}
    - require:
        - pkg: subversion
        - file: /opt/apache-repo
```

The `name` attribute specifies the URL of the repository to be fetched. The `target` attribute specifies the local directory on the minion, where the fetched repository is to be placed.

The `user` attribute specifies the user for which the fetch needs to be performed, that is, the user who will run the `svn` command on the server. The `username` and `password` attributes are used to fetch the username and password of the Subversion server from the pillar data and then used to authenticate with the Subversion server.

See also

▶ http://docs.saltstack.com/en/latest/ref/states/all/salt.states.svn.html#module-salt.states.svn, to learn more about the svn module and its options

▶ The *Configuring alternatives* recipe, to learn about how to configure alternatives

Configuring alternatives

Infrastructures are often configured in a manner where multiple files providing the same binary exists, and we configure alternatives to set the correct file that should provide the required binary and they are known as alternatives. In this recipe, we will learn how to configure alternatives in Salt.

How to do it...

We will use the same minion as the previous recipe. We will assume that there is a local web server in our environment, which provides an archived file containing a hotspot version of Java from Oracle:

1. Create a new state directory called `alternatives`.

2. Create and edit the `/opt/salt-cookbook/staging/alternatives/init.sls` file to have the following entries:

```
extract_jdk_archive:
  archive:
    - extracted
    - name: /opt/
    - source: http://reposerver/jdk-7u71-linux-x64.gz
    - source_hash: md5=22761b214b1505f1a9671b124b0f44f4
    - archive_format: tar
    - if_missing: /opt/jdk1.7.0_71


/opt/java:
  file.symlink:
    - target: jdk1.7.0_71
    - require:
      - archive: extract_jdk_archive


install_java_alternative:
  alternatives.install:
    - name: java
    - link: /usr/bin/java
    - path: /opt/java/bin/java
    - priority: 1
    - require:
      - file: /opt/java


set_java_alternative:
  alternatives.set:
    - name: java
    - path: /opt/java/bin/java
    - require:
      - alternatives: install_java_alternative
```

3. Apply the state to the minion by running the following command:

```
[root@salt-master ~]# salt 'salt-minion' state.sls alternatives
saltenv=staging --state-output=terse

salt-minion:
  Name: /opt/ - Function: archive.extracted - Result: Changed
  Name: /opt/java - Function: file.symlink - Result: Changed
  Name: java - Function: alternatives.install - Result:
  Changed
  Name: java - Function: alternatives.set - Result: Changed
```

```
Summary
------------
Succeeded: 4 (changed=4)
Failed:    0
------------
Total states run:     4


Test on the minion:
[root@salt-minion ~]# java -version
java version "1.7.0_71"
Java(TM) SE Runtime Environment (build 1.7.0_71-b14)
Java HotSpot(TM) 64-Bit Server VM (build 24.71-b01, mixed
mode)
```

How it works...

In this recipe, we demonstrated the ability of Salt to configure `alternatives`. Often in Linux systems, the default version of installed Java is the OpenJDK Java, which is available from the repository. However, most developers prefer the Hotspot Java version available from Oracle. The objective of this recipe is to fetch the package for the Oracle Java and set the Java alternative to point to the Java binary from this package.

First, we fetched the Java archive from a locally hosted server and extracted the archive using the `archive` module. Next, we set a symlink called Java to point to the `jdk` directory that is complexly named for ease of access.

We then installed the new alternative in the minion:

```
install_java_alternative:
  alternatives.install:
    - name: java
    - link: /usr/bin/java
    - path: /opt/java/bin/java
    - priority: 1
    - require:
      - file: /opt/java
```

The `alternatives.install` module function is used for this purpose. The `name` attribute specifies the master name for the alternative group.

The `link` attribute specifies the path of the binary, which is visible to the system, but is actually a symlink pointing to /etc/alternatives/<master-name>:

```
- link: /usr/bin/java
```

```
[root@salt-minion ~]# ls -l /usr/bin/java
lrwxrwxrwx. 1 root root 22 Dec 11 05:06 /usr/bin/java ->
/etc/alternatives/java
```

The `path` attribute specifies the actual location of the new binary, which is about to be set as the main binary:

```
- path: /opt/java/bin/java
```

Finally, we set the newly installed alternative as the main alternative with the `alternative.set` module function.

See also

▶ http://docs.saltstack.com/en/latest/ref/states/all/salt.states.alternatives.html#module-salt.states.alternatives, to learn more about configuring alternatives

▶ *Chapter 6, Managing Application Servers*, to learn how to configure application servers

6
Managing Application Servers

In this chapter, you will cover:

- ▶ Apache web server packages and services
- ▶ Managing web server modules
- ▶ Adding web server configuration
- ▶ Web server security with htpasswd
- ▶ Setting up Java for Apache Tomcat
- ▶ Apache Tomcat packages, files, and services
- ▶ Deploying the WAR file in Apache Tomcat

Introduction

One of the most important components of any infrastructure is the application server. With loads of Enterprise and open source options available, it really depends on the requirements of the administrators and engineers as to which application server should be used in a particular environment. After extensive proofs of concepts, trials and errors, a decision can be reached as to which is the ideal choice.

Of all the options available, there are a few that are widely accepted and used as the primary application server in most environments. In this chapter, we will learn how Salt can help us to configure and manage some of the most widely used open source application servers.

In this chapter, we will not only learn the generic procedures to install and configure the servers, but also how Salt provides us with some extremely useful modules with which we can configure very explicit details and parameters for an application server.

Apache web server packages and services

Apache web server is one of the most widely used web server software packages that supports a wide range of back ends, such as Ruby, and Python-based frameworks. It can serve a wide range of dynamic and static pages and applications. In this recipe, we will learn how to configure Apache web server packages and services.

How to do it...

1. Configure a new minion called `salt-minion-ubuntu` as having the Ubuntu server operating system in the `development` environment.

2. Create a new state directory in the `development` environment called `apache`.

3. Create and edit `/opt/salt-cookbook/development/apache/init.sls` to have the following entries:

```
apache_packages:
  pkg.installed:
    - pkgs:
      - apache2

apache_service:
  service:
    - name: apache2
    - running
    - enable: True
    - require:
      - pkg: apache_packages
```

4. Apply the state to the minion, using the following command:

```
[root@salt-master ~]# salt 'salt-minion-ubuntu' state.sls
apache saltenv=development

salt-minion-ubuntu:
----------
          ID: apache_packages
    Function: pkg.installed
      Result: True
     Comment: The following packages were installed/updated:
apache2.
     Started: 02:16:27.105662
    Duration: 39479.427 ms
```

```
Changes:
    ----------
    apache2:
        ----------
        new:
            2.2.22-1ubuntu1.7
        old:

    apache2-mpm:
        ----------
        new:
            1
        old:

    apache2-mpm-worker:
        ----------
        new:
            2.2.22-1ubuntu1.7
        old:

    httpd:
        ----------
        new:
            1
        old:

    httpd-cgi:
        ----------
        new:
            1
        old:

----------
        ID: apache_service
  Function: service.running
      Name: apache2
```

```
          Result: True
         Comment: Service apache2 is already enabled, and is
      running
         Started: 02:17:47.302851
        Duration: 97.703 ms
         Changes:
                  ----------
                  apache2:
                      True

      Summary
      ------------
      Succeeded: 2 (changed=2)
      Failed:    0
      ------------
      Total states run:      2
```

How it works...

In this recipe, we demonstrated the generic ability of Salt to install packages and configure services to implement the Apache web server software. The objective of the recipe is to install the web server, and make sure that the service is running and enabled to start at boot time.

First, we used the `pkg` module to install the `apache2` package, which is the default package for the Apache web server in Ubuntu. In CentOS, it will be `httpd`:

```
apache_packages:
  pkg.installed:
    - pkgs:
      - apache2
```

We can also see a few dependencies being automatically fetched and installed during the install process.

Next we used the `service` module to make sure that the `apache2` service is running and is configured to start at boot time:

```
apache_service:
  service:
    - name: apache2
    - running
```

```
        - enable: True
      - require:
        - pkg: apache_packages
```

Here, we made sure that the `apache2` service is running, and we also made the service dependent on the `apache2` package installation.

See also

▸ The *Managing packages using the default package manager* recipe, in *Chapter 5, Advanced Administration Tasks*, to learn more about installing packages

▸ The *Managing services* recipe, in *Chapter 5, Advanced Administration Tasks*, to learn about service management

Managing web server modules

During the configuration of the Apache web server, we often have to install Apache modules for various different tasks, and they have to be loaded explicitly so that Apache web server can use them and do the respective tasks. In this recipe, we will learn how to enable and disable Apache web server modules using Salt.

How to do it...

We will use the same minion as in the previous chapter.

1. Edit `/opt/salt-cookbook/development/apache/init.sls` to have the following entries:

```
apache_packages:
  pkg.installed:
    - pkgs:
      - apache2

enable_rewrite_module:
  apache_module.enable:
    - name: rewrite
    - require:
      - pkg: apache_packages
    - watch_in:
      - service: apache_service
```

```
apache_service:
  service:
    - name: apache2
    - running
    - enable: True
    - require:
      - pkg: apache_packages
```

2. Apply the state to the minion, using the following command:

```
[root@salt-master ~]# salt 'salt-minion-ubuntu' state.sls
apache saltenv=development

salt-minion-ubuntu:
----------
          ID: apache_packages
    Function: pkg.installed
      Result: True
     Comment: All specified packages are already installed.
     Started: 01:23:20.714205
    Duration: 5936.48 ms
     Changes:
----------
          ID: enable_rewrite_module
    Function: apache_module.enable
        Name: rewrite
      Result: True
     Comment:
     Started: 01:23:26.651159
    Duration: 323.882 ms
     Changes:
              ----------
              new:
                  rewrite
              old:
                  None
----------
          ID: apache_service
    Function: service.running
        Name: apache2
```

```
        Result: True

        Comment: Service apache2 is already enabled, and is in
    the desired state

        Started: 01:23:26.975470

        Duration: 89.565 ms

        Changes:


    Summary
    ------------

    Succeeded: 3 (changed=1)

    Failed:    0
    ------------

    Total states run:     3
```

How it works...

In this recipe, we demonstrated the ability of Salt to enable and disable Apache web server modules. The Apache web server supports a lot of modules to perform a wide range of tasks. Although some of the modules are installed and enabled by default, many are not. The objective of this recipe is to enable an already installed module. For many others, the module needs to be installed first, using the `pkg` module, before it can be enabled.

Here we used the `apache_module` state module to enable the rewrite module in Apache web server:

```
enable_rewrite_module:
  apache_module.enable:
    - name: rewrite
    - require:
      - pkg: apache_packages
    - watch_in:
      - service: apache_service
```

We used the `enable` function to make sure that the module is enabled. The name of the module is mentioned using the `name` attribute. We also made this module dependent on the Apache packages definition.

This module makes use of the `a2enmod` binary that is available in Ubuntu to perform these tasks on the modules. The `disable` function may also be used to disable an already enabled module.

There's more...

The `a2enmod` binary is only available in Ubuntu and its variants, and is not available in CentOS and similar distributions. As a result of this, the `apache_module` state module only works on Ubuntu and its variants.

For CentOS and similar distributions, the modules will need to be manually entered into the configuration file, and the `file` module can be used with the `managed` function to achieve this task.

See also

▶ The *Apache web server packages and services* recipe, to learn how to install and configure the Apache web server

▶ `http://docs.saltstack.com/en/latest/ref/states/all/salt.states.`
`apache_module.html#module-salt.states.apache_module`, to learn more about the `apache_module` state module

Adding web server configuration

One of the most important tasks of Apache web server management is to make sure that the proper configuration file for the website or the application is in place. In this recipe, we will learn how to configure this file with a lot of details and parameters using Salt.

How to do it...

We will use the same minion as in the previous recipe.

1. Edit `/opt/salt-cookbook/development/apache/init.sls` to have the following entries:

```
apache_packages:
  pkg.installed:
    - pkgs:
      - apache2

enable_rewrite_module:
  apache_module.enable:
    - name: rewrite
    - require:
      - pkg: apache_packages
```

```
/etc/apache2/sites-enabled/salt-cookbook.conf:
  apache.configfile:
    - config:
      - VirtualHost:
          this: '*:80'
          ServerName:
            - salt-cookbook.com
          ServerAlias:
            - www.salt-cookbook.com
          ErrorLog: /var/log/apache2/salt-cookbook.com-
error_log
          CustomLog: /var/log/apache2/salt-cookbook.com-
access_log combined
          DocumentRoot: /var/www/vhosts/salt-cookbook.com
          Directory:
            this: /var/www/vhosts/salt-cookbook.com
            Order: Allow,Deny
            Allow from: all
            Options:
              - +Indexes
              - FollowSymlinks
            AllowOverride: All

apache_service:
  service:
    - name: apache2
    - running
    - enable: True
    - require:
      - pkg: apache_packages
```

2. Apply the state to the minion, using the following command:

```
[root@salt-master ~]# salt 'salt-minion-ubuntu' state.sls
apache saltenv=development

salt-minion-ubuntu:
----------
  .

  .

  .

  .

----------
          ID: /etc/apache2/sites-enabled/salt-cookbook.conf
```

```
Function: apache.configfile
  Result: True
 Comment: Successfully created configuration.
 Started: 01:29:15.880379
Duration: 1.043 ms
 Changes:
            ----------
            new:
                <VirtualHost *:80>
                ServerName salt-cookbook.com
                ServerAlias www.salt-cookbook.com
                ErrorLog /var/log/apache2/salt-cookbook.com-
error_log
                CustomLog /var/log/apache2/salt-
cookbook.com-access_log combined
                DocumentRoot /var/www/vhosts/salt-
cookbook.com
                <Directory /var/www/vhosts/salt-
cookbook.com>
                Order Allow,Deny
                Allow from all
                Options +Indexes FollowSymlinks
                AllowOverride All
                </Directory>
                </VirtualHost>
            old:

----------
    .
    .
    .
    .


Summary
------------
Succeeded: 4 (changed=1)
Failed:    0
------------
Total states run:     4
```

How it works...

In this recipe, we demonstrated the ability of Salt to implement the configuration file for a particular website or application. This module can easily be termed as one of the most important modules as it makes web server configuration much more flexible.

First, we used the name of the configuration file that will be implemented, and then we made use of the apache module with the configfile function to add the subsequent parameters and attributes:

```
/etc/apache2/sites-enabled/salt-cookbook.conf:
  apache.configfile:
    - config:
```

The config attribute is important as it tells Salt that all the attributes after it are the Apache web server-specific configuration parameters.

Next we mentioned the entire configuration of our website or application:

```
        - VirtualHost:
            this: '*:80'
            ServerName:
              - salt-cookbook.com
            ServerAlias:
              - www.salt-cookbook.com
            ErrorLog: /var/log/apache2/salt-cookbook.com-error_log
            CustomLog: /var/log/apache2/salt-cookbook.com-access_log
  combined
            DocumentRoot: /var/www/vhosts/salt-cookbook.com
            Directory:
              this: /var/www/vhosts/salt-cookbook.com
              Order: Allow,Deny
              Allow from: all
              Options:
                - +Indexes
                - FollowSymlinks
              AllowOverride: All
```

The first attribute is the VirtualHost attribute. In Apache web server configuration files, there are lots of configurations that are enclosed in blocks. The block starts with an attribute enclosed in <> and also ends the same way, but with an extra / in the enclosure. An example is as follows, where we see how the VirtualHost block looks in the configuration file:

```
<VirtualHost *:80>
  .
  .
  .
</VirtualHost>
```

In our Salt configuration, immediately after the `VirtualHost` attribute, we see the following entry:

```
this: '*:80'
```

The `this` attribute mentions that the value that it holds will be in the enclosure, which precedes this attribute: that is, the `VirtualHost` attribute comes before this entry. So, in the Apache configuration file, it will look like this:

```
<VirtualHost *:80>
```

Where the `*:80` is taken from the `this` attribute.

Next we mentioned all the common parameters that come under the `VirtualHost` block in the Apache configuration file, such as `ServerName`, `ServerAlias`, `ErrorLog`, `CustomLog`, and `DocumentRoot`.

We have a similar entry to the `VirtualHost` entry that we have seen previously; here, it is the `Directory` parameter. Inside the `VirtualHost` block there can be other nested blocks, one of which is the `Directory` block, others being `Location`, `Files`, `IfModule`, and so on. We again see the `this` attribute, which tells us that the configuration will look like the following:

```
<Directory /var/www/vhosts/salt-cookbook.com>
```

All subsequent attributes after this entry, which have similar indentations, will be under the `Directory` block in the configuration file.

The entries shown in this example are just some of the parameters which can be configured using Salt. Almost all the parameters seen in an Apache web server configuration file can be configured using Salt.

See also

> ▸ The *Apache web server packages and services* recipe, to learn how to install and configure the Apache web server

> ▸ The *Managing web server modules* recipe, to learn how to enable Apache web server modules

> ▸ `http://docs.saltstack.com/en/latest/ref/states/all/salt.states.apache.html#module-salt.states.apache`, to learn more about the `apache` state module

Web server security with htpasswd

After the server has been configured and services have been started, the next step is to implement security for the server to perform access control. In this recipe, we will learn how to configure security for the Apache web server using Salt.

How to do it...

We will use the same minion as in the previous recipe.

1. Edit `/opt/salt-cookbook/development/apache/init.sls` to have the following entries:

```
apache_packages:
  pkg.installed:
    - pkgs:
      - apache2
      - apache2-utils

enable_rewrite_module:
  apache_module.enable:
    - name: rewrite
    - require:
      - pkg: apache_packages

/etc/apache2/sites-enabled/salt-cookbook.conf:
  apache.configfile:
    - config:
    - VirtualHost:
        this: '*:80'
        ServerName:
          - salt-cookbook.com
        ServerAlias:
          - www.salt-cookbook.com
        ErrorLog: logs/salt-cookbook.com-error_log
        CustomLog: logs/salt-cookbook.com-access_log
combined
        DocumentRoot: /var/www/vhosts/salt-cookbook.com
        Directory:
          this: /var/www/vhosts/salt-cookbook.com
          Order: Allow,Deny
          Allow from: all
```

```
                    Options:
                      - +Indexes
                      - FollowSymlinks
                    AllowOverride: All

        website_directory:
          file.directory:
            - name: /var/www/vhosts/salt-cookbook.com
            - makedirs: True

        salt-cookbook:
          webutil.user_exists:
            - password: 'saltc00kb00k'
            - htpasswd_file: /etc/apache2/.htpasswd
            - options: d
            - force: true

        htaccess_file:
          file.managed:
            - name: /var/www/vhosts/salt-cookbook.com/.htaccess
            - source: salt://apache/files/htaccess
            - mode: 400
            - require:
              - file: website_directory
              - webutil: salt-cookbook

        apache_service:
          service:
            - name: apache2
            - running
            - enable: True
            - require:
              - pkg: apache_packages
```

2. Create a directory called `files` in the `apache` state directory. Create and edit `/opt/salt-cookbook/development/apache/files/htaccess` to have the following entries:

```
AuthType Basic
AuthName "Restricted Access"
AuthUserFile /etc/apache2/.htpasswd
Require user salt-cookbook
```

3. Apply the state to the minion, using the following command:

```
[root@salt-master ~]# salt 'salt-minion-ubuntu' state.sls
apache saltenv=development
salt-minion-ubuntu:
----------
    .
    .
    .
    .
----------
          ID: website_directory
    Function: file.directory
        Name: /var/www/vhosts/salt-cookbook.com
      Result: True
     Comment: Directory /var/www/vhosts/salt-cookbook.com
updated
     Started: 01:38:52.084826
    Duration: 1.418 ms
     Changes:
              ----------
              /var/www/vhosts/salt-cookbook.com:
                  New Dir
----------
          ID: salt-cookbook
    Function: webutil.user_exists
      Result: True
     Comment: Warning: Password truncated to 8 characters by
CRYPT algorithm.
              Adding password for user salt-cookbook
     Started: 01:38:52.086366
    Duration: 21.269 ms
     Changes:
              ----------
              salt-cookbook:
                  True
```

```
          - - - - - - - - - -
                ID: htaccess_file
          Function: file.managed
              Name: /var/www/vhosts/salt-cookbook.com/.htaccess
            Result: True
           Comment: File /var/www/vhosts/salt-cookbook.com/.htaccess
updated
           Started: 01:38:52.108549
          Duration: 297.826 ms
           Changes:
                    - - - - - - - - - -
                    diff:
                        New file
                    mode:
                        0400
          - - - - - - - - - -
              .
              .
              .
              .


Summary
- - - - - - - - - - - -
Succeeded: 7 (changed=3)
Failed:    0
- - - - - - - - - - - -
Total states run:      7
```

How it works...

In this recipe, we demonstrated the ability of Salt to configure authentication in an Apache web server configuration using the htpasswd username and password configuration. The objective of this recipe is to generate an htpasswd file, which is the default authentication mechanism for Apache web server, and then make sure that the file is referenced correctly when the web page is accessed.

We introduced three new definitions in the file. First, we created the directory which is the DocumentRoot directory for this website or application. In a production implementation, this directory will be populated with the website data and either the Git or the svn module can be used to fetch the data from a repository.

```
website_directory:
  file.directory:
    - name: /var/www/vhosts/salt-cookbook.com
    - makedirs: True
```

We used the file module with the directory function to create the directory.

Next we used the webutil module with the user_exists function to create the htpasswd file, which contains the username and password with which we authenticate when accessing the website.

```
salt-cookbook:
  webutil.user_exists:
    - password: 'saltc00kb00k'
    - htpasswd_file: /etc/apache2/.htpasswd
    - options: d
    - force: true
```

The first salt-cookbook entry is the username which will be used to authenticate. The password attribute mentions the password which will be used; this value can also be fetched from pillar data. The htpasswd_file attribute mentions the location of the file where the username and password are stored. The options attribute can be used to mention options available in the htpasswd command. Here, we mentioned the -d option, which forces CRYPT encryption of the password.

Next we used the file module to place a .htaccess file in the directory, which acts as the DocumentRoot for the website:

```
htaccess_file:
  file.managed:
    - name: /var/www/vhosts/salt-cookbook.com/.htaccess
    - source: salt://apache/files/htaccess
    - mode: 400
    - require:
      - file: website_directory
      - webutil: salt-cookbook
```

This file contains the path to the htpasswd file that we configured in the previous definition and also mentions the username that will be used for authentication when we try to access this website.

We made this definition dependent on the file definition to create the directory and also the htpasswd file.

See also

▶ The *Apache web server packages and services* recipe, to learn how to configure Apache web server

▶ The *Managing web server modules* recipe, to learn how to enable Apache web server modules

▶ The *Adding web server configuration* recipe, to learn how to implement the Apache web server configuration file

▶ `http://docs.saltstack.com/en/latest/ref/states/all/salt.states.htpasswd.html#module-salt.states.htpasswd`, to learn more about the `htpasswd/webutil` state module

Setting up Java for Apache Tomcat

Apache Tomcat is undoubtedly the most widely used open source application server for Java-based applications, and it depends on Java to run successfully. In this recipe, we will learn how to set up Java for Tomcat.

How to do it...

1. Configure a new minion called `salt-minion` in the `development` environment.

2. Download the Java archive file from the following link; it should be something like `jdk-7u71-linux-x64.gz`. The md5 hash for the file should also be available from the same location: `http://www.oracle.com/technetwork/java/javase/downloads/jdk7-downloads-1880260.html`

3. Next we hosted the Java archive file on a local node, called `repo`, via a web server: the link for this should be something like `http://repo/jdk-7u71-linux-x64.gz`.

4. Create a new state directory called `tomcat` in the `development` environment.

5. Create and edit `/opt/salt-cookbook/development/tomcat/java.sls` to have the following entries:

```
java_package:
  archive:
    - extracted
    - name: /opt/
    - source: http://repo/jdk-7u71-linux-x64.gz
    - source_hash: md5=22761b214b1505f1a9671b124b0f44f4
    - archive_format: tar
    - if_missing: /opt/jdk1.7.0_71/
```

```
java_symlink:
  file.symlink:
    - name: /opt/java
    - target: jdk1.7.0_71
    - require:
      - archive: java_package

install_java_alternative:
  alternatives.install:
    - name: java
    - link: /usr/bin/java
    - path: /opt/java/bin/java
    - priority: 1
    - require:
      - file: java_symlink

set_java_alternative:
  alternatives.set:
    - name: java
    - path: /opt/java/bin/java
    - require:
      - alternatives: install_java_alternative
```

6. Apply the state to the minion, using the following command:

```
[root@salt-master ~]# salt 'salt-minion' state.sls tomcat.java
saltenv=development
salt-minion:
----------
          ID: java_package
    Function: archive.extracted
        Name: /opt/
      Result: True
     Comment: http://repo/jdk-7u71-linux-x64.gz extracted in
/opt/
     Started: 03:50:10.127188
    Duration: 38140.209 ms
     Changes:
              ----------
              directories_created:
                  - /opt/
                  - /opt/jdk1.7.0_71/
```

```
                extracted_files:
                    - jdk1.7.0_71

    .

    .

    .

    .

----------
              ID: java_symlink
        Function: file.symlink
            Name: /opt/java
          Result: True
         Comment: Created new symlink /opt/java -> jdk1.7.0_71
         Started: 03:50:48.279877
        Duration: 60.181 ms
         Changes:
                    ----------
                    new:
                        /opt/java
----------
              ID: install_java_alternative
        Function: alternatives.install
            Name: java
          Result: True
         Comment: Setting alternative for java to
/opt/java/bin/java with priority 1
         Started: 03:50:48.341002
        Duration: 370.984 ms
         Changes:
                    ----------
                    link:
                        /usr/bin/java
                    name:
                        java
                    path:
                        /opt/java/bin/java
```

```
           priority:
               1
- - - - - - - - - -
             ID: set_java_alternative
       Function: alternatives.set
           Name: java
         Result: True
        Comment: Alternative for java already set to
/opt/java/bin/java
        Started: 03:50:48.714373
       Duration: 2.116 ms
        Changes:

Summary
- - - - - - - - - - - -
Succeeded: 4 (changed=3)
Failed:    0
- - - - - - - - - - - -
Total states run:     4
```

How it works...

In this recipe, we demonstrated the ability of Salt to use many of its modules and configured Java to be used by Tomcat. The objective of the recipe is to fetch the Java archive file from a local source, extract it, set required links for the directory, and install required alternatives for the Java binary to make them available to the system.

First, we downloaded the Java archive file from the following link:

```
http://www.oracle.com/technetwork/java/javase/downloads/jdk7-
downloads-1880260.html
```

Next we hosted the file on a local node, called `repo`, via a web server, and used the `archive` module to fetch the file and extract it to the desired location:

```
java_package:
  archive:
    - extracted
    - name: /opt/
    - source: http://repo/jdk-7u71-linux-x64.gz
```

```
        - source_hash: md5=22761b214b1505f1a9671b124b0f44f4
        - archive_format: tar
        - if_missing: /opt/jdk1.7.0_71/
```

We also included a condition with the `if_missing` attribute so as to execute this state only if the required directory does not exist.

Next we used the `file` module to create a symbolic link to point to the extracted Java directory using a simpler name for that directory.:

```
java_symlink:
  file.symlink:
    - name: /opt/java
    - target: jdk1.7.0_71
    - require:
      - archive: java_package
```

Finally, we used the `alternatives` module to install and configure the alternative for Java, ensuring that the `java` binary is available to the system and correctly points to the source we configured, that is to `/opt/java`:

```
install_java_alternative:
  alternatives.install:
    - name: java
    - link: /usr/bin/java
    - path: /opt/java/bin/java
    - priority: 1
    - require:
      - file: java_symlink

set_java_alternative:
  alternatives.set:
    - name: java
    - path: /opt/java/bin/java
    - require:
      - alternatives: install_java_alternative
```

Now that Java is configured, we will look at how to install and configure Apache Tomcat in the next recipe.

See also

- ▶ The *Handling archive files* recipe, in *Chapter 4, General Administration Tasks*, to learn how to manage archive files
- ▶ The *Managing files* and *Configuring alternatives* recipes, in *Chapter 5, Advanced Administration Tasks*, to learn how to configure files and alternatives

Apache Tomcat packages, files, and services

In this recipe, we will learn how to install Tomcat packages, configure the appropriate files needed for Tomcat to function, and configure the Tomcat service.

How to do it...

We will use the same minion as in the previous recipe.

1. Create and edit `/opt/salt-cookbook/development/tomcat/init.sls` to have the following entries:

```
include:
  - tomcat.java

tomcat-server:
  archive:
    - extracted
    - name: /opt/
    - source:
http://mirror.nus.edu.sg/apache/tomcat/tomcat-
6/v6.0.43/bin/apache-tomcat-6.0.43.tar.gz
    - source_hash: md5=0abbb1852a608c8b4ccb7003c700337b
    - archive_format: tar
    - if_missing: /opt/apache-tomcat-6.0.43/
    - require:
      - alternatives: set_java_alternative

tomcat_symlink:
  file.symlink:
    - name: /opt/tomcat
    - target: apache-tomcat-6.0.43
    - require:
      - archive: tomcat-server

tomcat_init_script:
  file.managed:
    - name: /etc/init.d/tomcat
    - source: salt://tomcat/files/tomcat_init_script
    - mode: 0755
    - require:
      - archive: tomcat-server
```

```
        add_tomcat_service:
          cmd.wait:
            - name: 'chkconfig --add tomcat'
            - shell: /bin/bash
            - stateful: False
            - require:
              - file: tomcat_init_script
            - watch:
              - file: tomcat_init_script

        tomcat_service_start:
          cmd.run:
            - name: 'service tomcat start'
            - shell: /bin/bash
            - unless: 'ps -ef | grep apache.catalina.startup.Bootstra[p]'
            - require:
              - file: tomcat_init_script
```

2. Create a directory called `files` in the `tomcat` state directory.

3. Copy over the `tomcat_init_script` file from the code base to the `files` directory.

4. Apply the state to the minion, using the following command:

```
[root@salt-master ~]# salt 'salt-minion' state.sls tomcat
saltenv=development

salt-minion:
----------
          ID: tomcat-server
    Function: archive.extracted
        Name: /opt/
      Result: True
     Comment: http://mirror.nus.edu.sg/apache/tomcat/tomcat-
6/v6.0.43/bin/apache-tomcat-6.0.43.tar.gz extracted in /opt/
     Started: 02:48:25.666002
    Duration: 25893.675 ms
     Changes:
              ----------
              directories_created:
                  - /opt/
                  - /opt/apache-tomcat-6.0.43/
```

```
            extracted_files:
                - apache-tomcat-6.0.43/bin/catalina.sh

    .

    .

    .

    .

----------
          ID: tomcat_symlink
    Function: file.symlink
        Name: /opt/tomcat
      Result: True
     Comment: Created new symlink /opt/tomcat -> apache-
tomcat-6.0.43
     Started: 02:48:51.560532
    Duration: 2.588 ms
     Changes:
                ----------
                new:
                    /opt/tomcat
----------
          ID: tomcat_init_script
    Function: file.managed
        Name: /etc/init.d/tomcat
      Result: True
     Comment: File /etc/init.d/tomcat updated
     Started: 02:48:52.989985
    Duration: 389.405 ms
     Changes:
                ----------
                diff:
                    New file
                mode:
                    0755
----------
          ID: add_tomcat_service
```

```
Function: cmd.wait
    Name: chkconfig --add tomcat
  Result: True
 Comment: Command "chkconfig --add tomcat" run
 Started: 02:48:53.381505
Duration: 22.883 ms
 Changes:
          ----------
          pid:
              3756
          retcode:
              0
          stderr:

          stdout:


----------
      ID: tomcat_service_start
Function: cmd.run
    Name: service tomcat start
  Result: True
 Comment: Command "service tomcat start" run
 Started: 02:48:54.404930
Duration: 180.711 ms
 Changes:
          ----------
          pid:
              3760
          retcode:
              0
          stderr:

          stdout:
              Starting tomcat
```

```
Summary
------------
Succeeded: 5 (changed=5)
Failed:    0
------------
Total states run:    5
```

How it works...

In this recipe, we demonstrated how to install and configure the Apache Tomcat application server. The objective of the recipe is to download and extract the Apache Tomcat archive file from the official source repository, create a symbolic link, install a startup script for the server, and make sure the service is up and running.

First, we included the `java` SLS file in the new `init.sls` file so that we can make the Tomcat installation dependent on the Java installation. We then used the `archive` module to fetch the file from the official location, and then we compared it with the md5 hash to confirm the download:

```
include:
  - tomcat.java

tomcat-server:
  archive:
    - extracted
    - name: /opt/
    - source: http://mirror.nus.edu.sg/apache/tomcat/tomcat-
6/v6.0.43/bin/apache-tomcat-6.0.43.tar.gz
    - source_hash: md5=0abbb1852a608c8b4ccb7003c700337b
    - archive_format: tar
    - if_missing: /opt/apache-tomcat-6.0.43/
    - require:
      - alternatives: set_java_alternative
```

We also configured a condition to execute this module only if the directory does not exist, and made the definition dependent on the Java installation.

Next we used the `file` module to create a symbolic link to create a simpler name for the Tomcat directory:

```
tomcat_symlink:
  file.symlink:
    - name: /opt/tomcat
    - target: apache-tomcat-6.0.43
    - require:
      - archive: tomcat-server
```

Next we copied over a Tomcat startup script from the code base to the Salt repository, so that it could be used, in turn, in the definition to copy it over to the minion used in the Tomcat installation.

```
tomcat_init_script:
  file.managed:
    - name: /etc/init.d/tomcat
    - source: salt://tomcat/files/tomcat_init_script
    - mode: 0755
    - require:
      - archive: tomcat-server
```

We then used the cmd module to execute a command to install the tomcat service into the chkconfig list, so that it can be configured to start at boot time:

```
add_tomcat_service:
  cmd.wait:
    - name: 'chkconfig --add tomcat'
    - shell: /bin/bash
    - stateful: False
    - require:
      - file: tomcat_init_script
    - watch:
      - file: tomcat_init_script
```

Finally, we again used the cmd module to execute a command to start the service if it is not running already. We put in a condition using the unless attribute to verify if the Tomcat process is running:

```
tomcat_service_start:
  cmd.run:
    - name: 'service tomcat start'
    - shell: /bin/bash
    - unless: 'ps -ef | grep apache.catalina.startup.Bootstra[p]'
    - require:
      - file: tomcat_init_script
```

See also

▶ The *Handling archive files* and *Running commands* recipes, in *Chapter 4, General Administration Tasks*, to learn how to manage archive files and run commands

▶ The *Managing files* recipe, in *Chapter 5, Advanced Administration Tasks*, to learn how to configure files

Deploying the WAR file in Apache Tomcat

After all the configurations have been completed, the final step is to deploy the WAR files, which contain all the application-related files and are served by the application server. In this recipe, we will learn how to deploy WAR files using Salt.

How to do it...

We will use the same minion as in the previous recipe.

For this example, we will use a sample WAR file called `sample.war`. Many such example application WAR files can be found online, for example at this location `https://tomcat.apache.org/tomcat-6.0-doc/appdev/sample/sample.war`.

The file is downloaded and located in the `/opt/salt-cookbook/development/tomcat/files/sample.war` location.

1. Create and edit `/opt/salt-cookbook/development/tomcat/deploy.sls` to have the following entries:

   ```
   include:
     - tomcat

   sample_war:
     file.managed:
       - name: /opt/tomcat/webapps/sample.war
       - source: salt://tomcat/files/sample.war
       - mode: 0644
       - require:
         - file: /opt/tomcat
   ```

2. Apply the state to the minion, using the following command:

   ```
   [root@salt-master ~]# salt 'salt-minion' state.highstate
   saltenv=development
   salt-minion:
   ----------
       .
       .
       .
       .
   ----------
             ID: sample_war
   ```

```
Function: file.managed
    Name: /opt/tomcat/webapps/sample.war
  Result: True
 Comment: File /opt/tomcat/webapps/sample.war updated
 Started: 05:05:01.309881
Duration: 316.716 ms
 Changes:
          ----------
          diff:
              New file
          mode:
              0644


Summary
------------
Succeeded: 8 (changed=1)
Failed:    0
------------
Total states run:     8
```

How it works...

In this recipe, we demonstrated the procedure to deploy a WAR file in Tomcat. WAR files contain all of the files needed to serve the application in Tomcat, and can be simply copied over to the webapps directory in the Tomcat base directory.

We included the init.sls file in the deploy.sls file to make the definition dependent on the Tomcat installation:

```
include:
  - tomcat

sample_war:
  file.managed:
    - name: /opt/tomcat/webapps/sample.war
    - source: salt://tomcat/files/sample.war
    - mode: 0644
    - require:
      - file: /opt/tomcat
```

We then used the file module to copy over a WAR file called sample.war, which is available in the official website of Apache Tomcat.

There's more...

To deploy a WAR file in Tomcat, there is another way to do the task using the `tomcat` module.

Using the `war_deployed` function of the `tomcat` module, WAR files can be deployed in Tomcat in the following manner:

```
sample_app:
  tomcat.war_deployed:
    - name: /sample
    - war: salt://tomcat/files/sample.war
    - require:
      - file: /opt/tomcat
```

The `war` attribute takes the source of the WAR file. However, this method is not known to work in all platforms or with all Java and Tomcat versions.

See also

- ▶ The *Managing files* recipe, in *Chapter 5, Advanced Administration Tasks*, to learn how to manage files using Salt

- ▶ The *Apache Tomcat package, files, and services* recipe, to learn how to configure Tomcat

- ▶ `http://docs.saltstack.com/en/latest/ref/states/all/salt.states.tomcat.html#module-salt.states.tomcat`, to learn more about the Tomcat module

7

Managing Databases

In this chapter, you will cover:

- ▸ Using MySQL packages, files, and services
- ▸ Using MySQL databases
- ▸ Creating MySQL database users
- ▸ Running MySQL queries
- ▸ Providing MySQL user grants
- ▸ Using PostgreSQL packages, files, and services
- ▸ Setting up PostgreSQL groups and users
- ▸ Configuring PostgreSQL databases

Introduction

With the availability of so many types of databases in present times, it is a really complex task to design and implement infrastructure with lots of parameters to consider. Among the multiple options available, MySQL and Postgres seem to be most widely used, both in small business infrastructures as well as large enterprises, due to the flexibility and stability they offer.

The most common tasks that are generally performed by configuration management tools are installing the databases, making sure the configuration files are in place, and the service is running. However, Salt goes a step ahead, and enables us to configure databases and few more important configuration tasks on the database software, so that managing databases is much simpler and scalable.

In this chapter, you will learn how to configure these databases, and dive deeper into the procedures of using different Salt modules to implement advanced parameters and configurations on the database software.

Using MySQL packages, files, and services

In this recipe, you will learn about how to install the MySQL database. Make sure the proper configuration file for MySQL is present on the host, and the database service is running.

How to do it...

1. Configure a new minion in the staging environment called `salt-minion-mysql`. Create a new state directory called `mysql` in the staging environment.

2. Create and edit `/opt/salt-cookbook/staging/mysql/init.sls` to have the following entries:

```
mysql_package:
  pkg.installed:
    - name: mysql-server

mysql_conf:
  file.managed:
    - name: /etc/my.cnf
    - source: salt://mysql/files/my.cnf
    - user: root
    - group: root
    - mode: 0644
    - require:
      - pkg: mysql_package

mysql_service:
  service:
    - name: mysqld
    - running
    - enable: True
    - require:
      - file: mysql_conf
    - watch:
      - file: mysql_conf
```

3. Create a directory called `files` in the `mysql` state directory.

4. Create and edit `/opt/salt-cookbook/staging/mysql/files/my.cnf` to have the following entries:

```
[mysqld]
datadir=/var/lib/mysql
socket=/var/lib/mysql/mysql.sock
```

```
user=mysql
symbolic-links=0

[mysqld_safe]
log-error=/var/log/mysqld.log
pid-file=/var/run/mysqld/mysqld.pid
```

5. Apply the state to the minion, with the following command:

```
[root@salt-master ~]# salt 'salt-minion-mysql' state.sls mysql
saltenv=staging
salt-minion-mysql:
----------
          ID: mysql_package
    Function: pkg.installed
        Name: mysql-server
      Result: True
     Comment: The following packages were installed/updated:
mysql-server.
     Started: 23:02:58.327791
    Duration: 63413.884 ms
     Changes:
              ----------
              mysql:
                  ----------
                  new:
                      5.1.73-3.el6_5
                  old:

              mysql-libs:
                  ----------
                  new:
                      5.1.73-3.el6_5
                  old:
                      5.1.71-1.el6
              mysql-server:
                  ----------
                  new:
                      5.1.73-3.el6_5
```

```
                      old:

           perl-DBD-MySQL:
           ----------
              new:
                  4.013-3.el6
              old:

           perl-DBI:
           ----------
              new:
                  1.609-4.el6
              old:


----------
          ID: mysql_conf
    Function: file.managed
        Name: /etc/my.cnf
      Result: True
     Comment: File /etc/my.cnf is in the correct state
     Started: 23:04:01.742191
    Duration: 343.621 ms
     Changes:
----------
          ID: mysql_service
    Function: service.running
        Name: mysqld
      Result: True
     Comment: Service mysqld has been enabled, and is running
     Started: 23:04:02.086336
    Duration: 4796.126 ms
     Changes:
             ----------
             mysqld:
                 True
```

```
Summary
------------
Succeeded: 3  (changed=2)
Failed:     0
------------
Total states run:      3
```

How it works...

In this recipe, we demonstrated the procedure to install the database, and to implement its configuration file and the database service.

First, we used the `pkg` module to install the `mysql-server` package, which is the name of the MySQL server for CentOS:

```
mysql_package:
  pkg.installed:
    - name: mysql-server
```

The module automatically fetches the dependencies for this package, and installs them along with the main package.

Next, we used the `file` module to make sure that the proper MySQL configuration file is configured on the host:

```
mysql_conf:
  file.managed:
    - name: /etc/my.cnf
    - source: salt://mysql/files/my.cnf
    - user: root
    - group: root
    - mode: 0644
    - require:
      - pkg: mysql_package
```

We also created the file on the Salt master, which will be copied over to the host. The file configuration depends on the package installation using the `require` attribute.

Finally, we configured the MySQL service definition using the service module:

```
mysql_service:
  service:
    - name: mysqld
    - running
    - enable: True
```

```
    - require:
      - pkg: mysql_conf
    - watch:
      - pkg: mysql_conf
```

It ensures that the service is enabled to start at boot time, and is always running. It also depends on the MySQL configuration file and keeps a watch on the file for any changes.

See also

▶ The *Managing packages using the default package manager* recipe, from *Chapter 5, Advanced Administration Tasks*, to know more about installing packages

▶ The *Managing files* recipe from *Chapter 5, Advanced Administration Tasks* to learn about managing files

▶ The *Managing services* recipe, from *Chapter 5, Advanced Administration Tasks*, to learn about service management

Using MySQL databases

In this recipe, you will learn how to create and remove databases in MySQL. You will also learn how to interrelate these definitions with other Salt definitions, and make all the database components work together.

How to do it...

We will use the same minion as the previous recipe.

1. Create and edit `/opt/salt-cookbook/staging/mysql/database.sls` to have the following entries:

```
include:
  - mysql

MySQL-python:
  pkg.installed

stg_databases:
  mysql_database.present:
    - name: stagingdb
    - require:
      - pkg: MySQL-python
      - service: mysql_service
```

```
    databases_to_remove:
      mysql_database.absent:
        - name: test
        - require:
          - pkg: MySQL-python
          - service: mysql_service
```

2. Apply the state to the minion, using the following command:

```
[root@salt-master ~]# salt 'salt-minion-mysql' state.sls
mysql.database saltenv=staging
salt-minion-mysql:
----------
          ID: mysql_package
    Function: pkg.installed
        Name: mysql-server
      Result: True
     Comment: Package mysql-server is already installed.
     Started: 02:30:23.014093
    Duration: 644.129 ms
     Changes:
----------
          ID: mysql_conf
    Function: file.managed
        Name: /etc/my.cnf
      Result: True
     Comment: File /etc/my.cnf is in the correct state
     Started: 02:30:23.658423
    Duration: 278.91 ms
     Changes:
----------
          ID: mysql_service
    Function: service.running
        Name: mysqld
      Result: True
     Comment: Service mysqld is already enabled, and is in the
desired state
     Started: 02:30:23.937874
    Duration: 350.67 ms
```

```
        Changes:
----------
            ID: MySQL-python
      Function: pkg.installed
        Result: True
       Comment: Package MySQL-python is already installed.
       Started: 02:30:24.289292
      Duration: 4.867 ms
        Changes:
----------
            ID: stg_databases
      Function: mysql_database.present
          Name: stagingdb
        Result: True
       Comment: The database stagingdb has been created
       Started: 02:20:59.289944
      Duration: 425.321 ms
        Changes:
                  ----------
                  stagingdb:
                      Present
----------
            ID: databases_to_remove
      Function: mysql_database.absent
          Name: test
        Result: True
       Comment: Database test has been removed
       Started: 02:20:59.715780
      Duration: 304.277 ms
        Changes:
                  ----------
                  test:
                      Absent
Summary
------------
```

```
Succeeded: 6 (changed=2)

Failed:    0

------------

Total states run:    6
```

How it works...

In this recipe, we demonstrated the ability of Salt to configure databases on a MySQL database setup. Each MySQL installation has a database, called `test` by default. For security reasons, it is standard practice to remove this database after the installation. The objective of this recipe is to create a new database, and remove the `test` database.

First, we included the `mysql` state's `init.sls` file in the new SLS file, using the `include` attribute:

```
include:
  - mysql
```

Next, we used the `pkg` module to install the `MySQL-python` package on the system. This package is required for the `mysql` modules to work in Salt. Without this package, we will get an error as follows:

```
State 'mysql_database.absent' found in SLS 'mysql.database' is
unavailable
```

Next, we used the `mysql_database` module to create a database using the `present` function, and then to remove the `test` database using the `absent` function:

```
stg_databases:
  mysql_database.present:
    - name: stagingdb
    - require:
      - pkg: MySQL-python
      - service: mysql_service

databases_to_remove:
  mysql_database.absent:
    - name: test
    - require:
      - pkg: MySQL-python
      - service: mysql_service
```

We also made these definitions dependent on the `MySQL-python` package and the MySQL service daemon.

In MySQL, after the server package is installed, it is possible for the `root` user to connect to the database without using a password from the local system. If a password is implemented for this access, the Salt `mysql` modules will no longer work, as they use this feature of MySQL to make the necessary changes to the databases. In that case, the MySQL credentials should be passed as the connection arguments in the `/etc/salt/minion` file. To know more about this, please refer to the following link, `http://docs.saltstack.com/en/latest/ref/modules/all/salt.modules.mysql.html`.

See also

▶ `http://docs.saltstack.com/en/latest/ref/states/all/salt.states.mysql_database.html#module-salt.states.mysql_database`, to know more about the `mysql_database` module

▶ The *Using MySQL packages, files, and services* recipe, to learn how to install and configure MySQL

Creating MySQL database users

Setting up users and giving them proper permissions to access databases is one of the most critical tasks in database management. In this recipe, you will learn how to create database users and manage their access from different servers.

How to do it...

We will use the same minion as the previous recipe.

1. Create and edit `/opt/salt-cookbook/pillar/staging/mysql/init.sls` to have the following entries:

```
mysql:
  stg-passwd-hash:
'*CAC560C0ED394C2D89B7A1F08422B200B2FFBC26'
```

2. Edit `/opt/salt-cookbook/pillar/staging/top.sls` to have the following entries:

```
staging:
  '*':
    - mysql
```

3. Create and edit `/opt/salt-cookbook/staging/mysql/users.sls` to have the following entries:

```
include:
  - mysql.database
```

```
db_user:
  mysql_user.present:
    - name: stg-db
    - host: '*'
    - password_hash: '{{ pillar['mysql']['stg-passwd-hash']
}}'
    - connection_charset: utf8
    - saltenv:
      - LC_ALL: "en_US.utf8"
    - require:
      - mysql_database: stg_databases
```

4. Edit `/opt/salt-cookbook/staging/top.sls` to have the following entries:

```
staging:
  '*':
    - mysql.users
```

5. Apply the state to the minion, using the following command:

[root@salt-master ~]# salt 'salt-minion-mysql' state.highstate saltenv=staging

salt-minion-mysql:

  .

  .

  .

  .

  - - - - - - - - - -

```
          ID: stg_databases
    Function: mysql_database.present
        Name: stagingdb
      Result: True
     Comment: Database stagingdb is already present
     Started: 03:36:33.605435
    Duration: 6.428 ms
     Changes:
```
  - - - - - - - - - -
```
          ID: databases_to_remove
    Function: mysql_database.absent
        Name: test
      Result: True
```

```
        Comment: Database test is not present, so it cannot be
removed
        Started: 03:36:33.612201
       Duration: 1.71 ms
        Changes:
----------
             ID: db_user
       Function: mysql_user.present
           Name: stg-db
         Result: True
        Comment: The user stg-db@* has been added
        Started: 03:36:33.614404
       Duration: 212.046 ms
        Changes:
                ----------
                stg-db:
                    Present


Summary
------------
Succeeded: 7 (changed=1)
Failed:    0
------------
Total states run:     7
```

How it works...

In this recipe, we demonstrated the ability of Salt to configure database users in MySQL. The objective of the recipe is to create a user and configure additional parameters for it, which helps the user to connect and communicate with the database.

First, we included the database.sls file in the new users.sls file, so that the database definitions are available to the user definitions:

```
include:
  - mysql.database
```

Next, we created the definitions for the MySQL user, using the `mysql_user` module and the `present` function:

```
db_user:
  mysql_user.present:
    - name: stg-db
    - host: '*'
    - password_hash: '{{ pillar['mysql']['stg-passwd-hash'] }}'
    - connection_charset: utf8
    - saltenv:
      - LC_ALL: "en_US.utf8"
    - require:
      - mysql_database: stg_databases
```

Here, we used the `mysql_user` module and its `present` function to create the user. The host attribute mentions the host from which the connection originates to the database. We have mentioned it as `*`, which means that it can originate from any host.

We saved a MySQL password hash in a pillar and mentioned the same hash with the `password_hash` attribute. We also mentioned the character set that the user is supposed to use when connecting to the database.

We then added the state to the minion in the `top.sls` file, and applied the state to the minion using the `state.highstate` module.

Users can also be removed using the `absent` function.

See also

- ► http://docs.saltstack.com/en/latest/ref/states/all/salt.states.mysql_user.html#module-salt.states.mysql_user, to know more about the `mysql_user` module

- ► The *Using MySQL packages, files, and services* and *Using MySQL databases* recipes, to learn how to configure MySQL databases

Running MySQL queries

Apart from managing configuration tasks in MySQL, Salt enables us to run SQL queries on databases using appropriate modules, in turn, providing us with a lot of flexibility for database management. In this recipe, you will learn how to run queries on MySQL databases using Salt.

How to do it...

We will use the same minion as the previous recipe.

1. Create and edit `/opt/salt-cookbook/staging/mysql/query.sls` to have the following entries:

```
include:
  - mysql.database
```

2. Create the first table:

```
mysql_query.run:
  - database: stagingdb
  - query: "create table first_table(id INT NOT NULL
AUTO_INCREMENT, name VARCHAR(100) NOT NULL, PRIMARY KEY (
id ));"
  - output:    "/tmp/create_first_table.txt"
  - require:
    - mysql_database: stg_databases
```

3. Create the second table:

```
mysql_query.run:
  - database: stagingdb
  - query: "create table second_table(id INT, address
VARCHAR(100));"
  - output:    "/tmp/create_second_table.txt"
  - require:
    - mysql_database: stg_databases
```

4. Apply the state to the minion with the following command:

```
[root@salt-master ~]# salt 'salt-minion-mysql' state.sls
mysql.query saltenv=staging

salt-minion-mysql:
----------
  .
  .
  .
  .
----------
          ID: create_first_table
    Function: mysql_query.run
      Result: True
```

```
        Comment: {'rows affected': 0L, 'query time': {'raw':
'0.1006', 'human': '100.6ms'}}
        Started: 22:55:13.317832
       Duration: 103.458 ms
        Changes:
                 ----------
               query:
                     Executed. Output into
/tmp/create_first_table.txt
----------
            ID: create_second_table
      Function: mysql_query.run
        Result: True
        Comment: {'rows affected': 0L, 'query time': {'raw':
'0.00536', 'human': '5.4ms'}}
        Started: 22:55:13.421609
       Duration: 8.536 ms
        Changes:
                 ----------
               query:
                     Executed. Output into
/tmp/create_second_table.txt

Summary
------------
Succeeded: 8 (changed=2)
Failed:    0
------------
Total states run:      8
```

How it works...

In this recipe, we demonstrated the ability of Salt to run SQL queries on the MySQL database. The objective of the recipe is to create two different tables with different columns in the database that we had created earlier in the recipe MySQL databases.

First, we included the `database.sls` file in the new `query.sls` file, so that we can reference the `stagingdb` database that we had created.

```
include:
  - mysql.database
```

Next, we created a definition for a MySQL query, using the `mysql_query` module and the `run` function.

```
create_first_table:
  mysql_query.run:
    - database: stagingdb
    - query: "create table first_table(id INT NOT NULL
AUTO_INCREMENT, name VARCHAR(100) NOT NULL, PRIMARY KEY ( id ));"
    - output:    "/tmp/create_first_table.txt"
    - require:
      - mysql_database: stg_databases
```

The `database` attribute mentions the name of the database on which to run the query. The `query` attribute determines the actual SQL query to run on the database. Here, we created a table with two different columns.

The `output` attribute mentions the place where the query output should be stored or displayed. Here, we mentioned a file where the output of the query needs to be stored. If the `output` attribute is not used, the output will only be shown during the Salt command run. The output can also be stored in `grain`, in which case, the attribute should be configured as follows:

```
- output: grain
- grain: table_output
```

Here, `table_output` is the name of the grain where the output needs to be stored.

We also made the query dependent on the `mysql_database` module definition, without which this definition will not succeed.

We made a second query definition, which is similar to the first one. The only difference is that the options in the column or fields definition are different from the first one.

See also

▶ The *Using MySQL packages, files, and services* and *Using MySQL databases* recipes to learn how to configure MySQL databases

▶ http://docs.saltstack.com/en/latest/ref/states/all/salt.states.mysql_query.html#module-salt.states.mysql_query, to learn more about the `mysql_query` module

Providing MySQL user grants

In this recipe, you will learn about how to provide grants to MySQL users, that is, the permissions that a user has to perform operations on the databases, and how to relate them with other MySQL definitions.

How to do it...

We will use the same minion as the previous recipe.

1. Modify /opt/salt-cookbook/staging/mysql/users.sls to have the following entries:

```
include:
  - mysql.database

first_db_user:
  mysql_user.present:
    - name: stg-admin
    - password_hash: '{{ pillar['mysql']['stg-passwd-hash']
}}'
    - host: '%'
    - connection_charset: utf8
    - saltenv:
      - LC_ALL: "en_US.utf8"
    - require:
      - mysql_database: stg_databases

second_db_user:
  mysql_user.present:
    - name: stg-db
    - password_hash: '{{ pillar['mysql']['stg-passwd-hash']
}}'
    - host: '%'
    - connection_charset: utf8
    - saltenv:
      - LC_ALL: "en_US.utf8"
    - require:
      - mysql_database: stg_databases
```

2. Create and edit `/opt/salt-cookbook/staging/mysql/grants.sls` to have the following entries:

```
include:
  - mysql.database
  - mysql.users
  - mysql.query

first_table_grants:
  mysql_grants.present:
    - grant: all privileges
    - database: stagingdb.*
    - user: stg-admin
    - host: '%'
    - require:
      - mysql_user: first_db_user

second_table_grants:
  mysql_grants.present:
    - grant: select,insert,update
    - database: stagingdb.second_table
    - user: stg-db
    - host: '%'
    - require:
      - mysql_user: second_db_user
```

3. Edit `/opt/salt-cookbook/staging/top.sls` to have the following entries:

```
staging:
  '*':
    - mysql.grants
```

4. Apply the state to the minion, using the following command:

```
[root@salt-master ~]# salt 'salt-minion-mysql' state.highstate
saltenv=staging

salt-minion-mysql:
----------

    .

    .

    .

    .

----------
          ID: first_db_user
    Function: mysql_user.present
```

```
         Name: stg-admin
       Result: True
      Comment: The user stg-admin@% has been added
      Started: 23:53:00.041526
     Duration: 31.712 ms
      Changes:
                  ----------
              stg-admin:
                  Present
----------
           ID: second_db_user
     Function: mysql_user.present
         Name: stg-db
       Result: True
      Comment: The user stg-db@% has been added
      Started: 23:53:00.073514
     Duration: 6.947 ms
      Changes:
                  ----------
              stg-db:
                  Present
----------
           ID: create_first_table
     Function: mysql_query.run
       Result: True
      Comment: {}
      Started: 23:39:26.170935
     Duration: 3.695 ms
      Changes:
                  ----------
              query:
                  Executed. Output into
/tmp/create_first_table.txt
----------
           ID: create_second_table
     Function: mysql_query.run
```

```
         Result: True
        Comment: {}
        Started: 23:39:26.174977
       Duration: 3.628 ms
        Changes:

                  ----------
                  query:
                      Executed. Output into
/tmp/create_second_table.txt
----------
             ID: first_table_grants
       Function: mysql_grants.present
         Result: True
        Comment: Grant all privileges on stagingdb.* to stg-
admin@% has been added
        Started: 23:53:47.314533
       Duration: 10.513 ms
        Changes:

                  ----------
                  first_table_grants:
                      Present
----------
             ID: second_table_grants
       Function: mysql_grants.present
         Result: True
        Comment: Grant select,insert,update on
stagingdb.second_table to stg-db@% has been added
        Started: 23:53:47.325578
       Duration: 10.092 ms
        Changes:

                  ----------
                  second_table_grants:
                      Present
```

```
Summary

- - - - - - - - - - - - -

Succeeded: 12  (changed=6)

Failed:      0

- - - - - - - - - - - - -

Total states run:      12
```

How it works...

In this recipe, we demonstrated the ability of Salt to configure grants for users in the MySQL database. The objective of the recipe is to configure two different definitions for different types of grants, on two different tables in a database.

First, we included the already configured SLS files for the `mysql` state in the new file `grants.sls`:

```
include:
  - mysql.database
  - mysql.users
  - mysql.query
```

Although only including the `users.sls` file will be enough, including all the SLS files, and then applying only the `grants.sls` file to the minion will make sure that all the `mysql` definitions are applied to the minion.

Next, we configured a grant definition, using the `mysql_grants` module:

```
first_table_grants:
  mysql_grants.present:
    - grant: all privileges
    - database: stagingdb.*
    - user: stg-admin
    - host: '%'
    - require:
      - mysql_user: first_db_user
```

The `grant` attribute defines the permissions that a user will have for a database. Here, we mentioned the user to have all privileges. The database attribute determines which tables in a database the user will have permissions for. Here, we mentioned that the user will have permissions for all tables of the `stagingdb` database.

The `user` attribute determines the MySQL user, for which we are setting up the grants. The host attribute determines the host or network from which the connection will originate. We mentioned %, which means that the connection can originate from any host.

Finally, we made the definition dependent on the `mysql_user` definition, without which the grant definition will not succeed.

In the second definition, we perform the same task of providing grants for a different user, on a different table, with different permissions. That is, we configured the grants for the `stg-db` user to have the select, insert, and update permissions on the `second_table` table of the `stagingdb` database.

See also

▸ The *Using MySQL packages, files, and services*, *Using MySQL databases*, *Creating MySQL database users*, and *Running MySQL queries* recipes, to learn how to configure MySQL database

▸ `http://docs.saltstack.com/en/latest/ref/states/all/salt.states.mysql_grants.html#module-salt.states.mysql_grants`, to know more about the mysql_grants module

Using PostgreSQL packages, files, and services

PostgreSQL is an extremely important relational database solution, and it has made its way into lot of important infrastructure setups and organizations. In this recipe, you will learn how to configure PostgreSQL by installing the respective packages, setting up the proper configuration file, and configuring the database service.

How to do it...

1. Configure a new minion in the staging environment called `salt-minion-postgresql`.

2. Create a new state directory in the staging environment called `postgresql`, and create a directory called `files` in this directory.

3. Create and edit `/opt/salt-cookbook/staging/postgresql/init.sls` to have the following entries:

```
pg_repo_pkg:
  pkg.installed:
    - sources:
      - pgdg-centos94:
http://yum.postgresql.org/9.4/redhat/rhel-6-x86_64/pgdg-
centos94-9.4-1.noarch.rpm
```

```
postgresql_server_pkg:
  pkg.installed:
    - pkgs:
      - postgresql94-server
      - postgresql94

postgresql_config_cmd:
  cmd.run:
    - name: /sbin/service postgresql-9.4 initdb
    - creates: /var/lib/pgsql/9.4/data/postgresql.conf
    - require:
      - pkg: postgresql_server_pkg

postgresql_config_file:
  file.managed:
    - name: /var/lib/pgsql/9.4/data/postgresql.conf
    - source: salt://postgresql/files/postgresql.conf
    - user: postgres
    - group: postgres
    - mode: 0600
    - require:
      - pkg: postgresql_server_pkg

postgresql_service:
  service:
    - name: postgresql-9.4
    - running
    - enable: True
    - watch:
      - file: postgresql_config_file
    - require:
      - file: postgresql_config_file
```

4. Copy over a proper configuration file from a PostgreSQL 9.4 installation to the
   `/opt/salt-cookbook/staging/postgresql/files` directory, and name it
   `postgresql.conf`. Edit the file to have the following entry:

   ```
   listen_addresses = '*'
   ```

5. Apply the state to the minion with the following command:

   ```
   [root@salt-master ~]# salt 'salt-minion-postgresql' state.sls
   postgresql saltenv=staging
   salt-minion-postgresql:
   ----------
   ```

```
          ID: pg_repo_pkg
    Function: pkg.installed
      Result: True
     Comment: The following packages were installed/updated:
pgdg-centos94.
     Started: 03:21:43.835111
    Duration: 19938.093 ms
     Changes:
                 ----------
                 pgdg-centos94:
                     ----------
                     new:
                         9.4-1
                     old:


----------
          ID: postgresql_server_pkg
    Function: pkg.installed
      Result: True
     Comment: 2 targeted packages were installed/updated.
     Started: 03:22:03.773509
    Duration: 62422.648 ms
     Changes:
                 ----------
                 postgresql94:
                     ----------
                     new:
                         9.4.0-1PGDG.rhel6
                     old:

                 postgresql94-libs:
                     ----------
                     new:
                         9.4.0-1PGDG.rhel6
                     old:
```

```
                    postgresql194-server:
                        ----------
                        new:
                            9.4.0-1PGDG.rhel6
                        old:


----------
              ID: postgresql_config_cmd
        Function: cmd.run
            Name: /sbin/service postgresql-9.4 initdb
          Result: True
         Comment: Command "/sbin/service postgresql-9.4 initdb"
run
         Started: 03:23:06.196961
        Duration: 14806.122 ms
         Changes:
                    ----------
                    pid:
                        8974
                    retcode:
                        0
                    stderr:

                    stdout:
                        Initializing database: [  OK  ]
----------
              ID: postgresql_config_file
        Function: file.managed
            Name: /var/lib/pgsql/9.4/data/postgresql.conf
          Result: True
         Comment: File /var/lib/pgsql/9.4/data/postgresql.conf
updated
         Started: 03:23:21.003803
        Duration: 502.896 ms
         Changes:
                    ----------
```

```
            diff:
                ---
                +++
                @@ -56,7 +56,7 @@


                # - Connection Settings -


                -#listen_addresses = 'localhost' # what IP
address(es) to listen on;
                +listen_addresses = '*'                   # what
IP address(es) to listen on;
                                                          #
comma-separated list of addresses;
                                                          #
defaults to 'localhost'; use '*' for all
                                                          #
(change requires restart)


----------
          ID: postgresql_service
    Function: service.running
        Name: postgresql-9.4
      Result: True
     Comment: Service postgresql-9.4 has been enabled, and is
running
     Started: 03:23:21.508080
    Duration: 2619.602 ms
     Changes:
                ----------
                postgresql-9.4:
                    True


Summary
------------
Succeeded: 5 (changed=5)
Failed:    0
------------
Total states run:     5
```

How it works...

In this recipe, we demonstrated the ability of Salt to configure service stacks, using the `pkg`, `file`, `cmd`, and `service` modules. The objective of the recipe is to install the files for the PostgreSQL `yum` repository, install the required server packages, initialize the database, propagate the appropriate configuration file, and make sure the service is up and running.

First, we used the `pkg` module to install the `pgdg-centos94-9.4-1.noarch.rpm` package from a web URL, which provides the repository information for `yum  repo` of PostgreSQL database.

```
pg_repo_pkg:
  pkg.installed:
    - sources:
      - pgdg-centos94: http://yum.postgresql.org/9.4/redhat/rhel-
6-x86_64/pgdg-centos94-9.4-1.noarch.rpm
```

Next, we installed the PostgreSQL server and client packages, using the `pkg` module.

We have the used the `cmd` module to run a command for initializing the database and generating the PostgreSQL configuration files:

```
postgresql_config_cmd:
  cmd.run:
    - name: /sbin/service postgresql-9.4 initdb
    - creates: /var/lib/pgsql/9.4/data/postgresql.conf
    - require:
      - pkg: postgresql_server_pkg

postgresql_config_file:
  file.managed:
    - name: /var/lib/pgsql/9.4/data/postgresql.conf
    - source: salt://postgresql/files/postgresql.conf
    - user: postgres
    - group: postgres
    - mode: 0600
    - require:
      - pkg: postgresql_server_pkg
```

The `create` attribute makes sure that the command is only run if the mentioned file is not present, as the command generates this file.

We also propagated a standard PostgreSQL configuration file with the parameter for the database to listen on all network interfaces, instead of the default configuration to listen only on the loopback interface.

Finally, we configured the PostgreSQL service daemon to be running at all times, and to be enabled to start at boot time.

```
postgresql_service:
  service:
    - name: postgresql-9.4
    - running
    - enable: True
    - watch:
      - file: postgresql_config_file
    - require:
      - file: postgresql_config_file
```

We have also made the service dependent on the configuration file, without which it will not be able to start.

See also

▸ The *Managing packages using the default package manager* recipe in *Chapter 5, Advanced Administration Tasks*, to know more about installing packages

▸ The *Managing files* recipe, in *Chapter 5, Advanced Administration Tasks*, to learn about managing files

▸ The *Managing services* recipe in *Chapter 5, Advanced Administration Tasks*, to learn about service management

Setting up PostgreSQL groups and users

After setting up our PostgreSQL environment, the next important task is to set up the authentication process for users and groups. In this recipe, you will learn how to create groups and users in PostgreSQL database.

How to do it...

We will use the same minion as the previous recipe.

1. Create and edit `/opt/salt-cookbook/staging/postgresql/users.sls` to have the following entries:

```
postgres_db_grp:
  postgres_group.present:
    - name: stggrp
    - login: True
```

```
postgres_db_user:
  postgres_user.present:
    - name: stgdb
    - password: {{ pillar['postgresql']['passwd'] }}
    - encrypted: True
    - groups: stggrp
    - require:
      - postgres_group: postgres_db_grp

postgres_admin_user:
  postgres_user.present:
    - name: stgadmin
    - password: {{ pillar['postgresql']['passwd'] }}
    - encrypted: True
    - createdb: True
    - createroles: True
    - createuser: True
    - login: True
```

2. Create and edit /opt/salt-cookbook/pillar/staging/postgresql/init. sls to have the following entries:

```
postgresql:
  passwd: 'saltcookbook'
```

3. Edit /opt/salt-cookbook/pillar/staging/top.sls to have the following entries:

```
staging:
  '*':
    - postgresql
```

4. Edit /opt/salt-cookbook/staging/top.sls to have the following entries:

```
staging:
  '*':
    - postgresql.users
```

5. Apply the state to the minion, with the following command:

```
[root@salt-master ~]# salt 'salt-minion-postgresql'
state.highstate saltenv=staging
salt-minion-postgresql:
----------

          ID: postgres_db_grp
    Function: postgres_group.present
        Name: stggrp
```

```
          Result: True
         Comment: The group stggrp has been created
         Started: 03:23:47.752628
        Duration: 834.775 ms
         Changes:
----------
              ID: postgres_db_user
        Function: postgres_user.present
            Name: stgdb
          Result: True
         Comment: The user stgdb has been created
         Started: 03:23:48.588486
        Duration: 482.232 ms
         Changes:
                  ----------
                  stgdb:
                      Present
----------
              ID: postgres_admin_user
        Function: postgres_user.present
            Name: stgadmin
          Result: True
         Comment: The user stgadmin has been created
         Started: 03:23:49.071548
        Duration: 439.224 ms
         Changes:
                  ----------
                  stgadmin:
                      Present

Summary
------------
Succeeded: 3 (changed=2)
Failed:    0
------------
Total states run:      3
```

How it works...

In this recipe, we demonstrated the ability of Salt to configure groups and users for the PostgreSQL database. The objective of the recipe is to create a general database group, to create a general user, add it to this group, and finally to create an admin user for the database.

First, we used the `postgres_group` module to create a PostgreSQL database group called `stggrp`:

```
postgres_db_grp:
  postgres_group.present:
    - name: stggrp
    - login: True
```

Next, we created a user using the `postgres_user` module:

```
postgres_db_user:
  postgres_user.present:
    - name: stgdb
    - password: {{ pillar['postgresql']['passwd'] }}
    - encrypted: True
    - groups: stggrp
    - require:
      - postgres_group: postgres_db_grp
```

The password of the user has been fetched from the pillar configuration, which we also configured. The `encrypted` attribute is a handy option to convert a plain password to an encrypted one when adding the user.

The `groups` attribute takes a list of comma-separated group names, in which the user is supposed to be in. In this case, it is the `stggrp` group.

We also created an admin user called `stgadmin`, and have given the user some additional permissions to manage databases with the `createdb`, `createroles`, and `createuser` attributes.

See also

▶ The *Using PostgreSQL packages, files, and services* recipe, to learn how to install and configure PostgreSQL database

▶ To learn more about the `postgres_group` and `postgres_user` modules, go to the links `http://docs.saltstack.com/en/latest/ref/states/all/salt.states.postgres_group.html#module-salt.states.postgres_group` and `http://docs.saltstack.com/en/latest/ref/states/all/salt.states.postgres_user.html#module-salt.states.postgres_user`

Configuring PostgreSQL databases

Once the groups and users are set up in the PostgreSQL database, it is then time to configure some databases and extensions. In this recipe, we will learn how to configure databases and extensions, and relate them with the groups and users we have already configured.

How to do it...

We will use the same minion as the previous recipe.

1. Create and edit `/opt/salt-cookbook/staging/postgresql/database.sls` to have the following entries:

```
include:
  - postgresql.users

postgres_staging_db:
  postgres_database.present:
    - name: stagingdb
    - owner: stgdb
    - require:
      - postgres_user: postgres_db_user
```

2. Edit `/opt/salt-cookbook/staging/top.sls` to have the following entries:

```
staging:
  '*':
    - postgresql.database
```

3. Apply the state to the minion, using the following command:

```
[root@salt-master ~]# salt 'salt-minion-postgresql'
state.highstate saltenv=staging
salt-minion-postgresql:
----------
          .
          .
          .
          .
----------
          ID: postgres_staging_db
    Function: postgres_database.present
        Name: stagingdb
```

```
     Result: True
    Comment: The database stagingdb has been created
    Started: 04:15:31.374239
   Duration: 870.76 ms
    Changes:
              ----------
            stagingdb:
                Present


Summary
------------
Succeeded: 4 (changed=1)
Failed:    0
------------
Total states run:    4
```

How it works...

In this recipe, we demonstrated the ability of Salt to configure PostgreSQL databases. The objective of the recipe is to create a PostgreSQL database, and provide the ownership of the database to the user that we created in the previous recipe.

First, we included the `users.sls` file in the new `database.sls` file, so that the database definition can be made dependent on the user definition:

```
include:
  - postgresql.users
```

Next, we used the `postgres_database` module to create the database:

```
postgres_staging_db:
  postgres_database.present:
    - name: stagingdb
    - owner: stgdb
    - require:
      - postgres_user: postgres_db_user
```

The `owner` attribute enables us to define the ownership of the database to the user that we had created in the previous recipe.

There are few other attributes that can be used to define the encoding of the database:

```
- encoding: UTF-8
- lc_ctype: en_US.UTF-8
- lc_collate: en_US.UTF-8
```

The `absent` function in this module can also be used to remove databases from PostgreSQL.

See also

- The *Using PostgreSQL packages, files, and services* and *Setting up PostgreSQL groups and users* recipes, to learn more about configuring the PostgreSQL database
- `http://docs.saltstack.com/en/latest/ref/states/all/salt.states.postgres_database.html#module-salt.states.postgres_database`, to know more about the postgres_database module

8

Configuring Salt Cloud

In this chapter, you will cover:

- ▸ Configuring Salt cloud environment
- ▸ Configuring cloud providers
- ▸ Configuring cloud profiles
- ▸ Extending profiles and providers
- ▸ Configuring cloud maps
- ▸ Using post-install scripts
- ▸ Launching, querying, and destroying instances
- ▸ Performing general cloud functions

Introduction

Until now, we have seen how Salt can help us configure our infrastructure, such as servers, applications, databases, and so on. However, the capabilities of Salt don't just stop here. Salt has extensive support for all the major cloud service providers available today, and can interact with the cloud provider to provide a scalable and flexible cloud deployment method.

Salt cloud makes use of all the parameters and options available in the service provider API services, and provides us with a common interface to interact with as many environments as we wish to. As of now, Salt cloud supports cloud providers, such as Amazon EC2, Rackspace, Google Compute Engine, Azure, HP cloud, OpenStack, DigitalOcean, GoGrid, Linode, and many others.

In this chapter, we will start with the basics of the Salt cloud functionality, move on to its terminologies and features one at a time, explore each feature in depth, and move toward the successful deployment of a Amazon EC2 infrastructure.

Configuring the Salt cloud environment

Before learning the features of Salt cloud in detail, it is important to know about its core components and how they work with each other to provide the service. In this recipe, you will learn about the core components and configuration of the Salt cloud environment.

How to do it...

We will use Amazon EC2 to demonstrate the cloud capabilities of Salt. To configure a Salt master node in Amazon EC2, we will use a **Virtual Private Cloud** (**VPC**) in Amazon EC2.

1. Create the following directories and files in the base configuration directory of Salt, that is, /etc/salt:

   Directories:

   - /etc/salt/cloud.providers.d
   - /etc/salt/cloud.profiles.d

   Files:

   - /etc/salt/cloud
   - /etc/salt/cloud.providers
   - /etc/salt/cloud.profiles
   - /etc/salt/cloud.map

2. Edit /etc/salt/cloud to have the following entries:

   ```
   pool_size: 5
   minion:
        master: salt-master.teknification.com
        environment: production
   ```

3. Execute the following commands:

   ```
   [root@salt-master ~]# which salt-cloud
   /usr/bin/salt-cloud

   [root@salt-master ~]# yum provides /usr/bin/salt-cloud
   Loaded plugins: fastestmirror
   Determining fastest mirrors

   .
   .
   .
   .
   ```

```
salt-cloud-2014.7.0-3.el6.noarch : Cloud provisioner for Salt,
a parallel remote execution system
Repo         : epel
Matched from:
Filename     : /usr/bin/salt-cloud


salt-master-2014.1.10-4.el6.noarch : Management component for
salt, a parallel remote execution system
Repo         : installed
Matched from:
Other        : Provides-match: /usr/bin/salt-cloud
```

How it works...

In this recipe, we created the basic directories and files used in the Salt cloud environment. Let's look at each of them in detail.

The cloud operation of Salt involves few directories and files.

- ▸ `/etc/salt/cloud`: This is the basic file that contains some of the core configuration parameters of Salt, such as `pool_size`, which determines how many instances Salt cloud can launch at a time. It also contains minion-specific configurations, which are read when launching minions and configuring them. When Salt cloud was first launched, this file contained all of the configurations; however, the configurations have been distributed over a few other files, that we will look at next.

- ▸ `/etc/salt/cloud.providers`: This file contains some cloud provider-specific parameters, such as the authentication keys and other parameters, such as key file location and key filename, cloud provider location, and so on.

- ▸ `/etc/salt/cloud.profiles`: This file contains more parameters and options specific to the cloud service provider and constitutes most of the information needed to configure the cloud instances.

- ▸ `/etc/salt/cloud.map`: This file contains the list as to which profile is used to launch which instances. This is the file read when launching instances, and can be of any name, as the user explicitly mentions this file when executing the Salt cloud command.

- ▸ `/etc/salt/cloud.providers.d`: This directory contains multiple files consisting of different cloud provider configurations. We can create one file for each service provider if we use multiple providers, and all of these files will be read when running Salt cloud.

▶ `/etc/salt/cloud.profiles.d`: This directory contains multiple files consisting of different cloud profile configurations. We can create different files for each cloud service provider we use, or different files can be created for each region, availability zone, and environments that we use. All the files will be read when running Salt cloud.

Next, we look at the binary, which provides the Salt cloud capability that is `salt-cloud`. This binary, as we see, is provided by the `salt-cloud` package and also the `salt-master` package. If the `salt-master` package has been installed, this binary gets installed along with it. In Ubuntu, the Salt cloud package needs to be installed explicitly.

If we want to use only the Salt cloud capability, without using the Salt master package, we can install only the `salt-cloud` package.

These are the basic files, packages, and binaries that we need to get started with Salt cloud.

See also

▶ The *Installing and configuring the Salt master* recipe in *Chapter 1, Salt Architecture and Components*, to know about how to configure Salt master

▶ The *Installing and configuring the Salt minion* and *Configuring environments and grains on the minion* recipes, in *Chapter 1, Salt Architecture and Components*, to know more about minion configuration and options

Configuring cloud providers

Salt cloud providers are the components that provide the cloud service provider specific configuration options and parameters while using Salt cloud. In this recipe, you will learn how to use cloud provider configurations in Salt.

How to do it...

Edit `/etc/salt/cloud.providers` to have the following entries:

```
cookbook_ec2_us_west_2:

  ssh_interface: private_ips

  id: <access_key>
  key: '<secret_key>'

  keyname: common
  private_key: /etc/salt/key/common.pem
```

```
location: us-west-2
availability_zone: us-west-2b

size: t2.micro
del_root_vol_on_destroy: True
ssh_username: ec2-user
rename_on_destroy: True
provider: ec2
```

How it works...

In this recipe, we demonstrated the procedure to configure a basic provider file for Salt cloud.

First, we have given a name to the provider, which is `cookbook_ec2_us_west_2:`, ending with a colon, which is very important. All the attributes and their values that come next will be indented, to make sure that they belong to the provider. Basically, the file needs to be in the proper YAML format.

```
cookbook_ec2_us_west_2:
```

The `ssh_interface` attribute mentions the IP address, which will be used by the Salt master to communicate with the minions; here, we mention it as `private_ips`, as we are using the VPC feature of Amazon EC2.

```
ssh_interface: private_ips
```

The next attributes are `id` and `key`, which mentions the access and secret key of Amazon EC2 required for authentication with the service provider. Please refer to the following link for more information on Amazon EC2:

`http://salt-cloud.readthedocs.org/en/latest/topics/aws.html`

```
id: <access_key>
key: '<secret_key>'
```

The `keyname` attribute mentions the name of the SSH key that we generated in EC2, and which will be used in the newly launched instances. The `private_key` attribute mentions the path to the private key file that Salt cloud uses to log in to the minions. This file should reside on the master node:

```
keyname: common
private_key: /etc/salt/key/common.pem
```

The `location` attribute mentions the Amazon region that will be used to launch the instances, and the `availability_zone` mentions the availability zone to be used. Different providers can be configured to launch instances in different availability zones using different values for this attribute.

```
location: us-west-2
availability_zone: us-west-2b
```

The `size` attribute determines the instance type of the instance to be launched, which in this case is `t2.micro`, one of the lowest configurations available with minimum resources. The `del_root_vol_on_destroy` attribute makes sure that if the instance is backed by EBS volumes, then the volume is destroyed when the instance is terminated permanently.

```
size: t2.micro
del_root_vol_on_destroy: True
```

The `ssh_username` parameter determines the user as which the Salt master will log in to the minions to configure them. Usually, this user will have sudo access to perform administrative tasks on the instances. The `rename_on_destroy` attribute makes sure that the `Name` tag of the instances is changed to a different value when the instances are terminated. This helps in identifying the correct active instance, when a new instance is created with the same name as a terminated one.

The `provider` attribute mentions the name of the cloud service provider which, in this case, is `ec2` (Amazon EC2):

```
ssh_username: ec2-user
rename_on_destroy: True
provider: ec2
```

These are some of the attributes and parameters, which can be configured in Salt cloud providers file. These configurations can also be done in files located in the `/etc/salt/cloud.providers.d` directory.

See also

> ▶ The *Configuring the Salt cloud environment* recipe, to learn how to configure Salt cloud
> ▶ The *Configuring cloud profiles* recipe, to learn how to configure Salt cloud profiles

Configuring cloud profiles

Salt cloud profiles are the components that provide more cloud service provider-specific configuration options, and also minion-specific parameters when using Salt cloud. In this recipe, you will learn how to use cloud profile configurations in Salt.

How to do it...

Edit `/etc/salt/cloud.profiles` to have the following entries:

```
cookbook_ec2_prod_db:
  provider: cookbook_ec2_us_west_2
  minion:
    master: salt-master
    environment: production
  image: ami-721b7b42
  script: bootstrap-salt
  sync_after_install: all

  network_interfaces:
    - DeviceIndex: 0
      PrivateIpAddresses:
        - Primary: True
      AssociatePublicIpAddress: False
      SubnetId: subnet-4236c535
      SecurityGroupId:
        - sg-5b35a03e
  grains:
    server_type: db
    environment: production
  tag: {'Environment': 'Production', 'Role': 'Database'}
```

How it works...

In this recipe, we demonstrated the procedure to configure Salt cloud profiles, and the various attributes involved.

The first configuration is the name of the profile, which is the unique identifier for this profile, which is:

```
cookbook_ec2_prod_db:
```

The `provider` attribute mentions the name of the Salt cloud provider that we configured in the previous recipe *Configuring cloud providers*, and inherits all the attributes configured in it for this profile.

```
provider: cookbook_ec2_us_west_2
```

The `minion` attribute determines that all the indented attributes after it will be minion configurations, which will be set in the newly launched instances' Salt minion configuration file. Here, we set the values for the `master` and `environment` parameters.

```
minion:
    master: salt-master
    environment: production
```

The `image` attribute mentions the image ID of the AMI image, which will be used to launch the new instances. The `script` attribute mentions the name of the script that will be run on the newly launched minions to configure them. We will learn more about scripts in the recipe *Using post-install scripts* later in this chapter.

The `sync_after_install` attribute makes sure that all the Salt components like grains, pillars, and so on are synchronized with the Salt master on the minion.

```
image: ami-721b7b42
script: bootstrap-salt
sync_after_install: all
```

The `network_interfaces` attribute tells Salt that all the indented attributes after it are network configurations for the newly launched instances, and are specific to VPC.

```
network_interfaces:
    - DeviceIndex: 0
      PrivateIpAddresses:
        - Primary: True
      AssociatePublicIpAddress: False
      SubnetId: subnet-4236c535
      SecurityGroupId:
        - sg-5b35a03e
```

The `DeviceIndex` attribute mentions the position of the interface in the instance, that is, a value of `0` means that it will be the `eth0` interface. The `PrivateIpAddresses` and its subsequent attribute `Primary`, make sure that this private interface is the primary interface to communicate with the Salt master.

The `AssociatePublicIpAddress` attribute makes sure that a public IP address is configured for this interface; in our case, we disabled it by the value of `False`. The `SubnetId` attribute is used to mention the subnet ID, which will be used to configure the instance, and the IP address will be fetched from the range configured for this subnet. The `SecurityGroupId` attribute mentions a single or a list of security groups, which will ensure traffic filtering for the instances. These information can be found on the VPC page in the AWS management console.

The `grains` attribute makes sure that the indented grains and their values mentioned after them will be configured in the `/etc/salt/grains` file of the newly launched instances.

```
grains:
  server_type: db
  environment: production
```

The `tag` attribute determines a list of EC2 tags, which will be configured for the instances after they are launched.

```
tag: {'Environment': 'Production', 'Role': 'Database'}
```

See also

▸ The *Configuring cloud providers* recipe, to learn about configuring Salt cloud providers

▸ The *Using post-install scripts* recipe, to learn about how to configure post-install scripts in Salt cloud

Extending profiles and providers

To ensure efficient use of providers and profiles in Salt cloud, the feature of extending enables providers and profiles to extend other providers and profiles, so that their attributes can be inherited and configurations can be made more organized. In this recipe, you will learn how to configure the extend feature in Salt cloud.

How to do it...

Edit `/etc/salt/cloud.profiles` to add the following entries:

```
cookbook_ec2_prod_common_app:
  provider: cookbook_ec2_us_west_2
  minion:
    master: salt-master
    environment: production
  image: ami-721b7b42
  grains:
    server_type: app
    environment: production
  tag: {'Environment': 'Production', 'Role': 'Application'}
  del_root_vol_on_destroy: True
  script: bootstrap-salt
  sync_after_install: all
```

```
cookbook_ec2_prod_app_us-west-2b:

  availability_zone: us-west-2b

  network_interfaces:
    - DeviceIndex: 0
      PrivateIpAddresses:
        - Primary: True
      AssociatePublicIpAddress: False
      SubnetId: subnet-4236c535
      SecurityGroupId:
        - sg-2a35a04f
  extends: cookbook_ec2_prod_common_app

cookbook_ec2_prod_app_us-west-2a:

  availability_zone: us-west-2a

  network_interfaces:
    - DeviceIndex: 0
      PrivateIpAddresses:
        - Primary: True
      AssociatePublicIpAddress: False
      SubnetId: subnet-a9fb26cc
      SecurityGroupId:
        - sg-2a35a04f
  extends: cookbook_ec2_prod_common_app
```

How it works...

In this recipe, we demonstrated the procedure of how Salt cloud profiles can extend other profiles, and inherit their attributes to act as their own.

The objective of the recipe is to configure profiles for a set of application instances. We configured two different profiles for instances in two different availability zones. We also created a profile for attributes, which are common to instances in both availability zones. The two profiles will extend this common profile and inherit its attributes.

First, we configured a profile called `cookbook_ec2_prod_common_app`. We used the provider that we had configured in the *Configuring cloud providers* recipe previously in this chapter. The rest of the attributes have been described in the *Configuring cloud profiles* recipe previously in this chapter.

```
cookbook_ec2_prod_common_app:
  provider: cookbook_ec2_us_west_2
```

```
minion:
  master: salt-master
  environment: production
image: ami-721b7b42
grains:
  server_type: app
  environment: production
tag: {'Environment': 'Production', 'Role': 'Application'}
del_root_vol_on_destroy: True
script: bootstrap-salt
sync_after_install: all
```

The attributes configured in this profile are common to the instances, irrespective of their location of launch, and this profile definition will be inherited in the following profiles.

We have then configured two other profiles:

```
cookbook_ec2_prod_app_us-west-2b:

  availability_zone: us-west-2b

  network_interfaces:
    - DeviceIndex: 0
      PrivateIpAddresses:
        - Primary: True
      AssociatePublicIpAddress: False
      SubnetId: subnet-4236c535
      SecurityGroupId:
        - sg-2a35a04f
    extends: cookbook_ec2_prod_common_app


cookbook_ec2_prod_app_us-west-2a:

  availability_zone: us-west-2a

  network_interfaces:
    - DeviceIndex: 0
      PrivateIpAddresses:
        - Primary: True
      AssociatePublicIpAddress: False
      SubnetId: subnet-a9fb26cc
      SecurityGroupId:
        - sg-2a35a04f
    extends: cookbook_ec2_prod_common_app
```

The two profiles configured are different, in terms of the location where the instances using them will be launched. The availability zones configured and the subnet IDs being used are different because in EC2, a subnet corresponds to a specific availability zone.

At the end of each of these profiles, we added an extra attribute called `extend`. This attribute has the name of the common profile as its value, and inherits all the attributes defined in the common profile. In this way, the extend feature prevents the use of repetitive code and provides efficient management of Salt code.

Similarly, Salt cloud providers can also extend other providers and inherit their attributes.

See also

- The *Configuring cloud providers* recipe, to learn about Salt cloud providers
- The *Configuring cloud profiles* recipe, to learn about Salt cloud profiles
- The *Configuring cloud maps* recipe, to learn how to create maps for Salt cloud deployments

Configuring cloud maps

After cloud providers and profiles have been created, it has to be mentioned as to which instances will use which profile. To achieve this task, cloud maps are used. In this recipe, you will learn how to configure cloud maps, and relate profiles with instances.

How to do it...

Edit `/etc/salt/cloud.map` to have the following entries:

```
cookbook_ec2_prod_db:
  - cookbookdb01

cookbook_ec2_prod_app_us-west-2a:
  - cookbookapp01
  - cookbookapp03

cookbook_ec2_prod_app_us-west-2b:
  - cookbookapp02
  - cookbookapp04
```

How it works...

In this recipe, we demonstrated the procedure to configure cloud maps in Salt cloud. The objective of the recipe is to relate the already configured cloud profiles with actual instances, which will be launched in EC2.

The cloud map file can be of any name; here, we named it `cloud.map`. This file can also be placed under `/etc/salt/cloud.map.d/cookbook.conf`. The map created is of simple YAML format with the name of the profile first, followed by the host names of the instances to be launched as its keys.

```
cookbook_ec2_prod_db:
  - cookbookdb01

cookbook_ec2_prod_app_us-west-2a:
  - cookbookapp01
  - cookbookapp03
```

The profile name, that is, `cookbook_ec2_prod_app_us-west-2a` has been mentioned first, followed by a list of host names as keys in YAML format. It is as simple as that.

However, there are a few other things that can be done with cloud maps. We can add additional options for the minions in the map file, as follows:

```
cookbook_ec2_prod_app_us-west-2a:
  - cookbookapp01
      minion:
        log_level: warn
      grains:
        location: dc1
        app_name: cookbook-app
  - cookbookapp03
```

Options for the minion configuration file can be set in the cloud map file, as well as grains and their values. The instances, for which these parameters are not set in the map file, will continue to use the parameters available from the providers and profiles.

We can also make new instances being launched from the map file act as the Salt master in the following method:

```
cookbook_ec2_prod_app_us-west-2a:
  - cookbookapp01
      minion:
        master: salt-master
        log_level: warn
```

```
        grains:
          location: dc1
          app_name: cookbook-app
    - cookbookapp03
        make_master: True
    - cookbookapp05
```

Here, we made the instance `cookbookapp03` a new Salt master. It is to be noted that if nothing else is mentioned, all the instances being launched from the same map file will have the new Salt master, that is, `cookbookapp03` as the Salt master.

We can make the instances have a Salt master other than the one in the map file, by explicitly mentioning the master attribute as done earlier for `cookbookapp01`. In the preceding example, `cookbookapp03` becomes the new Salt master, `cookbookapp05` launches with `cookbookapp03` as its Salt master, but `cookbookapp01` launches with the host `salt-master` as its master.

See also

- ▶ The *Configuring cloud providers* and *Configuring cloud profiles* recipes, to learn more about providers and profiles
- ▶ The *Launching, querying, and destroying instances* recipe, to learn how to launch instances using Salt cloud

Using post-install scripts

When Salt cloud is used to launch instances, they need to be configured to install the Salt minion package, and register themselves with the Salt master. This task is done by using post-install scripts. In this recipe, we will learn about the procedure to use post-install scripts in Salt cloud.

How to do it...

1. On the Salt master, execute the following command:

```
[root@salt-master ~]# ls -l /usr/lib/python2.6/site-packages/salt/
cloud/deploy/

total 248
-rw-r--r-- 1 root root    864 Jun 17  2014 Arch-git.sh
-rw-r--r-- 1 root root    677 Jun 17  2014 Arch.sh
-rw-r--r-- 1 root root 166951 Sep 19 11:52 bootstrap-salt.sh
-rw-r--r-- 1 root root    735 Aug  1  2014 curl-bootstrap-git.sh
-rw-r--r-- 1 root root    708 Aug  1  2014 curl-bootstrap.sh
```

```
-rw-r--r-- 1 root root    1297 Jun 17  2014 Debian-git.sh
-rw-r--r-- 1 root root    1049 Jun 17  2014 Debian.sh
-rw-r--r-- 1 root root    1187 Jun 17  2014 Fedora-git.sh
-rw-r--r-- 1 root root     982 Jun 17  2014 Fedora.sh
-rw-r--r-- 1 root root    1000 Jun 17  2014 FreeBSD-git.sh
-rw-r--r-- 1 root root     938 Jun 17  2014 FreeBSD.sh
-rw-r--r-- 1 root root     407 Jun 17  2014 None.sh
-rw-r--r-- 1 root root     807 Aug  1  2014 python-bootstrap.sh
-rw-r--r-- 1 root root     913 Jun 17  2014 RHEL5-git.sh
-rw-r--r-- 1 root root     725 Jun 17  2014 RHEL5.sh
-rw-r--r-- 1 root root     934 Jun 17  2014 RHEL6-git.sh
-rw-r--r-- 1 root root     751 Jun 17  2014 RHEL6.sh
-rw-r--r-- 1 root root    1031 Jun 17  2014 SmartOS.sh
-rw-r--r-- 1 root root    1464 Jun 17  2014 Ubuntu-git.sh
-rw-r--r-- 1 root root    1217 Jun 17  2014 Ubuntu.sh
-rw-r--r-- 1 root root     757 Aug  1  2014 wget-bootstrap-nocert.
sh
-rw-r--r-- 1 root root     711 Aug  1  2014 wget-bootstrap.sh
```

2. In the recipe called *Configuring cloud profiles*, earlier in this chapter, we have seen the following Salt code:

```
cookbook_ec2_prod_db:
  provider: cookbook_ec2_us_west_2
  minion:
    master: salt-master
    environment: production
  image: ami-721b7b42
  script: bootstrap-salt
  sync_after_install: all
```

How it works...

In this recipe, we mentioned the procedure to identify and use post-install scripts in Salt cloud. The objective of the recipe is to find the available scripts, and make sure that one of them is used to deploy instances with Salt cloud.

When Salt is installed, a number of preconfigured scripts are available with it, and are available at the `/usr/lib/python2.6/site-packages/salt/cloud/deploy` location, and there are scripts for a number of operating systems and platforms. It is up to the user as to which script they prefer to use.

The name of the script is then used when configuring the profile, and is mentioned with the `script` attribute:

```
script: bootstrap-salt
```

The name is mentioned without the extension of the file, and searches for the script in the `/usr/lib/python2.6/site-packages/salt/cloud/deploy` location.

If we choose not to run a script when instances are deployed, we need to change the value of the `script` attribute to `None`:

```
script: None
```

Also, there are methods to skip the script run when launching the instances, which we will see in the next recipe *Launching, querying, and destroying instances*.

It is to be noted that in a lot of cases, the scripts don't work perfectly during deployments. It is up to the user to perform some trial and error before finalizing on the correct script.

Users can also write their own script, place it in the mentioned location, and use it in the cloud profile configurations. The file module can be used to copy over the file in the Salt master.

A sample script has been provided in the code base with some tweaking to work with CentOS.

See also

▶ The *Configuring cloud providers* and *Configuring cloud profiles* recipes, to learn more about providers and profiles

▶ The *Launching, querying, and destroying instances* recipe, to learn how to launch instances using Salt cloud

Launching, querying, and destroying instances

Once all our configurations are done, it is time to actually use them and launch the instances. In this recipe, you will learn how to launch, query, and destroy instances.

How to do it...

1. Create a new file `/etc/salt/cloud.map.app`, and edit it to have the following entries:

```
cloudopen_ec2_prod_app_us-west-2a:
  - cookbookapp01
```

```
cloudopen_ec2_prod_app_us-west-2b:
  - cookbookapp02
```

2. Execute the following command to launch an instance without using the map file:

```
[root@salt-master ~]# salt-cloud -p cookbook_ec2_prod_db
cookbookdb08
```

```
[INFO    ] salt-cloud starting

[INFO    ] Creating Cloud VM cookbookdb08 in us-west-2

[INFO    ] Attempting to look up root device name for image id
ami-721b7b42 on VM cookbookdb08

[INFO    ] Found root device name: /dev/sda1

[INFO    ] Created node cookbookdb08

[INFO    ] Salt node data. Private_ip: 172.31.16.184
```

```
Warning: Permanently added '172.31.16.184' (RSA) to the list
of known hosts.
```

```
[INFO    ] Rendering deploy script: /usr/lib/python2.6/site-
packages/salt/cloud/deploy/bootstrap-salt.sh
```

```
Warning: Permanently added '172.31.16.184' (RSA) to the list
of known hosts.
```

```
.

.

.

 *  INFO: /bin/sh /tmp/.saltcloud-50421d3e-5813-4272-837d-
e77b41f1b61f/deploy.sh -- Version 2014.06.30


 *  INFO: System Information:
 *  INFO:    CPU:          GenuineIntel
 *  INFO:    CPU Arch:     x86_64
 *  INFO:    OS Name:      Linux
 *  INFO:    OS Version:   2.6.32-431.3.1.el6.x86_64
 *  INFO:    Distribution: CentOS 6.5


 *  INFO: Installing minion
 *  INFO: Found function install_centos_stable_deps
 *  INFO: Found function config_salt
 *  INFO: Found function install_centos_stable
 *  INFO: Found function install_centos_stable_post
 *  INFO: Found function install_centos_restart_daemons
```

```
    *   INFO: Found function daemons_running
    *   INFO: Found function install_centos_check_services
    *   INFO: Running install_centos_stable_deps()

    .

    .

    .

    .

    *   INFO: Running install_centos_stable_post()
    *   INFO: Running install_centos_check_services()
    *   INFO: Running install_centos_restart_daemons()
Starting salt-minion daemon:                    [OK  ]
    *   INFO: Running daemons_running()

    .

    .

    .

[INFO     ] Salt installed on cookbookdb08
[INFO     ] Created Cloud VM 'cookbookdb08'
cookbookdb08:
    ----------
    amiLaunchIndex:
        0

    .

    .

    .

    .

    virtualizationType:
        hvm
    vpcId:
        vpc-45f53420
```

3. Next, execute the following command to launch instances using the map file:

```
[root@salt-master ~]# salt-cloud -m /etc/salt/cloud.map.app -P
[INFO     ] salt-cloud starting
[INFO     ] Applying map from '/etc/salt/cloud.map.app'.
The following virtual machines are set to be created:
  cookbookapp01
  cookbookapp02
```

```
Proceed? [N/y] y

... proceeding

[INFO    ] Calculating dependencies for cookbookapp01

[INFO    ] Calculating dependencies for cookbookapp02

[INFO    ] Since parallel deployment is in use, ssh console output
is disabled. All ssh output will be logged though

[INFO    ] Cloud pool size: 2

[INFO    ] Creating Cloud VM cookbookapp02 in us-west-2

[INFO    ] Creating Cloud VM cookbookapp01 in us-west-2

[INFO    ] Attempting to look up root device name for image id
ami-721b7b42 on VM cookbookapp02

[INFO    ] Attempting to look up root device name for image id
ami-721b7b42 on VM cookbookapp01

[INFO    ] Found root device name: /dev/sda1

[INFO    ] Found root device name: /dev/sda1

[INFO    ] Created node cookbookapp02

[INFO    ] Salt node data. Private_ip: 172.31.28.87

[INFO    ] Created node cookbookapp01

[INFO    ] Salt node data. Private_ip: 172.31.36.126

[INFO    ] Rendering deploy script: /usr/lib/python2.6/site-
packages/salt/cloud/deploy/bootstrap-salt.sh

[INFO    ] Rendering deploy script: /usr/lib/python2.6/site-
packages/salt/cloud/deploy/bootstrap-salt.sh

[INFO    ] Salt installed on cookbookapp02

[INFO    ] Created Cloud VM 'cookbookapp02'

[INFO    ] Salt installed on cookbookapp01

[INFO    ] Created Cloud VM 'cookbookapp01'

cookbookapp01:

    ----------

    amiLaunchIndex:

        0

.

.

.

    vpcId:

        vpc-45f53420
```

```
        cookbookapp02:
            ----------
            amiLaunchIndex:
                0
        .

        .

        .

            vpcId:
                vpc-45f53420
```

4. To query the instances mentioned in a map file, execute the following command:

```
[root@salt-master ~]# salt-cloud -m /etc/salt/cloud.map -Q
[INFO     ] salt-cloud starting
[INFO     ] Applying map from '/etc/salt/cloud.map'.
cloudopen_ec2_us_west_2:
        ----------
        ec2:
            ----------
            cookbookapp01:
                ----------
                id:
                    i-ef7940e5
                image:
                    ami-721b7b42
                private_ips:
                    172.31.36.126
                public_ips:
                size:
                    t2.micro
                state:
                    running
            cookbookapp02:
                ----------
                id:
                    i-e50d5ae9
```

```
            image:
                ami-721b7b42
            private_ips:
                172.31.28.87
            public_ips:
            size:
                t2.micro
            state:
                running
```

5. Finally, execute the following command to destroy the instances:

```
[root@salt-master ~]# salt-cloud -m /etc/salt/cloud.map.app -d
[INFO    ] salt-cloud starting
[INFO    ] Applying map from '/etc/salt/cloud.map.app'.
[INFO    ] Destroying in non-parallel mode.
[INFO    ] Renaming cookbookapp01 to cookbookapp01-
DEL6b5a0c5f46b4407cb0b4fdcc16205eab
[INFO    ] Machine will be identified as cookbookapp01-
DEL6b5a0c5f46b4407cb0b4fdcc16205eab until it has been cleaned
up.
[INFO    ] [{'instanceId': 'i-ef7940e5', 'currentState':
{'code': '32', 'name': 'shutting-down'}, 'previousState':
{'code': '16', 'name': 'running'}}]
[INFO    ] Renaming cookbookapp02 to cookbookapp02-
DEL4b5f0d8223ad4340b2d03924b5613dd1
[INFO    ] Machine will be identified as cookbookapp02-
DEL4b5f0d8223ad4340b2d03924b5613dd1 until it has been cleaned
up.
[INFO    ] [{'instanceId': 'i-e50d5ae9', 'currentState':
{'code': '32', 'name': 'shutting-down'}, 'previousState':
{'code': '16', 'name': 'running'}}]
cloudopen_ec2_us_west_2:
    ----------
    ec2:
        ----------
        cookbookapp01:
            ----------
            currentState:
                ----------
```

```
                          code:
                              32
                          name:
                              shutting-down

              .

              .

              .


          cookbookapp02:
              - - - - - - - - - -
          currentState:
              - - - - - - - - - -
              code:
                  32
              name:
                  shutting-down

              .

              .

              .


          previousState:
              - - - - - - - - - -
              code:
                  16
              name:
                  running
```

How it works...

In this recipe, we demonstrated the ability of Salt to launch, query, and destroy instances.

First, we launched an instance without using a map file:

```
[root@salt-master ~]# salt-cloud -p cookbook_ec2_prod_db cookbookdb08
```

The -p option mentions the profile name that we previously configured, and at the end, we mention the name of the instance to be launched.

This command gives a long output, generating each step as they are applied on the instance.

Next, we launched multiple instances at the same time using a map file,

```
[root@salt-master ~]# salt-cloud -m /etc/salt/cloud.map.app -P
```

The -m option mentions the path to the map file, and the -P option tells Salt to use the parallel mode to launch instances; without which, instances will be launched one after the other, taking more time. There is one more option called -H, whose usage should be managed very cautiously as this option will terminate any instance not present in the map file.

Next, we queried the launched instances, using the following command:

```
[root@salt-master ~]# salt-cloud -m /etc/salt/cloud.map -Q
```

The -Q option tells Salt that this is a query on the instances mentioned in the map file. However, the output produced is much shorter, and does not include all the information. To get complete information about the instances, the -F option should be used.

Finally, we terminated the instance, using the following command:

```
[root@salt-master ~]# salt-cloud -m /etc/salt/cloud.map.app -d
```

All the instances mentioned in the map file will be terminated when this command is issued, the -d being the termination option.

To avoid running the post-install script after the instances are launched, the --no-deploy option has to be used with the salt-cloud command.

See also

▸ The *Configuring cloud providers* and *Configuring cloud profiles* recipes, to learn more about providers and profiles

▸ The *Configuring the Salt cloud environment* recipe, to learn how to configure Salt cloud

Performing general cloud functions

After the instances are launched, Salt cloud can help us perform a lot of cloud-specific functions on the instances. In this recipe, you will learn about a few such functions, and some resources where we can find more such options.

How to do it...

1. Execute the following command to get the tags associated with the instance:

```
[root@salt-master ~]# salt-cloud -y -a get_tags cookbookapp02
[INFO    ] salt-cloud starting
cloudopen_ec2_us_west_2:
    ----------
    ec2:
        ----------
```

```
            cookbookapp02:
                ----------
                - key:
                    Role
                - resourceId:
                    i-e50d5ae9
                - resourceType:
                    instance
                - value:
                    Application
                ----------

    .

    .

    .

                ----------
                - key:
                    Environment
                - resourceId:
                    i-e50d5ae9
                - resourceType:
                    instance
                - value:
                    Production
```

2. Execute the following command to show all the available information on the instance:

```
[root@salt-master ~]# salt-cloud -y -a show_instance
cookbookapp02

[INFO    ] salt-cloud starting

cloudopen_ec2_us_west_2:
        ----------
        ec2:
            ----------
            cookbookapp02:
                ----------
                amiLaunchIndex:
                    0
```

```
architecture:
    x86_64
.

.

.


virtualizationType:
    hvm
vpcId:
    vpc-45f53420
```

3. Execute the following command to enable termination protection for the instance, to avoid accidental termination:

```
[root@salt-master ~]# salt-cloud -y -a enable_term_protect
cookbookapp02
[INFO    ] salt-cloud starting
[INFO    ] Termination Protection is enabled for cookbookapp02
cloudopen_ec2_us_west_2:
    ----------
    ec2:
        ----------
        cookbookapp02:
            true
```

4. Execute the following command to create an EBS volume with some options:

```
[root@salt-master salt]# salt-cloud -f create_volume ec2
zone=us-west-2a size=10 type=standard
[INFO    ] salt-cloud starting
cloudopen_ec2_us_west_2:
    ----------
    ec2:
        ----------
        - requestId:
            20b976d4-034c-474d-bfe3-ffda545eceec
        ----------
        - volumeId:
            vol-4c8bff5d
```

```
          ----------

     .

     .

     .

     .

          ----------

          - volumeType:

               standard
```

5. Execute the following command to attach the created volume to an instance:

```
[root@salt-master ~]# salt-cloud -y -a attach_volume
cookbookapp01 volume_id=vol-4c8bff5d device=/dev/sdc

[INFO    ] salt-cloud starting

cloudopen_ec2_us_west_2:

     ----------

     ec2:

          ----------

          cookbookapp01:

               ----------

               - requestId:

                    48456026-e4ad-474d-bce1-5be6d7afe385

               ----------

               - volumeId:

                    vol-4c8bff5d

               ----------

               - instanceId:

                    i-ef7940e5

               ----------

               - device:

                    /dev/sdc

               ----------

               - status:

                    attaching

               ----------

               - attachTime:

                    2015-02-04T21:11:19.670Z
```

How it works...

In this recipe, we demonstrated the ability of Salt to interact with the cloud service provider, and perform all sorts of functions and tasks on the instances and other components of the cloud.

The basic structure of the commands used to perform the tasks is to use the `salt-cloud` binary, followed by the `-a` or `-f` option with the function name, and then other options depending on the component being worked on and the instance or any other components we are working with, such as the EBS volume.

We used few functions such as `get_tags`, `show_instance`, `enable_term_protect`, `create_volume`, and `attach_volume`.

There are numerous other options and functions available in Salt cloud, used to act on cloud components.

> To find out more about EC2-specific functions, go to the link:
>
> `http://docs.saltstack.com/en/latest/topics/cloud/aws.html`
>
> To find out more about other cloud providers, go to the link:
>
> `http://docs.saltstack.com/en/latest/topics/cloud`

See also

▶ The *Configuring cloud providers* and *Configuring cloud profiles* recipes, respectively, to learn more about providers and profiles

▶ The *Launching, querying, and destroying instances* recipe, to learn how to launch instances using Salt cloud

9
Managing Amazon Web Services

In this chapter, we will cover the following topics:

- ▸ Implementing security groups
- ▸ Using elastic load balancers
- ▸ Configuring DNS with Route53
- ▸ Configuring Simple Queue Service
- ▸ Deploying ElastiCache clusters
- ▸ Configuring CloudWatch alarms

Introduction

Now that we are aware of how to utilize Salt to create resources on a cloud service provider's platform, it is time now to get into more details about the various other resources that are configurable on a cloud provider with Salt.

Any cloud service is incomplete without continuous development in the cloud offerings provided, and with a lot of competition emerging in the cloud service industry, it is extremely important to provide more features in order to stay ahead of the competition.

Salt not only helps us to spin up instances and compute resources in the cloud, but also enables us to configure various other important cloud offerings provided by the service providers, such as load balancers, security components, monitoring and alerts, DNS services, and so on. In this chapter, we will look into a few such important cloud offerings provided by Amazon Web Services and how we can utilize Salt in configuring these resources.

Implementing security groups

Before compute resources can be configured, it is extremely important to configure the proper security measures to be taken to avoid unwanted access. In this recipe, we will learn about how to configure security groups using Salt in AWS.

How to do it...

1. Configure a new state called `aws` in the production environment. Create `/opt/salt-cookbook/production/aws/secgroup.sls` to have the following entries:

```
cookbooksecgroup:
    boto_secgroup.present:
        - description: Cookbook security group
        - rules:
            - ip_protocol: tcp
              from_port: 80
              to_port: 80
              cidr_ip:
                - 172.31.0.0/20
                - 172.31.16.0/20
        - vpc_id: vpc-45f53420
        - region: us-west-2
        - keyid: <access-key>
        - key: '<secret-key>'
```

2. Apply the state to the Salt master by running the following command:

```
[root@salt-master ~]# salt 'salt-master' state.sls
aws.secgroup saltenv=production

salt-master:
----------
          ID: cookbooksecgroup
    Function: boto_secgroup.present
      Result: True
     Comment: Security group cookbooksecgroup created.
Created rules on cookbooksecgroup security group.
     Started: 18:44:52.400517
    Duration: 958.162 ms
     Changes:
              ----------
              new:
```

```
          ----------
          rules:
              |_
                ----------
                cidr_ip:
                    172.31.0.0/20
                from_port:
                    80
                ip_protocol:
                    tcp
                to_port:
                    80
              |_
                ----------
                cidr_ip:
                    172.31.16.0/20
                from_port:
                    80
                ip_protocol:
                    tcp
                to_port:
                    80
        secgroup:
          ----------
          description:
              Cookbook security group
          group_id:
              sg-c41130a1
          name:
              cookbooksecgroup
          owner_id:
              808429213833
          rules:
    old:
      ----------
      rules:
```

```
                     secgroup:

                         None


    Summary

    - - - - - - - - - - - -

    Succeeded: 1 (changed=1)

    Failed:    0

    - - - - - - - - - - - -

    Total states run:    1
```

How it works...

In this recipe, we have demonstrated Salt's ability to configure security groups in AWS. The objective of the recipe is to create a new security group and configure it with the required rules.

```
cookbooksecgroup:
    boto_secgroup.present:
        - description: Cookbook security group
```

First, we have named the security group that needs to be created and then we have used the boto_secgroup module and the present function to make sure that the security group is created. We have also mentioned a description for the security group with the description attribute.

The boto Python module is needed for the EC2 Salt modules and can be installed with the following commands:

[root@salt-master ~]# yum -y install python-pip

[root@salt-master ~]# pip install boto

For Ubuntu, the same can be achieved by installing the python-boto package.

Next, we have mentioned the rules for the security groups, that is, the ports for which the inbound traffic needs to be filtered and the network subnets from which access needs to be provided:

```
        - rules:
            - ip_protocol: tcp
              from_port: 80
              to_port: 80
              cidr_ip:
                 - 172.31.0.0/20
                 - 172.31.16.0/20
```

Next, we have mentioned the EC2 VPC ID for our account with the `vpc_id` attribute. Do note that this attribute is compulsory, without which there is a possibility of a failure in the module:

```
- vpc_id: vpc-45f53420
```

The next three attributes are also known as the profile attributes and can be common to all EC2 Salt modules. The `keyid` and the `key` attributes take the AWS access and secret key, respectively, for the Amazon account being used to deploy the infrastructure, and the `region` attribute mentions the region:

```
- region: us-west-2
- keyid: <access-key>
- key: '<secret-key>'
```

Also, do note that we have applied the state to the Salt master itself that is named `salt-master` in this recipe and has its master configured as itself. This is because the resources that are being worked on are not present in any minion, they are present on the cloud provider's infrastructure. The states can be applied to any minion for the actions to take place, but we have chosen to apply it to the Salt master itself and we will do the same for the rest of the recipes.

There's more...

The profile can also be configured in pillar data or the minion configuration file. The three profile attributes that are common to the different AWS modules can be saved in a pillar file or the minion configuration file as follows and should be made available to the minions:

```
cookbookprofile:
  region: us-west-2
  keyid: <access-key>
  key: '<secret-key>'
        - key: '<secret-key>'
```

In the EC2 module's definitions, this profile can then be mentioned with the `profile` attribute instead of the three different attributes as follows:

```
- profile: cookbookprofile
```

This helps to reduce lines of Salt code and prevents mentioning a repetitive `profile` attribute.

See also

▶ http://docs.saltstack.com/en/latest/ref/states/all/salt.states.boto_secgroup.html#module-salt.states.boto_secgroup, to find out more about the `boto_secgroup` module

▶ The *Using elastic load balancers* recipe, to learn how to configure AWS load balancers

Using elastic load balancers

For a highly available infrastructure, in most modern production environments, load balancers are one of the most important components. In this recipe, we will learn how to configure AWS elastic load balancers using Salt modules.

How to do it...

1. Create and edit /opt/ salt-cookbook/production/aws/elb.sls to have the following entries:

```
salt-cookbook:
    boto_elb.present:
        - region: us-west-2
        - availability_zones:
            - us-west-2a
            - us-west-2c
        - keyid: <access-key>
        - key: '<secret-key>'
        - listeners:
            - elb_port: 80
              instance_port: 80
              elb_protocol: HTTP
        - attributes:
            cross_zone_load_balancing:
              enabled: true
        - health_check:
            target: 'HTTP:80/'
        - cnames:
            - name: lb1.salt-cookbook.com.
              zone: salt-cookbook.com.
              ttl: 60
```

2. Apply the state to the Salt master by running the following command:

```
[root@salt-master ~]# salt 'salt-master' state.sls aws.elb
saltenv=production

salt-master:
----------
          ID: salt-cookbook
    Function: boto_elb.present
      Result: True
```

Comment: ELB salt-cookbook present. Availability zones already set on ELB salt-cookbook. Set attributes on ELB salt-cookbook. Set health check on ELB salt-cookbook.

Started: 03:16:29.542518

Duration: 115133.924 ms

Changes:
```
          ----------
          new:
              ----------
              attributes:
                  ----------
                  cross_zone_load_balancing:
                      ----------
                      enabled:
                          True
              cnames:
                  |_
                    ----------
                    name:
                        lb1.salt-cookbook.com.
                    ttl:
                        60
                    zone:
                        salt-cookbook.com.
              health_check:
                  ----------
                  healthy_threshold:
                      3
                  interval:
                      30
                  target:
                      HTTP:80/
                  timeout:
                      5
                  unhealthy_threshold:
                      5
```

```
                    old:
                        ----------
                        attributes:
                            ----------
                            access_log:
                                ----------
                                emit_interval:
                                    None
                                enabled:
                                    False
                                s3_bucket_name:
                                    None
                                s3_bucket_prefix:
                                    None
                            cross_zone_load_balancing:
                                ----------
                                enabled:
                                    False
                        health_check:
                            ----------
                            healthy_threshold:
                                10
                            interval:
                                30
                            target:
                                TCP:80
                            timeout:
                                5
                            unhealthy_threshold:
                                2

    Summary
    ------------
    Succeeded: 1 (changed=1)
    Failed:    0
    ------------
    Total states run:    1
```

How it works...

In this recipe, we have demonstrated Salt's ability to configure **elastic load balancers** (**ELB**) on AWS. The objective of the recipe is to create a new load balancer with some of the important configuration options.

First, we have named the load balancer, which is `salt-cookbook` here, and then used the `boto_elb` module and its present function to make sure that the ELB is created:

```
salt-cookbook:
    boto_elb.present:
```

Next, we have mentioned the profile attributes which can also be replaced by the `profile` attribute, as demonstrated earlier:

```
        - region: us-west-2
        - keyid: <access-key>
        - key: '<secret-key>'
```

We have then mentioned the availability zones that the load balancer will be configured with. If using VPC, the `subnets` attribute is very important and should be used to mention which subnets will be used by the load balancer:

```
        - availability_zones:
            - us-west-2a
            - us-west-2c
```

Next, the listeners for the load balancer are configured with the `listeners` attribute. The details of the listener are configured using the `port` and the `protocol` attributes, as shown:

```
        - listeners:
            - elb_port: 80
              instance_port: 80
              elb_protocol: HTTP
```

The features available in the load balancer are then mentioned using the `attributes` attribute. The health check to be performed by the load balancer on the underlying servers is mentioned by the `health_check` attribute:

```
        - attributes:
            cross_zone_load_balancing:
              enabled: true
        - health_check:
            target: 'HTTP:80/'
```

Finally, a CNAME DNS record is added for the load balancer. The definition mentions that a CNAME record called `lb1.salt-cookbook.com` will be configured in the `salt-cookbook.com` hosted domain and should point to the DNS name generated by Amazon for the ELB when it is created. The DNS zone should be hosted on Amazon Route53 for this to work:

```
- cnames:
    - name: lb1.salt-cookbook.com.
      zone: salt-cookbook.com.
      ttl: 60
```

There are numerous other options that can be configured for Amazon ELB; we have demonstrated a few of them here.

See also

▸ http://docs.saltstack.com/en/latest/ref/states/all/salt.states. boto_elb.html#module-salt.states.boto_elb, to learn more about the boto_elb module

▸ The *Configuring DNS with Route53* recipe, to know how to configure DNS zones in AWS

Configuring DNS with Route53

The DNS naming service is one of the core components of infrastructure management, and Amazon provides an excellent service to host and manage DNS zones. In this recipe, we will learn how to manage DNS in AWS using Salt modules.

How to do it...

1. Create and edit /opt/ salt-cookbook/production/aws/dns.sls to have the following entries:

```
cookbookcname:
    boto_route53.present:
        - name: cookbook.salt-cookbook.com.
        - value: cookbookelb-440144868.us-west-
2.elb.amazonaws.com.
        - zone: salt-cookbook.com.
        - ttl: 60
        - record_type: CNAME
        - region: us-west-2
        - keyid: <access-key>
        - key: '<secret-key>'
```

2. Apply the state to the Salt master by running the following command:

```
[root@salt-master ~]# salt 'salt-master' state.sls aws.dns
saltenv=production
salt-master:
----------
              ID: cookbookcname
        Function: boto_route53.present
            Name: cookbook.salt-cookbook.com.
          Result: True
         Comment:
         Started: 18:50:05.292446
        Duration: 0.332 ms
         Changes:

Summary
------------
Succeeded: 1
Failed:    0
------------
Total states run:     1
```

How it works...

In this recipe, we have demonstrated Salt's ability to configure DNS records using the Route53 service of AWS. The objective of the recipe is to configure a specific record given the required information.

First, we gave a generic name to the definition, which is `cookbookcname` here, and used the `boto_route53` module and its present function to create the record:

```
cookbookcname:
    boto_route53.present:
```

Next, we mentioned the name of the record that we need to add to the zone using the `name` attribute. As this is a CNAME record, the `value` attribute points to an Amazon-generated DNS name. If it was an *A* record, it would point to an IP address.

The zone where the record needs to be added is mentioned by the `zone` attribute. This zone needs to be preconfigured in Amazon Route53 for this definition to work.

We then specify the TTL value for the record using the `ttl` attribute, which is 60 seconds here, and then we mention the record type using the `record_type` attribute, which is CNAME here:

```
        - name: cookbook.salt-cookbook.com.
        - value: cookbookelb-440144868.us-west-
    2.elb.amazonaws.com.
        - zone: salt-cookbook.com.
        - ttl: 60
        - record_type: CNAME
```

Finally, we have mentioned the profile attributes that can also be replaced by the `profile` attribute:

```
        - region: us-west-2
        - keyid: <access-key>
        - key: '<secret-key>'
```

DNS records can also be removed from zones using the same module and the `absent` function.

See also

▶ http://docs.saltstack.com/en/latest/ref/states/all/salt.states.boto_route53.html#module-salt.states.boto_route53, to find out more about the `boto_route53` module

▶ The *Configuring Simple Queue Service* recipe, to learn about using Simple Queue Service in Amazon

Configuring Simple Queue Service

Message queuing is considered to be one of the integral parts of application management in the modern world. AWS provides a feature for this task called **Simple Queue Service** (**SQS**). In this recipe, we will learn how to configure SQS using Salt modules.

How to do it...

1. Create and edit `/opt/ salt-cookbook/production/aws/sqs.sls` to have the following entries:

```
saltcookbookqueue:
    boto_sqs.present:
        - region: us-west-2
        - keyid: <access-key>
```

```
        - key: '<secret-key>'
        - attributes:
            ReceiveMessageWaitTimeSeconds: 20
```

2. Apply the state to the Salt master by using the following command:

```
[root@salt-master aws]# salt 'salt-master' state.sls aws.sqs
saltenv=production
salt-master:
----------
          ID: saltcookbookqueue
    Function: boto_sqs.present
      Result: True
     Comment: Setting ReceiveMessageWaitTimeSeconds
  attribute(s).
     Started: 21:42:42.478834
    Duration: 635.271 ms
     Changes:
              ----------
              new:
                  ----------
                  attributes_set:
                      - ReceiveMessageWaitTimeSeconds
                  queue:
                      saltcookbookqueue
              old:
                  None

Summary
------------
Succeeded: 1 (changed=1)
Failed:    0
------------
Total states run:     1
```

How it works...

In this recipe, we have demonstrated Salt's ability to configure SQS queues in AWS.

This is one of the simplest services to be configured using Salt modules.

First, we have provided the name of the queue to be created, which here is `saltcookbookqueue`. We have then used the `boto_sqs` module and the `present` function to make sure that the queue exists:

```
saltcookbookqueue:
    boto_sqs.present:
```

Next, we have used the profile attributes to mention the credentials and region of the queue to be created:

```
        - region: us-west-2
        - keyid: <access-key>
        - key: '<secret-key>'
```

We have then used the `attributes` attribute to specify a parameter of the SQS queue that we are creating. There are lots of other such parameters that can be configured using this attribute:

```
        - attributes:
            ReceiveMessageWaitTimeSeconds: 20
```

See also

▶ http://docs.saltstack.com/en/latest/ref/states/all/salt.states. boto_sqs.html#module-salt.states.boto_sqs, to find out more about the boto_sqs module

▶ The *Deploying ElastiCache clusters* recipe, to learn how to configure the AWS ElastiCache service

Deploying ElastiCache clusters

One more important feature in present day application management is caching services, and Amazon provides a service for this task called **ElastiCache**. In this recipe, we will learn how to configure ElastiCache using Salt modules.

How to do it...

1. Create and edit /opt/ `salt-cookbook/production/aws/elasticache.sls` to have the following entries:

```
cookbook-elasticache:
  boto_elasticache.present:
    - engine: redis
    - cache_node_type: cache.t1.micro
    - num_cache_nodes: 1
    - notification_topic_arn: arn:aws:sns:us-west-
2:808429213833:salt-cookbook
    - region: us-west-2
    - keyid: <access-key>
    - key: '<secret-key>'
```

2. Apply the state to the Salt master by running the following command:

```
[root@salt-master aws]# salt 'salt-master.teknification.com'
state.sls aws.elasticache saltenv=production

salt-master.teknification.com:
----------
          ID: cookbook-elasticache
    Function: boto_elasticache.present
      Result: True
     Comment:
     Started: 20:48:48.158433
    Duration: 1045.662 ms
     Changes:
              ----------
              new:
                  ----------
                  address:
                      None
                  auto_minor_version_upgrade:
                      True
                  cache_cluster_id:
                      cookbook-elasticache
                  cache_cluster_status:
                      creating
                  cache_node_type:
```

```
                    cache.t1.micro
         cache_parameter_group:
             default.redis2.8
         cache_security_groups:
         cache_subnet_group_name:
             default
         engine:
             redis
         engine_version:
             2.8.6
         notification_topic_arn:
             arn:aws:sns:us-west-2:808429213833:salt-
cookbook

         num_cache_nodes:
             1
         port:
             None
         preferred_availability_zone:
             None
         preferred_maintenance_window:
             thu:07:30-thu:08:30
         replication_group_id:
             None
         security_groups:
             None
     old:
         None


Summary
------------
Succeeded: 1 (changed=1)
Failed:    0
------------
Total states run:    1
```

How it works...

In this recipe, we have demonstrated Salt's ability to configure ElastiCache caching services. The objective of the recipe is to configure an ElastiCache cluster using the available Salt module and attributes.

First, we have mentioned the name of the cluster, which here is `cookbook-elasticache`, and then we have used the `boto_elasticache` module along with the `present` function to make sure that the cluster gets created:

```
cookbook-elasticache:
  boto_elasticache.present:
```

Next, we have specified the engine to use, which is `redis` here. We can also use `memchached`, which is also supported by ElastiCache. The node type has been mentioned by the `cache_node_type` attribute. The number of nodes in the cluster is configured by the `num_cache_nodes` attribute. To configure notification services, the `notification_topic_arn` attribute is used along with the value of a preconfigured Amazon SNS topic:

```
    - engine: redis
    - cache_node_type: cache.t1.micro
    - num_cache_nodes: 1
    - notification_topic_arn: arn:aws:sns:us-west-
2:808429213833:salt-cookbook
```

Finally, we have mentioned the profile attributes that can also be configured by using the `profile` attribute:

```
    - region: us-west-2
    - keyid: <access-key>
    - key: '<secret-key>'
```

See also

- ▶ http://docs.saltstack.com/en/latest/ref/states/all/salt.states. boto_elasticache.html#module-salt.states.boto_elasticache, to find out more about the `boto_elasticache` module

- ▶ The *Configuring CloudWatch alarms* recipe, to learn more about configuring CloudWatch alarms

Configuring CloudWatch alarms

Once cloud resources are configured, the next step is to configure monitoring and alerts for them to be aware of important notifications about issues and problems in the ever-growing infrastructure. Amazon provides **CloudWatch** for this type of requirement. In this recipe, we will learn about how to configure CloudWatch alarms for AWS resources.

How to do it...

1. Create and edit /opt/ salt-cookbook/production/aws/cloudwatch.sls to have the following entries:

```
salt-cookbook-alarm:
  boto_cloudwatch_alarm.present:
    - name: 'salt-cookbook UnHealthyHostCount'
    - attributes:
        metric: UnHealthyHostCount
        namespace: AWS/ELB
        statistic: Average
        comparison: '>='
        threshold: 1.0
        period: 300
        evaluation_periods: 4
        unit: null
        description: salt-cookbook UnHealthyHostCount
        dimensions:
          LoadBalancerName: [salt-cookbook]
        alarm_actions: ['arn:aws:sns:us-west-
2:808429213833:salt-cookbook']
        ok_actions: ['arn:aws:sns:us-west-
2:808429213833:salt-cookbook']
        insufficient_data_actions: []
    - region: us-west-2
    - keyid: <access-key>
    - key: '<secret-key>'
```

2. Apply the state to the Salt master by using the following command:

```
[root@salt-master ~]# salt 'salt-master' state.sls
aws.cloudwatch saltenv=production

salt-master:
----------

          ID: salt-cookbook-alarm
    Function: boto_cloudwatch_alarm.present
```

```
     Name: salt-cookbook UnHealthyHostCount
   Result: True
  Comment:
  Started: 20:43:59.568222
 Duration: 214.601 ms
  Changes:
           ----------
           new:
               ----------
           alarm_actions:
               - arn:aws:sns:us-west-
2:808429213833:salt-cookbook
           comparison:
               >=
           description:
               salt-cookbook UnHealthyHostCount
           dimensions:
               ----------
               LoadBalancerName:
                   - salt-cookbook
           evaluation_periods:
               6
           insufficient_data_actions:
           metric:
               UnHealthyHostCount
           namespace:
               AWS/ELB
           ok_actions:
               - arn:aws:sns:us-west-
2:808429213833:salt-cookbook
           period:
               600
           statistic:
               Average
           threshold:
               1.0
```

```
              unit:
                  None


    Summary
    ------------
    Succeeded: 1 (changed=1)
    Failed:    0
    ------------
    Total states run:    1
```

How it works...

In this recipe, we have demonstrated the Salt's ability to configure a CloudWatch alarm. The objective of the recipe is to configure a CloudWatch alarm for a certain metric of an elastic load balancer in AWS.

First, we mentioned a generic name for the alarm called salt-cookbook-alarm and then we used the boto_cloudwatch_alarm module and its present function to make sure that the alarm was created. We have then mentioned the name of the alarm with the name attribute:

```
salt-cookbook-alarm:
  boto_cloudwatch_alarm.present:
    - name: 'salt-cookbook UnHealthyHostCount'
```

Next, we have used the attributes attribute to configure the various parameters for the alarm in AWS. The metric attribute mentions the name of the parameter for which we are configuring the alarm. Various other parameters are configured after that, using AWS specific parameter names.

Next, the dimensions attribute is used along with the LoadBalancerName attribute to mention the load balancer name for which the alarm is being configured:

```
    - attributes:
        metric: UnHealthyHostCount
        namespace: AWS/ELB
        statistic: Average
        comparison: '>='
        threshold: 1.0
        period: 300
        evaluation_periods: 4
        unit: null
        description: salt-cookbook UnHealthyHostCount
        dimensions:
          LoadBalancerName: [salt-cookbook]
```

We have then mentioned the SNS topics that we have already configured to process the notifications for this alarm by using the `alarm_actions` and `ok_actions` attributes:

```
    alarm_actions: ['arn:aws:sns:us-west-2:808429213833:salt-
cookbook']
    ok_actions: ['arn:aws:sns:us-west-2:808429213833:salt-
cookbook']
    insufficient_data_actions: []
```

Finally, we have mentioned the profile attributes to provide the region and credentials for the deployment:

```
    - region: us-west-2
    - keyid: <access-key>
    - key: '<secret-key>'
```

See also

▸ http://docs.saltstack.com/en/latest/ref/states/all/salt.states. boto_cloudwatch_alarm.html#module-salt.states.boto_cloudwatch_ alarm, to find out more about the `boto_cloudwatch_alarm` module

10
Salt Event and Reactor System

In this chapter, you will cover:

- ▶ Learning the basics of the event system
- ▶ Listening to events
- ▶ Firing events
- ▶ Identifying and working with Salt event types
- ▶ Integrating and configuring the reactor system
- ▶ Using reactors for Salt tasks

Introduction

Apart from providing a structured method for configuration management, Salt also provides various other features such as the event system. The event system in Salt uses a publisher and subscribe model and is used to pass events between the master and the minions. Based on the data being passed through these events, specific types of actions can be configured.

The two components of Salt that mainly take part in this type of communication are the event system and the reactor system. The event system acts as the base of the communication method and the reactor system uses the functionality of the event system and combines it with the YAML-based configuration procedure of Salt to achieve desired results.

In this chapter, we will start with a basic understanding of the event system and its main components. We will move on to learn about how they work with each other to make sense of the event system. We will then move on to understanding the reactor system and how we can use the knowledge of the event system and integrate it with YAML-based Salt configurations to make changes on minions or the infrastructure.

Learning the basics of the event system

In this recipe, we will learn the basics of what the event system is and how to see the events in action and identify its various components.

How to do it...

Run the following command on the Salt master:

```
[root@salt-master ~]# salt-run state.event pretty=True
salt/auth          {
    "_stamp": "2015-02-23T04:13:55.299418",
    "act": "accept",
    "id": "salt-minion-1",
    "pub": "-----BEGIN PUBLIC KEY-----
\nMIICIjANBgkqhkiG9w0BAQEFAAOCAg8AMIICCgKCAgEApGyOzGPpQpOAXL6rnMl3\n5
Pk0q9bmBfB7Oci8b1Z4I920pcNmh+A9bWoJWqr6c80tXjZ2VbShzRqybQ0mRfdm\nEm1
juhF9vfRgfvN+GNQmw/8aNHEf6BAmggy7zxfiLpSzar8soaMEr9AVkqH7Q9e\nT4hgQ0W
boS1LbH7+O6iUFn66zkK49kapzEkVRH47QO1L0b/H9zgDFsoFKgc1Hbp7\nPZlpYU5NpQ
vSTQV0AFRVbazdw9apMrNwjVi69FZrFRzMqruKCnIvzlzcjFYTwwaH\...........==\n
-----END PUBLIC KEY-----\n",
    "result": true
}
minion_ping          {
    "_stamp": "2015-02-23T04:13:55.419117",
    "cmd": "_minion_event",
    "data": "ping",
    "id": "salt-minion-1",
    "pretag": null,
    "tag": "minion_ping"
}
salt/auth          {
    "_stamp": "2015-02-23T04:14:55.702166",
    "act": "accept",
    "id": "salt-minion-2",
```

```
    "pub": "-----BEGIN PUBLIC KEY-----
\nA+7OEFa4BOPbopiIUUbRBhELWXpVDzgzHf1QB\nBjffn9P49vd++wZ+1jZGLqvYFAtW
7eJBdUnKc5qJu7nGv55c8+cpl0NbYegP2pT8\nj7k8l3+jC9hh/rvE5/rcBIj/UDvszqM
Oq/iVJ6DabNBVZKXEgA8rsjZL83yOTWzk\nseclACp9jOicUKrWbDUE7wYhj42raC/fmK
LCU5sjolEJuws09VFcNyiZl2wvtA+m\nX3vg7yn/2MarJMW+1uTf9sNKHrwSvjwdZZXIE
D9OhbZx+BUOfN8OsFN6uH7/gySk\nsefhbtIoYf3yKO9RrMStQpRaFKlFnO0UIQykuzb0
H4IG8W+7Rz6EgH5F+m003HtY\nnv1e9X/jLtvkkbKke7amKU1kCAwEAAQ............=
=\n-----END PUBLIC KEY-----\n",
    "result": true
}
minion_ping     {
    "_stamp": "2015-02-23T04:14:55.810511",
    "cmd": "_minion_event",
    "data": "ping",
    "id": "salt-minion-2",
    "pretag": null,
    "tag": "minion_ping"
}
^C
```

```
Exiting gracefully on Ctrl-c
[root@devdc1srv01 ~]#
```

How it works...

In this recipe, we have demonstrated the basic idea of the event system in Salt. The objective of the recipe is to provide an understanding of how the event bus works in Salt and how we can identify the types of data available to us from the output received.

The event system in Salt is used to pass the desired data between minions and masters using an event bus. The event system is just the framework for the data to be passed and identified between the nodes—that is, the event system is not able to do any specific tasks based on the data being passed. To take actions on the data, the reactor system is used, about which we will learn later in this chapter.

The event system comprises two main components: the **event sockets**, which publish the data from a node, and the **event library**, which can listen for these data, identify them, and act on this data to pass information to the Salt system to be acted on.

The Salt minions keep sending data to the master to make sure that the authentication works correctly and the master is able to make sure that the minions under it are alive and responding. The data being sent to the master from the minions can be viewed by using the `state.event` runner on the Salt master and by using the `salt-run` command:

```
[root@salt-master ~]# salt-run state.event pretty=True
salt/auth       {
    "_stamp": "2015-02-23T04:13:55.299418",
    "act": "accept",
    "id": "salt-minion-1",
    "pub": "-----BEGIN PUBLIC KEY-----
\nMIICIjANBgkqhkiG9w0BAQEFAAOCAg8AMIICCgKCAgEApGyOzGPpQpOAXL6rnM13\n5
Pk0q9bmBfB7Oci8b1Z4I920pcNmh+A9bWoJWqr6c80tXjZ2VbShzRqybQ0mRfdm\neEm1
juhF9vfRgfvN+GNQmw/8aNHEf6BAmggy7zxfiLpSzar8soaMEr9AVkqH7Q9e\nT4hgQ0W
boS1LbH7+O6iUFn66zkK49kapzEkVRH47QO1L0b/H9zgDFsoFKgc1Hbp7\nPZ1pYU5NpQ
vSTQV0AFRVbazdw9apMrNwjVi69FZrFRzMqruKCnIvzlzcjFYTwwaH\..........==\n
-----END PUBLIC KEY-----\n",
    "result": true
}
minion_ping     {
    "_stamp": "2015-02-23T04:13:55.419117",
    "cmd": "_minion_event",
    "data": "ping",
    "id": "salt-minion-1",
    "pretag": null,
    "tag": "minion_ping"
}
```

In this example, we have used the default listening capability of the Salt system by using the `salt.event` runner. The Salt events can also be listened by using Python scripts and a REST API system.

The preceding output is an example of an event being sent from a minion to the master. The `salt/auth` output, which is also known as a `tag`, states that this event is an authentication event. It determines the ID of the minion from the received data and also identifies the key presented by the minion so that the master can verify whether this key authenticates correctly with the keys that it stores in its repository.

An event has various components, two of the most important being the `tag`, which helps to identify the type of data being passed, and the `data`, which actually stores the content being passed through the event.

There are many more types of events used in Salt and there are various ways that they can be identified and fired from nodes. We will learn about these procedures later in this chapter.

See also

▶ http://docs.saltstack.com/en/latest/topics/event/index.html, to know more about the event system

▶ The *Listening to events* recipe, to learn how to listen to events on a node

Listening to events

Out of the two procedures of a Salt event system, one is listening to Salt events. In this chapter, we will learn about the different procedures to listen for Salt events.

How to do it...

1. On the Salt master, create a file anywhere called cookbookeventslisten.py and edit it so it has the following content:

```python
#!/usr/bin/python

import salt.config
import salt.utils.event
import time
import pprint

opts = salt.config.client_config('/etc/salt/master')

event = salt.utils.event.get_event(
        'master',
        sock_dir=opts['sock_dir'],
        transport=opts['transport'],
        opts=opts)

response = event.get_event(wait=30, tag='cookbook/test')
print('Event fired at {0}'.format(time.asctime()))
print('*' * 25)
print('Tag: {0}'.format(response['tag']))
print('Data:')
pprint.pprint(response['data'])
```

2. Run the script in either of the following ways; however, there will be no output as no events have been sent yet:

```
[root@salt-master ~]# ./cookbookeventslisten.py


[root@salt-master ~]# python cookbookeventslisten.py
```

How it works...

In this recipe, we have demonstrated the procedure to listen for Salt events. There is no compulsion about which node can fire or listen to events—that is, the minion or the master. Either of the nodes can do both tasks but only the master can use the data to perform Salt tasks using the reactor system.

In the previous recipe *Learning the basics of the event system*, we have already seen how we can use the Salt runner command to listen for Salt events:

```
[root@salt-master ~]# salt-run state.event pretty=True
```

In this recipe, we have demonstrated the procedure to listen for Salt events by writing a Python script.

First, we mentioned that the script is going to be a Python script and then imported all the required libraries. The most important library here is the `salt.utils.event`, which helps us to receive the event data; the `salt.config` library helps us to read the Salt configuration file:

```
#!/usr/bin/python

import salt.config
import salt.utils.event
import time
import pprint
```

We then created a `salt.config` object using `salt.config.client_config` to read the Salt master configuration file. We have then created a `SaltEvent` object called `event` using the `get_event` function. One of the most important parameter that we are reading from the file is the `sock_dir` parameter that by default points to `/var/run/salt/master` and it is the location where Salt Unix sockets are stored:

```
opts = salt.config.client_config('/etc/salt/master')

event = salt.utils.event.get_event(
        'master',
        sock_dir=opts['sock_dir'],
        transport=opts['transport'],
        opts=opts)
```

Using the `SaltEvent` object, we then used the `get_event` function to listen to a single event. The `wait` option enables us to mention a wait period in seconds and the `tag` option helps us to mention only the events that we need to receive by filtering the tag value. The function can also be used without these values, in which case all the events will be listed and the first event that is received will be printed as it only listens for a single event:

```
response = event.get_event(wait=30, tag='cookbook/test')
print('Event fired at {0}'.format(time.asctime()))
```

```
print('*' * 25)
print('Tag: {0}'.format(response['tag']))
print('Data:')
pprint.pprint(response['data'])
```

There's more...

The Python script can also be modified to create a continuously listening service. This can be achieved by using the `iter_events` function. In this case, the script can be modified to look as follows:

```
for response in event.iter_events(tag='cookbook/test'):
  print('Event fired at {0}'.format(time.asctime()))
  print('*' * 25)
  print('Tag: {0}'.format(response['tag']))
  print('Data:')
  pprint.pprint(response['data'])
```

In this case, we have used a for loop in Python to create a continuous iteration and look for events with the `cookbook/test` tag. Do note that, when iteration is used, we will not be able to mention the wait period for the function.

We can also use the `fnmatch` Python library to filter the event tags and look for patterns in tags. The `fnmatch` library needs to be imported in the script first:

```
import fnmatch
```

Next, we can add a condition to look for a certain tag pattern and perform a function if it matches as follows:

```
if fnmatch.fnmatch(response['tag'], 'cookbook/test/*/events/*'):
        print(response['data'])
```

See also

- ▶ http://docs.saltstack.com/en/latest/topics/event/index.html#listening-for-events, to know more about configuring listeners for events
- ▶ The *Learning the basics of the event system* recipe, to know the basics of the event system
- ▶ The *Firing events* recipe, to know how to fire events from Salt nodes

Firing events

The second important component of the Salt event system is the **publisher** that fires an event from a Salt node to be captured by the target node. In this recipe, we will look at the various methods to fire events on Salt nodes.

How to do it...

1. On the Salt master, edit the event listener script that we created in the recipe *Listening to events* earlier in this chapter to have the following lines:

```
response = event.get_event(wait=30, tag='cookbook/test')
print response
```

2. Start the event listener script by running the following command:

```
[root@salt-master ~]# ./cookbookeventslisten.py
```

3. On the minion, run the following command:

```
[root@salt-minion ~]# salt-call event.fire_master '{"data":
"Cookbook events test"}' 'cookbook/test'
local:
    True
```

4. Observe the events listener script on the master; it should have an output similar to the following:

```
[root@salt-master ~]# ./cookbookeventslisten.py
```

```
{'_stamp': '2015-02-23T05:11:20.262723', 'pretag': None,
'cmd': '_minion_event', 'tag': 'cookbook/test', 'data':
{'data': 'Cookbook events test'}, 'id': 'salt-minion'}
```

5. Edit the cookbookeventslisten.py script to have the following entries:

```
response = event.get_event(wait=30, tag='cookbook/test')
print('Event fired at {0}'.format(time.asctime()))
print('=' * 25)
print('Minion ID: {0}'.format(response['id']))
print('Tag: {0}'.format(response['tag']))
print('Data:')
pprint.pprint(response['data'])
```

6. Create a script called cookbookeventsfire.py on the minion and edit it to have the following entries:

```
#!/usr/bin/python

import salt.client
```

```
caller = salt.client.Caller()

caller.sminion.functions['event.send'](
    'cookbook/test',
    {
        'data': "Cookbook events test",
    }
)
```

7. Start the `cookbookeventslisten.py` script on the master and then run the `cookbookeventsfire.py` script on the minion:

   [root@salt-minion ~]# ./cookbookeventsfire.py

8. Observe the script output on the master, it should have an output similar to the following:

   [root@salt-master ~]# ./cookbookeventslisten.py

   Event fired at Mon Feb 23 05:16:54 2015

   ========================

   Minion ID: salt-minion

   Tag: cookbook/test

   Data:

   {'data': 'Cookbook events test'}

How it works...

In this recipe, we have demonstrated the procedure to fire Salt events from a node. The objective of the recipe is to demonstrate different methods to fire Salt events and also to listen and parse those events on the target nodes.

First, we edited the events listener script on the master to have the following entries. Here, we are listening for a single event and printing the data as received. We have also mentioned the tag that we are listening for and the wait period:

```
response = event.get_event(wait=30, tag='cookbook/test')
print response
```

We then fired an event from the minion to the master using the following command:

[root@salt-minion ~]# salt-call event.fire_master '{"data": "Cookbook events test"}' 'cookbook/test'

The command to use for this task is `salt-call` and the function used is `event.fire_master`. We also mentioned a dictionary containing the data to be passed and, at the end of the command, we mentioned the tag to be used for the event which is `cookbook/test`.

On the master, we can see the event that has been received and printed:

```
[root@salt-master ~]# ./cookbookeventslisten.py
{'_stamp': '2015-02-23T05:11:20.262723', 'pretag': None, 'cmd':
'_minion_event', 'tag': 'cookbook/test', 'data': {'data': 'Cookbook
events test'}, 'id': 'salt-minion'}
```

Next, we have modified the `cookbookeventslisten.py` script on the master to have the following entries:

```
response = event.get_event(wait=30, tag='cookbook/test')
print('Event fired at {0}'.format(time.asctime()))
print('=' * 25)
print('Minion ID: {0}'.format(response['id']))
print('Tag: {0}'.format(response['tag']))
print('Data:')
pprint.pprint(response['data'])
```

This is done to provide a cleaner output when the events are received on the master.

We then created a new script on the minion called `cookbookeventsfire.py` and populated it with the following entries:

```python
#!/usr/bin/python

import salt.client

caller = salt.client.Caller()

caller.sminion.functions['event.send'](
    'cookbook/test',
    {
        'data': "Cookbook events test",
    }
)
```

This is done to demonstrate one more method of firing events—that is, by the use of Python scripts. We used the `salt.client` library in this script and created a caller object by using the `Caller` function.

We then used the `sminion.functions` function with the object and the event type which is `event.send` here. This determines that it is an event publisher firing an event. The `event.send` type determines that the event will be fired to the master.

We then mentioned the tag for the event and the data to be passed in a dictionary format.

We then executed the script on the minion to actually fire the event, and, finally, the output received on the master has been displayed, which is a much better formatted output and more understandable than the previous version that we demonstrated:

```
[root@salt-master ~]# ./cookbookeventslisten.py
Event fired at Mon Feb 23 05:16:54 2015
=========================
Minion ID: salt-minion
Tag: cookbook/test
Data:
{'data': 'Cookbook events test'}
```

There's more...

There are different functions in the event module to fire events to different targets. In this recipe, we have demonstrated the method to fire events to the master from a minion. This can be done with either of the following two commands:

```
[root@salt-minion ~]# salt-call event.fire_master '{"data": "Cookbook
events test"}' 'cookbook/test'
```

```
[root@salt-minion ~]# salt-call event.send '{"data": "Cookbook events
test"}' 'cookbook/test'
```

The `event.send` and `event.fire_master` functions can both be used to fire events to the master. If a minion or master wants to fire an event on its local bus, the `event.fire` function can be used as follows:

```
[root@salt-minion ~]# salt-call event.fire '{"data": "Cookbook events
test"}' 'cookbook/test'
```

See also

- ▶ http://docs.saltstack.com/en/latest/topics/event/index.html#firing-events, to know more about firing Salt events
- ▶ The *Listening to events* recipe, to learn how to listen for events
- ▶ The *Learning the basics of the event system* recipe, to know the basics of the event system

Identifying and working with Salt event types

To work with Salt events, one of the most important aspects is to identify the type of Salt event. In this recipe, we will look at some of the Salt event types and how we can identify and work with them.

How to do it...

1. A preconfigured Python script is available to listen to Salt events continuously. Download the file from the following location on the Salt master and run it using the Python command:

```
[root@salt-master ~]# wget https://raw.github.com/saltstack/salt/
develop/tests/eventlisten.py
```

```
[root@salt-master ~]# python eventlisten.py
```

2. Configure a new minion and start the salt-minion service daemon on the minion.

3. Observe the events being captured on the Salt master; there should be outputs as follows:

```
Event fired at Tue Feb 24 13:42:49 2015
*************************
Tag: salt/auth
Data:
{'_stamp': '2015-02-24T13:42:49.444198',
 'act': 'accept',
 'id': 'salt-minion',
 'pub': '-----BEGIN PUBLIC KEY-----
\nMIICIjANBgkqhkiG9w0BAQEFAAOCA....==\n-----END PUBLIC KEY----
-\n',
 'result': True}
```

```
Event fired at Tue Feb 24 13:43:01 2015
*************************
Tag: salt/minion/salt-minion/start
Data:
{'_stamp': '2015-02-24T13:43:01.585294',
 'cmd': '_minion_event',
```

```
'data': 'Minion salt-minion started at Tue Feb 24 12:46:46
2015',
 'id': 'salt-minion',
 'pretag': None,
 'tag': 'salt/minion/salt-minion/start'}


Event fired at Tue Feb 24 13:42:42 2015
************************
Tag: salt/key
Data:
{'_stamp': '2015-02-24T13:42:42.789949',
 'act': 'accept',
 'id': 'salt-minion',
 'result': True}
```

4. Run the following command on the master to send a ping test to the minion:

```
[root@salt-master ~]# salt 'salt-minion' test.ping
```

5. Observe the events being captured on the master:

```
Event fired at Tue Feb 24 13:46:54 2015
************************
Tag: new_job
Data:
{'_stamp': '2015-02-24T13:46:54.007525',
 'arg': [],
 'fun': 'test.ping',
 'jid': '20150224134653928822',
 'minions': ['salt-minion'],
 'tgt': 'salt-minion',
 'tgt_type': 'glob',
 'user': 'root'}
Event fired at Tue Feb 24 13:46:54 2015
************************
Tag: salt/job/20150224134653928822/new
Data:
{'_stamp': '2015-02-24T13:46:54.009202',
 'arg': [],
```

```
'fun': 'test.ping',
'jid': '20150224134653928822',
'minions': ['salt-minion'],
'tgt': 'salt-minion',
'tgt_type': 'glob',
'user': 'root'}


Event fired at Tue Feb 24 13:46:54 2015
*************************
Tag: salt/job/20150224134653928822/ret/salt-minion
Data:
{'_stamp': '2015-02-24T13:46:54.366753',
 'cmd': '_return',
 'fun': 'test.ping',
 'fun_args': [],
 'id': 'salt-minion',
 'jid': '20150224134653928822',
 'retcode': 0,
 'return': True,
 'success': True}
```

How it works...

In this recipe, we have looked at the different event types available in the Salt event system. The objective of the recipe is to generate different types of Salt event, capture them, and analyze them to know about how we can work with them.

When a new Salt minion is configured and started, we observe three different types events being generated. The first event is a `salt/auth` event that takes place when a key-based authentication takes place between a minion and a master:

```
Event fired at Tue Feb 24 13:42:49 2015
*************************
Tag: salt/auth
Data:
{'_stamp': '2015-02-24T13:42:49.444198',
 'act': 'accept',
 'id': 'salt-minion',
```

```
'pub': '-----BEGIN PUBLIC KEY-----
\nMIICIjANBgkqhkiG9w0BAQEFAAOCA....==\n-----END PUBLIC KEY-----
\n',
 'result': True}
```

The `Tag` attribute of the output gives us the event type as its value.

The next event type is a `salt/minion/salt-minion/start` type. The actual syntax of the tag is `salt/minion/<minion-id>/start`. The `<minion-id>` field is replaced by the minion ID of the node on which this is being run. This event is generated when the `salt-minion` service daemon is started on a minion node:

Tag: salt/minion/salt-minion/start

The next event type generated is `salt/key`.

Event fired at Tue Feb 24 13:42:42 2015

****

```
Tag: salt/key
Data:
{'_stamp': '2015-02-24T13:42:42.789949',
 'act': 'accept',
 'id': 'salt-minion',
 'result': True}
```

This event is generated when a new minion is configured and it sends a request to the master. The master either accepts or rejects the key and this activity shows up as an event with the type as `salt/key`.

The next events demonstrated are the job type events.

We sent a test ping to the minion from the master using the ping function of the test module. This activity generates two different events. The first event is generated when the request is sent from the master to the minion, which is `salt/job/<job-id>/new` type of event:

Event fired at Tue Feb 24 13:46:54 2015

****

```
Tag: salt/job/20150224134653928822/new
Data:
{'_stamp': '2015-02-24T13:46:54.009202',
 'arg': [],
 'fun': 'test.ping',
 'jid': '20150224134653928822',
```

```
'minions': ['salt-minion'],
'tgt': 'salt-minion',
'tgt_type': 'glob',
'user': 'root'}
```

Each activity performed in Salt is a job and has a unique job ID. The `<job-id>` field in the event type is replaced by the unique job ID of the jobs.

The next event is generated when the minion returns a response for the request sent by the master. In this case, the event type is `salt/job/<job-id>/ret/<minion-id>`:

```
Event fired at Tue Feb 24 13:46:54 2015
*************************
Tag: salt/job/20150224134653928822/ret/salt-minion
Data:
{'_stamp': '2015-02-24T13:46:54.366753',
 'cmd': '_return',
 'fun': 'test.ping',
 'fun_args': [],
 'id': 'salt-minion',
 'jid': '20150224134653928822',
 'retcode': 0,
 'return': True,
 'success': True}
```

In this response event, there are two unique components: the job ID and the minion ID.

Apart from these event types, there are many other event types available in Salt. Two other set of events available are the presence and the cloud types of events.

We will learn how to use these event types to perform Salt actions in the next recipe.

See also

▶ http://docs.saltstack.com/en/latest/topics/event/master_events. html, to know more about the different event types

▶ The *Learning the basics of the event system* recipe, to know about the basics of the event system

▶ The *Integrating and configuring the reactor system* recipe, to know how to use events to perform Salt tasks

Integrating and configuring the reactor system

Some of the best use cases for the event system of Salt can be demonstrated by integration with the reactor system. In this recipe, we will learn about the reactor system in Salt and the procedure to configure it.

How to do it...

1. Configure a minion called `salt-minion-1`.

2. On the Salt master, create a new directory as follows:

    ```
    [root@salt-master ~]# mkdir -p /etc/salt/master.d
    ```

3. Create and edit `/etc/salt/master.d/reactor.conf` to have the following entries:

    ```
    reactor:

      - 'cookbook/test':
        - /opt/salt/staging/event/test.sls
    ```

4. Create and edit `/opt/salt/staging/event/test.sls` to have the following entries:

    ```
    command_run:
      local.cmd.run:
        - tgt: '*'
        - arg:
          - 'ls -l /* > /tmp/test_output'
    ```

5. Open a new terminal for the Salt master and run the `eventlisten.py` script:

    ```
    [root@salt-master ~]# python eventlisten.py
    ```

6. Open another terminal for the Salt master. Stop the `salt-master` service daemon and start the Salt master service in debug mode:

    ```
    [root@salt-master ~]# salt-master -l debug
    ```

7. Run the `cookbookeventsfire.py` script that we created in the *Firing events* recipe earlier in this chapter.

8. Observe the `eventlisten.py` script output:

    ```
    Event fired at Mon Mar 16 04:42:05 2015

    *************************

    Tag: cookbook/test
    ```

```
Data:
{'_stamp': '2015-03-16T04:42:05.620309',
 'cmd': '_minion_event',
 'data': {'data': 'Cookbook events test'},
 'id': 'salt-minion-1',
 'pretag': None,
 'tag': 'cookbook/test'}
Event fired at Mon Mar 16 04:42:05 2015
*************************
Tag: 20150316044205728497
Data:
{'_stamp': '2015-03-16T04:42:05.729357',
 'minions': ['salt-minion-1', 'salt-minion-2']}
```

9. The following are the events for a new job to run commands on the minions followed by the return events to confirm the successful run of the command on the minions:

```
Event fired at Mon Mar 16 04:42:05 2015
*************************
Tag: new_job
Data:
{'_stamp': '2015-03-16T04:42:05.731235',
 'arg': ['ls -l /* > /tmp/test_output'],
 'fun': 'cmd.run',
 'jid': '20150316044205728497',
 'minions': ['salt-minion-1', 'salt-minion-2'],
 'tgt': '*',
 'tgt_type': 'glob',
 'user': 'root'}
Event fired at Mon Mar 16 04:42:05 2015
*************************
Tag: salt/job/20150316044205728497/new
Data:
{'_stamp': '2015-03-16T04:42:05.734412',
 'arg': ['ls -l /* > /tmp/test_output'],
 'fun': 'cmd.run',
 'jid': '20150316044205728497',
```

```
  'minions': ['salt-minion-1', 'salt-minion-2'],
  'tgt': '*',
  'tgt_type': 'glob',
  'user': 'root'}


Event fired at Mon Mar 16 04:42:10 2015
*************************
Tag: 20150316044205728497
Data:
{'_stamp': '2015-03-16T04:42:10.516867',
 'cmd': '_return',
 'fun': 'cmd.run',
 'fun_args': ['ls -l /* > /tmp/test_output'],
 'id': 'salt-minion-1',
 'jid': '20150316044205728497',
 'retcode': 0,
 'return': '',
 'success': True}
Event fired at Mon Mar 16 04:42:10 2015
*************************
Tag: salt/job/20150316044205728497/ret/salt-minion-1
Data:
{'_stamp': '2015-03-16T04:42:10.517745',
 'cmd': '_return',
 'fun': 'cmd.run',
 'fun_args': ['ls -l /* > /tmp/test_output'],
 'id': 'salt-minion-1',
 'jid': '20150316044205728497',
 'retcode': 0,
 'return': '',
 'success': True}
```

10. Observe the `salt-master` debug output in the other terminal:

    ```
    [DEBUG   ] Sending event - data = {'_stamp': '2015-03-
    16T04:42:05.620309', 'pretag': None, 'cmd': '_minion_event',
    'tag': 'cookbook/test', 'data': {'data': 'Cookbook events
    test'}, 'id': 'salt-minion-1'}
    ```

```
[DEBUG    ] Gathering reactors for tag cookbook/test

[DEBUG    ] Compiling reactions for tag cookbook/test

[DEBUG    ] Jinja search path:
['/var/cache/salt/master/files/base']

[DEBUG    ] Rendered data from file:
/opt/salt/staging/event/test.sls:

highstate_run:

  local.cmd.run:

    - tgt: '*'

    - arg:

      - 'ls -l /* > /tmp/test_output'


[DEBUG    ] Results of YAML rendering:

OrderedDict([('highstate_run', OrderedDict([('local.cmd.run',
[OrderedDict([('tgt', '*')]), OrderedDict([('arg', ['ls -l /*
> /tmp/test_output'])])])])]))


[DEBUG    ] Sending event - data = {'_stamp': '2015-03-
16T04:42:05.729357', 'minions': ['salt-minion-1', 'salt-
minion-2']}


[DEBUG    ] Sending event - data = {'tgt_type': 'glob', 'jid':
'20150316044205728497', 'tgt': '*', '_stamp': '2015-03-
16T04:42:05.731235', 'user': 'root', 'arg': ['ls -l /* >
/tmp/test_output'], 'fun': 'cmd.run', 'minions': ['salt-
minion-1', 'salt-minion-2']}


[INFO    ] User root Published command cmd.run with jid
20150316044205728497

[DEBUG    ] Published command details {'tgt_type': 'glob',
'jid': '20150316044205728497', 'tgt': '*', 'ret': '', 'user':
'root', 'arg': ['ls -l /* > /tmp/test_output'], 'fun':
'cmd.run'}

[DEBUG    ] Gathering reactors for tag 20150316044205728497

[DEBUG    ] Gathering reactors for tag new_job

[DEBUG    ] Gathering reactors for tag
salt/job/20150316044205728497/new

    .

    .

    .
```

```
[INFO    ] Got return from salt-minion-1 for job
20150316044205728497

[DEBUG   ] Sending event - data = {'fun_args': ['ls -l /* >
/tmp/test_output'], 'jid': '20150316044205728497', 'return':
'', 'retcode': 0, 'success': True, 'cmd': '_return', '_stamp':
'2015-03-16T04:42:10.516867', 'fun': 'cmd.run', 'id': 'salt-
minion-1'} [DEBUG   ] LazyLoaded local_cache.returner

[DEBUG   ] Gathering reactors for tag 20150316044205728497

[DEBUG   ] Gathering reactors for tag
salt/job/20150316044205728497/ret/salt-minion-1
```

How it works...

In this recipe, we demonstrated the reactor system available in Salt. The basic functionality of the reactor system in Salt is to react in the form of a state run or command run based on the events received from minions.

First, we created a directory called /etc/salt/master.d and then created a file called reactor.conf in it, in which we mentioned the reactor configuration. This configuration can also be mentioned in the master configuration file—that is, /etc/salt/master. However, if the separate files are created in /etc/salt/master.d, the files can be given any name with a .conf extension and they will be read by the Salt master.

Next we mentioned the reactor configuration:

```
reactor:

  - 'cookbook/test':
    - /opt/salt/staging/event/test.sls
```

The first line suggests that this is a reactor configuration. The following line suggests that the subsequent files are to be executed for the mentioned tags:

```
  - 'cookbook/test':
```

Here, the reactor is looking for events with cookbook/test tag. The next line suggests that the Salt configuration in the /opt/salt/staging/event/test.sls file is to be executed if an event with the tag cookbook/test is received.

Next we mentioned the contents of the /opt/salt/staging/event/test.sls file:

```
command_run:
  local.cmd.run:
    - tgt: '*'
    - arg:
      - 'ls -l /* > /tmp/test_output'
```

Here `command_run` is a generic name for the configuration. The `local.cmd.run` module is equivalent to the `cmd.run` execution module when modules are run from the Salt command line. By using the `tgt` attribute, we are targeting all the authenticated minions under the master. The `arg` attribute mentions the command to be run using the `cmd.run` module.

To summarize, our objective is to run the `ls -l /* > /tmp/test_output` command on all the registered minions if an event with the `cookbook/test` tag is received on the master.

We then fired an event from the minion `salt-minion-1` with the `cookbook/test` tag.

Next we observed the outputs from the event listener script and the debug mode of the Salt master. From the event listener script, we can see the different type of events being received on the master such as the custom event that we have fired:

```
[DEBUG   ] Sending event - data = {'_stamp': '2015-03-
16T04:42:05.620309', 'pretag': None, 'cmd': '_minion_event', 'tag':
'cookbook/test', 'data': {'data': 'Cookbook events test'}, 'id':
'salt-minion-1'}
```

A new job to execute the command on the minions:

```
[DEBUG   ] Sending event - data = {'tgt_type': 'glob', 'jid':
'20150316044205728497', 'tgt': '*', '_stamp': '2015-03-
16T04:42:05.731235', 'user': 'root', 'arg': ['ls -l /* >
/tmp/test_output'], 'fun': 'cmd.run', 'minions': ['salt-minion-1',
'salt-minion-2']}
```

The job return event from the minion:

```
[INFO    ] Got return from salt-minion-1 for job 20150316044205728497

[DEBUG   ] Sending event - data = {'fun_args': ['ls -l /* >
/tmp/test_output'], 'jid': '20150316044205728497', 'return': '',
'retcode': 0, 'success': True, 'cmd': '_return', '_stamp': '2015-03-
16T04:42:10.516867', 'fun': 'cmd.run', 'id': 'salt-minion-1'}
```

See also

- http://docs.saltstack.com/en/latest/topics/reactor/, to know more about the Salt reactor system
- The *Learning the basics of the event system* recipe, to learn about the event system
- The *Using reactors for Salt tasks* recipe, to know how to use reactors to perform Salt tasks

Using reactors for Salt tasks

Now that we are aware of how the event and the reactor systems work in Salt, we can go ahead and look into some more advanced configurations involving using them to perform Salt tasks. In this recipe, we will learn how to perform a state run based on Salt events.

How to do it...

1. Configure two new minions called `salt-minion-1` and `salt-minion-2`.

2. On the master, configure a new state module called `cron` in the staging environment and populate the `/opt/salt/staging/cron/init.sls` file with the following entries:

```
find /var/log/ -mtime +30 -exec rm -rf {] \;:
    cron.present:
        - user: root
        - minute: 00
        - hour: 12
        - daymonth: '*'
        - month: '*'
        - dayweek: '*'
```

3. Edit the `/etc/salt/master.d/reactor.conf` file to have the following entries:

```
reactor:

    - 'salt/minion/*/start':
        - /opt/salt/staging/event/cron.sls
```

4. Create and edit `/opt/salt/staging/event/cron.sls` to have the following entries:

```
{% if data['id'] == 'salt-minion-1' %}
state_run:
  local.state.sls:
    - tgt: salt-minion-2
    - arg:
      - cron
    - kwarg:
        saltenv:
            staging
{% endif %}
```

5. Restart the Salt master in debug mode and then restart the `salt-minion` service daemon on `salt-minion-1`.

Observe the outputs of the event listener script and the debug output of the Salt master by following the method described in the *Using reactors for Salt tasks* recipe:

```
[DEBUG    ] Sending event - data = {'_stamp': '2015-03-
16T04:58:14.403724', 'pretag': None, 'cmd': '_minion_event',
'tag': 'salt/minion/salt-minion-1/start', 'data': 'Minion
salt-minion-1 started at Mon Mar 16 04:02:00 2015', 'id':
'salt-minion-1'}

[DEBUG    ] Gathering reactors for tag salt/minion/salt-minion-
1/start

[DEBUG    ] Compiling reactions for tag salt/minion/salt-
minion-1/start

[DEBUG    ] Jinja search path:
['/var/cache/salt/master/files/base']

[DEBUG    ] Rendered data from file:
/opt/salt/staging/event/cron.sls:


highstate_run:
  local.state.sls:
    - tgt: salt-minion-2
    - arg:
      - cron
    - kwarg:
        saltenv:
          staging



[DEBUG    ] Results of YAML rendering:
OrderedDict([('highstate_run',
OrderedDict([('local.state.sls', [OrderedDict([('tgt', 'salt-
minion-2')]), OrderedDict([('arg', ['cron'])]),
OrderedDict([('kwarg', OrderedDict([('saltenv',
'staging')]))])])]))])

[DEBUG    ] Sending event - data = {'_stamp': '2015-03-
16T04:58:14.600685', 'minions': ['salt-minion-2']}

[DEBUG    ] Sending event - data = {'tgt_type': 'glob', 'jid':
'20150316045814600106', 'tgt': 'salt-minion-2', '_stamp':
'2015-03-16T04:58:14.605909', 'user': 'root', 'arg': ['cron',
```

```
{'saltenv': 'staging', '__kwarg__': True}], 'fun':
'state.sls', 'minions': ['salt-minion-2']}
```

[INFO   ] User root Published command state.sls with jid
20150316045814600106

[DEBUG   ] Published command details {'tgt_type': 'glob',
'jid': '20150316045814600106', 'tgt': 'salt-minion-2', 'ret':
'', 'user': 'root', 'arg': ['cron', {'saltenv': 'staging',
'__kwarg__': True}], 'fun': 'state.sls'}

[DEBUG   ] Gathering reactors for tag 20150316045814600106

[DEBUG   ] Gathering reactors for tag new_job

[DEBUG   ] Gathering reactors for tag
salt/job/20150316045814600106/new

[INFO   ] Got return from salt-minion-2 for job
20150316045814600106

[DEBUG   ] Sending event - data = {'fun_args': ['cron',
{'saltenv': 'staging'}], 'jid': '20150316045814600106',
'return': {'cron_|-find /var/log/ -mtime +30 -exec rm -rf {}
\\;_|-find /var/log/ -mtime +30 -exec rm -rf {} \\;_|-
present': {'comment': "Cron find /var/log/ -mtime +30 -exec rm
-rf {} \\; added to root's crontab", 'name': 'find /var/log/ -
mtime +30 -exec rm -rf {} \\;', 'start_time':
'04:01:59.218652', 'result': True, 'duration':
385.24000000000001, '__run_num__': 0, 'changes': {'root':
'find /var/log/ -mtime +30 -exec rm -rf {} \\;'}}}, 'retcode':
0, 'success': True, 'cmd': '_return', '_stamp': '2015-03-
16T04:58:17.193713', 'fun': 'state.sls', 'id': 'salt-minion-
2', 'out': 'highstate'}

How it works...

In this recipe, we have demonstrated the ability of Salt to use the event and reactor system to perform advanced Salt functions. The objective of the recipe is to run a Salt state module on receiving a minion start event from one of the minions.

We first configured a state module called cron to add a cron job to the minion by adding the Salt configuration in the /opt/salt/staging/cron/init.sls file.

Next we implemented the reactor configuration:

```
reactor:

  - 'salt/minion/*/start':
    - /opt/salt/staging/event/cron.sls
```

This states that, whenever a minion starts, the Salt configuration in the `/opt/salt/staging/event/cron.sls` file will be executed.

Next, we configured the contents of the `/opt/salt/staging/event/cron.sls` file:

```
{% if data['id'] == 'salt-minion-1' %}
state_run:
  local.state.sls:
    - tgt: salt-minion-2
    - arg:
      - cron
    - kwarg:
        saltenv:
          staging
{% endif %}
```

This configuration states that, if the minion that has started is `salt-minion-1`, then the `cron` state module will be executed on the `salt-minion-2` minion. We have specified the target minion with the `tgt` attribute. The `arg` attribute mentions the name of the configured state and we configure other options using the `kwarg` attribute such as the `saltenv` option here.

The minions can also be targeted in the following manner:

```
- tgt: 'environment:staging'
- expr_form: grain
```

Once the `salt-minion` daemon is restarted on `salt-minion-1`, the master receives a start event for the minion and executes the Salt configuration in `/opt/salt/staging/event/cron.sls`, as shown in the output, and adds the cron job to the `crontab` of `salt-minion-2`:

```
[DEBUG   ] Rendered data from file: /opt/salt/staging/event/cron.sls:

highstate_run:
  local.state.sls:
    - tgt: salt-minion-2
    - arg:
      - cron
    - kwarg:
        saltenv:
          staging
```

```
[DEBUG    ] Results of YAML rendering:
OrderedDict([('highstate_run', OrderedDict([('local.state.sls',
[OrderedDict([('tgt', 'salt-minion-2')]), OrderedDict([('arg',
['cron'])]), OrderedDict([('kwarg', OrderedDict([('saltenv',
'staging')]))])])])])


[DEBUG    ] Sending event - data = {'_stamp': '2015-03-
16T04:58:14.600685', 'minions': ['salt-minion-2']}

[DEBUG    ] Sending event - data = {'tgt_type': 'glob', 'jid':
'20150316045814600106', 'tgt': 'salt-minion-2', '_stamp': '2015-03-
16T04:58:14.605909', 'user': 'root', 'arg': ['cron', {'saltenv':
'staging', '__kwarg__': True}], 'fun': 'state.sls', 'minions':
['salt-minion-2']}
```

Other functions can also be carried out similarly, such as highstate run with local.state.highstate.

This procedure can be used in continuous deployment scenarios where an event can be sent to the master to run a deploy task once the build job completes successfully.

See also

- http://docs.saltstack.com/en/latest/topics/reactor/, to know more about the reactor module
- The *Learning the basics of the event system* recipe, to know more about the event system

11
Troubleshooting

In this chapter, you will cover:

- ▶ Troubleshooting the Salt master
- ▶ Troubleshooting the Salt minion
- ▶ Dealing with too many open files
- ▶ Connectivity, DNS, and ports
- ▶ Dealing with YAML configuration problems

Introduction

All throughout this book, we have been looking at numerous techniques to configure and manage Salt and its components. However, like all other systems, breakdowns can and do happen with Salt. The procedures to troubleshoot and handle them should always be known by an engineer.

In this chapter, we will look at some possible problems and issues that may occur in a Salt environment, the methods to identify them, possible options to fix them, and making sure that the problem is handled for good.

Troubleshooting the Salt master

In this recipe, you will learn about the various ways to identify and troubleshoot situations when the Salt master stops responding and there is a problem with the configuration of the Salt master.

How to do it...

1. Run the following command from the Salt master on a minion, and when the command does not respond terminate the command using the *Ctrl + C* key combination:

   ```
   [root@salt-master ~]# salt 'salt-minion' test.ping
   ^C
   Exiting gracefully on Ctrl-c
   [root@salt-master ~]#
   ```

2. Stop the Salt master, using the following command:

   ```
   [root@salt-master ~]# service salt-master stop
   Stopping salt-master daemon:
   [  OK  ]
   ```

3. Start the Salt master, using the following command:

   ```
   [root@salt-master ~]# salt-master -l debug
   [DEBUG   ] Reading configuration from /etc/salt/master
   [DEBUG   ] Using cached minion ID from /etc/salt/minion_id:
   salt- master
   [DEBUG   ] Configuration file path: /etc/salt/master
   [INFO    ] Setting up the Salt Master
   [DEBUG   ] Loaded master key: /etc/salt/pki/master/master.pem
   [INFO    ] Preparing the root key for local communication
   [DEBUG   ] Removing stale keyfile: /var/cache/salt/master/.root_
   key
   [DEBUG   ] Created pidfile: /var/run/salt-master.pid
   [INFO    ] salt-master is starting as user 'root'
   [INFO    ] Current values for max open files soft/hard
   setting: 1024/4096
   [INFO    ] The value for the 'max_open_files' setting, 100000,
   is higher than what the user running salt is allowed to raise
   to, 4096. Defaulting to 4096.
   [INFO    ] Raising max open files value to 4096
   [INFO    ] New values for max open files soft/hard values:
   4096/4096
   ```

4. Check the following `sysctl` parameters:

   ```
   [root@salt-master ~]# cat /proc/sys/net/ipv4/tcp_rmem
   4096     87380     1900544
   [root@salt-master ~]# cat /proc/sys/net/ipv4/tcp_wmem
   ```

```
4096     16384    1900544
[root@salt-master ~]# cat /proc/sys/net/core/wmem_max
124928
[root@salt-master ~]# cat /proc/sys/net/core/rmem_max
124928
```

5. Set the values as follows:

```
[root@salt-master ~]# echo 16777216 >
/proc/sys/net/core/rmem_max
[root@salt-master ~]# echo 16777216 >
/proc/sys/net/core/wmem_max
[root@salt-master ~]# echo "4096 87380 16777216" >
/proc/sys/net/ipv4/tcp_rmem
[root@salt-master ~]# echo "4096 87380 16777216" >
/proc/sys/net/ipv4/tcp_wmem
```

How it works...

In this recipe, we followed different procedures to identify problems with the Salt master and how to troubleshoot them.

First, we demonstrated a situation when the Salt command is not providing an output or not responding:

```
[root@salt-master ~]# salt 'salt-minion' test.ping
^C
Exiting gracefully on Ctrl-c
[root@salt-master ~]#
```

The first step performed when this happened was to stop the salt-master daemon, as it was running, and then start it in debug mode to identify any problems with the master configuration file and the Salt service:

```
[root@salt-master ~]# salt-master -l debug
[DEBUG   ] Reading configuration from /etc/salt/master
[DEBUG   ] Using cached minion ID from /etc/salt/minion_id: salt-
master
[DEBUG   ] Configuration file path: /etc/salt/master
[INFO    ] Setting up the Salt Master
[DEBUG   ] Loaded master key: /etc/salt/pki/master/master.pem
[INFO    ] Preparing the root key for local communication
```

```
[DEBUG    ] Removing stale keyfile: /var/cache/salt/master/.root_key
[DEBUG    ] Created pidfile: /var/run/salt-master.pid
[INFO     ] salt-master is starting as user 'root'
[INFO     ] Current values for max open files soft/hard setting:
1024/4096
[INFO     ] The value for the 'max_open_files' setting, 100000, is
higher than what the user running salt is allowed to raise to, 4096.
Defaulting to 4096.
[INFO     ] Raising max open files value to 4096
[INFO     ] New values for max open files soft/hard values: 4096/4096
```

Here, we have provided a very small portion of the large amount of output that is created when the Salt master is started in debug mode. Any problems in the Salt service or the master configuration file will be visible in this output. Although the large amount of output may seem overwhelming, it is the key to finding the problem and require extensive parsing.

For certain ZeroMQ versions, there is a bug that causes the Salt master to not respond, mainly in versions earlier than 2.1.11. In such cases, we first check the following values in the sysctl configurations:

```
[root@salt-master ~]# cat /proc/sys/net/ipv4/tcp_rmem
4096    87380   1900544
[root@salt-master ~]# cat /proc/sys/net/ipv4/tcp_wmem
4096    16384   1900544
[root@salt-master ~]# cat /proc/sys/net/core/wmem_max
124928
[root@salt-master ~]# cat /proc/sys/net/core/rmem_max
124928
```

To solve the problem, the following values must be set for the sysctl parameters:

```
[root@salt-master ~]# echo 16777216 > /proc/sys/net/core/rmem_max
[root@salt-master ~]# echo 16777216 > /proc/sys/net/core/wmem_max
[root@salt-master ~]# echo "4096 87380 16777216" >
/proc/sys/net/ipv4/tcp_rmem
[root@salt-master ~]# echo "4096 87380 16777216" >
/proc/sys/net/ipv4/tcp_wmem
```

If the sysctl.conf file needs to be edited to make these changes permanent, the parameters to set are as follows:

```
net.core.rmem_max = 16777216
net.core.wmem_max = 16777216
net.ipv4.tcp_rmem = 4096 87380 16777216
net.ipv4.tcp_wmem = 4096 87830 16777216
```

In lot of the situations when the command does not respond, it may be due to a large amount of configurations being done at the backend and as a result the command may timeout. To prevent this from happening, the timeout parameter can be set in the `/etc/salt/master` file to increase the interval:

```
timeout: 60
```

These are some of the methods used to troubleshoot problems with the Salt master.

See also

▶ `http://docs.saltstack.com/en/latest/topics/troubleshooting/master.html`, to learn more about troubleshooting the Salt master

▶ The *Troubleshooting the Salt minion* recipe, to learn how to troubleshoot minions

Troubleshooting the Salt minion

Not only the Salt master but also the Salt minions can face a lot of problems. In this recipe, you will learn how to determine the problems with Salt minions and the procedures to troubleshoot and solve them.

How to do it...

1. Run the following command from the Salt master:

   ```
   [root@salt-master ~]# salt -vv 'salt-minion' test.ping
   Executing job with jid 20150220033703911853
   ----------------------------------------------

   salt-minion:
       Minion did not return. [Not connected]
   ```

2. On the minion, check if the `salt-minion` service is running. If not, start it.

3. If the preceding issue still persists, check the log file on the minion:

   ```
   [root@salt-minion ~]# cat /var/log/salt/minion
   2015-02-20 02:40:44,160 [salt.crypt
   ][CRITICAL] The Salt Master has rejected this minion's public
   key!
   ```

4. To repair this issue, either delete the public key for this minion on the Salt master and restart this minion, or restart the Salt master in open mode to clean out the keys. The Salt minion will now exit.

5. Remove the keys for the minion, on both the minion and the master, and restart the salt-minion service daemon:

```
[root@salt-master ~]# rm -rf
/etc/salt/pki/master/minions/salt-minion

[root@salt-master ~]# rm -rf
/etc/salt/pki/master/minions_denied/ salt-minion


[root@salt-minion ~]# rm -rf /etc/salt/pki/minion/*

[root@salt-minion ~]# service salt-minion restart

Stopping salt-minion daemon:
[FAILED]

Starting salt-minion daemon:
[  OK  ]


[root@salt-master ~]# salt -vv 'salt-minion' test.ping

Executing job with jid 20150220034522662177

-------------------------------------------


salt-minion:

     Minion did not return. [No response]


[root@salt-master ~]# salt -vv 'salt-minion' test.ping

Executing job with jid 20150220034535723449

-------------------------------------------


salt-minion:

     True
```

6. Run the following command on the minion to synchronize with the master:

```
[root@salt-minion ~]# salt-call -l debug state.highstate

[DEBUG   ] Reading configuration from /etc/salt/minion

[DEBUG   ] Using cached minion ID from /etc/salt/minion_id:
salt-minion

[DEBUG   ] Configuration file path: /etc/salt/minion

[DEBUG   ] Reading configuration from /etc/salt/minion

[DEBUG   ] Decrypting the current master AES key

[INFO    ] Loading fresh modules for state activity
```

```
[INFO    ] Fetching file from saltenv 'development', **
skipped ** latest already in cache 'salt://top.sls'

[DEBUG   ] Jinja search path:
['/var/cache/salt/minion/files/base']

[DEBUG   ] Rendered data from file:
/var/cache/salt/minion/files/development/top.sls:

development:

  '*':

    - tomcat

    - tomcat.deploy


[DEBUG   ] Results of YAML rendering:
```

7. Run the following command if all seems to be well but the `salt-minion` service is not starting up:

```
[root@salt-minion ~]# salt-minion -l debug

[DEBUG   ] Reading configuration from /etc/salt/minion

[DEBUG   ] Using cached minion ID from /etc/salt/minion_id:
salt-minion

[DEBUG   ] Configuration file path: /etc/salt/minion

[INFO    ] Setting up the Salt Minion "salt-minion"

[DEBUG   ] Created pidfile: /var/run/salt-minion.pid

[DEBUG   ] Reading configuration from /etc/salt/minion

[DEBUG   ] Attempting to authenticate with the Salt Master at
192.168.0.2

[DEBUG   ] Loaded minion key: /etc/salt/pki/minion/minion.pem

[DEBUG   ] Decrypting the current master AES key

[INFO    ] Authentication with master at 192.168.0.2
successful!
```

How it works...

In this recipe, we described various procedures to identify, troubleshoot, and solve problems related to the Salt minion.

First, we described a scenario where the basic communication between the minion and the master is not present:

```
[root@salt-master ~]# salt -vv 'salt-minion' test.ping
Executing job with jid 20150220033703911853
```

```
salt-minion:
    Minion did not return. [Not connected]
```

Many times, the output can also say `[No response]`, as we will see later. To troubleshoot this, we can check if the `salt-minion` service daemon has been started and is running on the minion.

If all is well, then the next thing to check is the log file on the minion:

```
[root@salt-minion ~]# cat /var/log/salt/minion
2015-02-20 02:40:44,160 [salt.crypt
] [CRITICAL] The Salt Master has rejected this minion's public key!
To repair this issue, delete the public key for this minion on the
Salt Master and restart this minion.
Or restart the Salt Master in open mode to clean out the keys. The
Salt Minion will now exit.
```

Here, what happened is that the master has a previous version of the minion's key, and the minion has generated a new set of keys, which the master is not able to authenticate due to the presence of the old key.

The solution to this problem is to remove the affected keys on the master and the minion as follows:

```
[root@salt-master ~]# rm -rf /etc/salt/pki/master/minions/salt-minion
[root@salt-master ~]# rm -rf /etc/salt/pki/master/minions_denied/
salt-minion

[root@salt-minion ~]# rm -rf /etc/salt/pki/minion/*
```

After this step, the `salt-minion` service daemon is restarted on the minion. As the minion was not able to authenticate the first time, the process was not running on the minion and gets started on restarting it:

```
[root@salt-minion ~]# service salt-minion restart
Stopping salt-minion daemon:                        [FAILED]
Starting salt-minion daemon:                        [  OK  ]
```

Next, we again try to test the communication between the master and the minion:

```
[root@salt-master ~]# salt -vv 'salt-minion' test.ping
Executing job with jid 20150220034522662177
```

```
salt-minion:

    Minion did not return.  [No response]


[root@salt-master ~]# salt -vv 'salt-minion' test.ping
Executing job with jid 20150220034535723449

-------------------------------------------


salt-minion:
    True
```

In the first attempt, it gives a [No response] output, as it takes some time for the authentication and the communication to take place after the minion is started. On the second attempt, we see a successful communication.

 The -vv option is very important, as without it there will be no output, resulting in no debugging.

If there is a problem with synchronization of the Salt states from the master and the minion, the salt-call command can produce a lot of useful outputs to debug:

```
[root@salt-minion ~]# salt-call -l debug state.highstate
[DEBUG    ] Reading configuration from /etc/salt/minion
[DEBUG    ] Using cached minion ID from /etc/salt/minion_id: salt-
minion
[DEBUG    ] Configuration file path: /etc/salt/minion
[DEBUG    ] Reading configuration from /etc/salt/minion
[DEBUG    ] Decrypting the current master AES key
[INFO     ] Loading fresh modules for state activity
[INFO     ] Fetching file from saltenv 'development', ** skipped **
latest already in cache 'salt://top.sls'
```

If there is a problem with the salt-minion service daemon itself and the service is having problems in starting up or staying up, the salt-minion command can be executed with the debug option to generate a lot of useful outputs for debugging:

```
[root@salt-minion ~]# salt-minion -l debug
[DEBUG    ] Reading configuration from /etc/salt/minion
[DEBUG    ] Using cached minion ID from /etc/salt/minion_id: salt-
minion
[DEBUG    ] Configuration file path: /etc/salt/minion
```

```
[INFO    ] Setting up the Salt Minion "salt-minion"
[DEBUG   ] Created pidfile: /var/run/salt-minion.pid
[DEBUG   ] Reading configuration from /etc/salt/minion
[DEBUG   ] Attempting to authenticate with the Salt Master at
192.168.0.2
[DEBUG   ] Loaded minion key: /etc/salt/pki/minion/minion.pem
[DEBUG   ] Decrypting the current master AES key
[INFO    ] Authentication with master at 192.168.0.2 successful!
```

These were some of the most important problems and solutions for the Salt minions.

See also

▶ http://docs.saltstack.com/en/latest/topics/troubleshooting/minion.html, to learn more about how to troubleshoot minions

▶ The *Dealing with too many open files* recipe, to learn more about troubleshooting steps

Dealing with too many open files

In this recipe, you will learn how to resolve a situation where the number of open files exceeds the maximum file limit set in the operating system.

How to do it...

1. On trying to add a new minion to the master, the following error may be noticed in the log:

```
[salt.master    ][INFO    ] Starting Salt worker process 38
Too many open files
sock != -1 (tcp_listener.cpp:335)
```

2. Check the limit of maximum open files in the system:

```
[root@salt-master ~]# ulimit -n
1024
```

3. Run the salt-master daemon in debug mode:

```
[root@salt-master ~]# salt-master -l debug
.
.
.
[INFO    ] salt-master is starting as user 'root'
```

```
[INFO    ] Current values for max open files soft/hard
setting: 1024/4096

[INFO    ] The value for the 'max_open_files' setting, 100000,
is higher than what the user running salt is allowed to raise to,
4096. Defaulting to 4096.

[INFO    ] Raising max open files value to 4096

[INFO    ] New values for max open files soft/hard values:
4096/4096
```

4. Edit the /etc/security/limits.conf file and add the following entries:

```
root         hard    nofile        8192
root         soft    nofile        8192
```

5. Check the maximum number of files limit in the Salt master configuration file:

    [root@salt-master ~]# grep -i max_open_files /etc/salt/master

    #max_open_files: 100000

How it works...

In this recipe, you learned about the procedure to troubleshoot the problem of exceeding the maximum number of open files.

In Salt, for each new minion, the Salt master needs two sockets for the communication: one for the publisher and one for the response port. In an operating system, the usual limit for the maximum number of open files is 1024, and when the Salt deployments grow to a certain scale, the numbers of open files exceed that limit for the system:

```
[salt.master    ][INFO    ] Starting Salt worker process 38
Too many open files
sock != -1 (tcp_listener.cpp:335)
```

The preceding error can be seen in the Salt master log file.

We can first verify the default limit of the operating system:

[root@salt-master ~]# ulimit -n

1024

Do note that, Salt, being aware of this problem, increases the limit to 4096 when the Salt service daemon starts, which can be seen by running the Salt master in debug mode:

[root@salt-master ~]# salt-master -l debug

.

.

[INFO   ] salt-master is starting as user 'root'

```
[INFO    ] Current values for max open files soft/hard setting:
1024/4096
[INFO    ] The value for the 'max_open_files' setting, 100000, is
higher than what the user running salt is allowed to raise to, 4096.
Defaulting to 4096.
[INFO    ] Raising max open files value to 4096
[INFO    ] New values for max open files soft/hard values: 4096/4096
```

However, to be safe, the values can be entered in the `/etc/security/limits.conf` file to make them persistent, and values are kept high:

```
    root        hard    nofile      8192
    root        soft    nofile      8192
```

It should also to noted that there is a maximum open files parameter in the Salt master configuration file:

```
[root@salt-master ~]# grep -i max_open_files /etc/salt/master
```

```
#max_open_files: 100000
```

However, this value cannot exceed the system default, so although the limit here is `100000`, it is not able to go beyond the system limit of **4096**, as seen in the debug output:

```
[INFO    ] The value for the 'max_open_files' setting, 100000, is
higher than what the user running salt is allowed to raise to,
4096. Defaulting to 4096.
```

See also

- ▶ The *Troubleshooting the Salt master* and *Troubleshooting the Salt minion* recipes, to learn how to troubleshoot the Salt master and minion
- ▶ The *Connectivity, DNS, and ports* recipe, to learn about troubleshooting network and network-service-related problems

Connectivity, DNS, and ports

In this recipe, you will learn about the network and network-service-related problems, which can affect both master and minions in Salt.

How to do it...

1. When communication between the Salt master and the minion fails, the log file on the minion tells us about the suspected problem:

   ```
   2015-02-20 03:46:32,765 [salt.utils        ][ERROR   ] DNS
   lookup of 'salt-master' failed.

   2015-02-20 03:46:32,765 [salt.minion       ][ERROR   ] Master
   hostname: 'salt-master' not found. Retrying in 30 seconds
   ```

2. Try to reach the Salt master:

   ```
   [root@salt-minion ~]# ping salt-master

   ping: unknown host salt-master
   ```

3. Add a DNS entry for the Salt master. If it is already present, check the /etc/resolv.conf file to see if the DNS servers are properly set. Also, the problem can be solved with an entry in the /etc/hosts file as follows:

   ```
   192.168.0.2 salt-master
   ```

4. If the Salt server is reachable, check the ports on the server as to whether or not they are up and listening:

   ```
   [root@salt-master ~]# netstat -ntlp | egrep '4505|4506'

   tcp         0      0 0.0.0.0:4505              0.0.0.0:*
   LISTEN      4754/python

   tcp         0      0 0.0.0.0:4506              0.0.0.0:*
   LISTEN      4766/python
   ```

5. Next, check the reachability of the ports from the minion:

   ```
   [root@salt-minion ~]# nc -v -z 192.168.0.2 4505

   Connection to 192.168.0.2 4505 port [tcp/*] succeeded!

   [root@salt-minion ~]# nc -v -z 192.168.0.2 4506

   Connection to 192.168.0.2 4506 port [tcp/*] succeeded!
   ```

How it works...

In this recipe, we demonstrated the procedures to identify and troubleshoot network and network-service-related problems in Salt.

The objective of the recipe is to find out the most probable reasons for minions not connecting to masters.

The first things to check on both the master and the minion are the log files. For the master the file is `/var/log/salt/master` and for the minion it is `/var/log/salt/minion`. Here, for the minion, we found the following errors:

```
2015-02-20 03:46:32,765 [salt.utils        ] [ERROR   ] DNS lookup
of 'salt-master' failed.
2015-02-20 03:46:32,765 [salt.minion       ] [ERROR   ] Master
hostname: 'salt-master' not found. Retrying in 30 seconds
```

It is quite clear that the minion is not able to find an IP address for the `salt-master` hostname in its configuration file.

If all the minions have the same issue, the reason can be a missing `salt-master` DNS entry.

If the problem is with a single minion, the problem can be improper DNS configuration on the host in the `/etc/resolv.conf` file, or a missing `salt-master` entry in the `/etc/hosts` file, if the minions don't use DNS. An entry can be added to `/etc/hosts` as follows:

```
192.168.0.2 salt-master
```

If the Salt master is reachable, the next things to check are the ports on the Salt master.

Salt uses port 4505 and 4506 for communication with minions, and the ports should be reachable on the master from the minions.

To check if the ports are up and listening on the master, we run the following command:

```
[root@salt-master ~]# netstat -ntlp | egrep '4505|4506'
tcp        0      0 0.0.0.0:4505            0.0.0.0:* LISTEN
4754/python
tcp        0      0 0.0.0.0:4506            0.0.0.0:* LISTEN
4766/python
```

If the ports are down, we need to check if the salt master process is running, and if, somehow, the ports are being used by a different process, we will need to make sure that the ports are made available to the Salt master process.

The next thing to check is the reachability of the ports from the minions. To find that out, the following commands are run:

```
[root@salt-minion ~]# nc -v -z 192.168.0.2 4505
Connection to 192.168.0.2 4505 port [tcp/*] succeeded!
[root@salt-minion ~]# nc -v -z 192.168.0.2 4506
Connection to 192.168.0.2 4506 port [tcp/*] succeeded!
```

The `nc` command (`netcat`) is used to find the reachability of ports from one host to another. Here, we can see that the port reachability is working fine and the communication succeeds.

If there is a problem in this communication, there is a high probability that a firewall or any other IP/port filtering service is blocking access from the minion to these ports on the master node, and the solution is to make sure that the ports are unblocked.

To avoid this kind of problem, the masterless minion can be configured where the minion gets its configuration from the files hosted on it.

These were some of the most common network and network-service-related problems seen in Salt deployments.

See also

▸ The *Installing and configuring Salt minion* recipe, in *Chapter 1, Salt Architecture and Components*, to learn more about configuring masterless minions

▸ The *Troubleshooting the Salt master* and *Troubleshooting the Salt minion* recipes, to learn how to troubleshoot master and minions

Dealing with YAML configuration problems

One of the most simple, but extremely important entities, which cause problems in Salt configurations is the YAML format, which has to be consistently maintained in all Salt configurations. In this chapter, you will learn about the most common mistakes and how to avoid them.

How to do it...

1. Run a misconfigured state file against a minion:

```
[root@salt-master ~]# salt 'salt-minion' state.sls apache
saltenv=development
salt-minion:
    Data failed to compile:
----------
    Rendering SLS apache failed, render error: while parsing a
    block mapping
  in "<unicode string>", line 6, column 4:
      service:
       ^
expected <block end>, but found '<block sequence start>'
  in "<unicode string>", line 8, column 5:
```

```
         - running
           ^



   .


   .


   .


ParserError: while parsing a block mapping
   in "<unicode string>", line 6, column 4:
         service:
           ^

expected <block end>, but found '<block sequence start>'
   in "<unicode string>", line 8, column 5:
           - running
             ^
```

2. Check the `/opt/salt/development/apache/init.sls` state file being applied:

    ```
    apache_packages:
      pkg.installed:
         - httpd


    apache_service:
       service:
       - name: httpd
        - running
        - enable: True
        - require:
          - pkg: apache_packages
    ```

3. Modify the file to look like the following, and apply the state again, which should succeed:

    ```
    apache_packages:
      pkg.installed:
         - httpd


    apache_service:
       service:
          - name: httpd
          - running
          - enable: True
          - require:
            - pkg: apache_packages
    ```

How it works...

In this recipe, we demonstrated some of the YAML configuration errors that can be committed while configuring Salt and writing state files.

In this recipe, we first tried to apply a state to a minion, resulting in the following output:

```
[root@salt-master ~]# salt 'salt-minion' state.sls apache
saltenv=development
salt-minion:
    Data failed to compile:
----------
    Rendering SLS apache failed, render error: while parsing a block
  mapping
  in "<unicode string>", line 6, column 4:
      service:
      ^
expected <block end>, but found '<block sequence start>'
  in "<unicode string>", line 8, column 5:
        - running
      ^
```

The mistake made here is that the proper indentation of the YAML format has not been followed, as can be seen here:

```
  apache_packages:
      pkg.installed:
          - httpd

  apache_service:
      service:
      - name: httpd
      - running
```

Here, we can see improper indentation leading to the preceding error message. This type of problem may look simple, but sometimes acts as the sole cause of problems leading to unnecessary troubleshooting and wasting valuable time.

The most common and important YAML mistakes are as follows:

1. **Only spaces, no tabs**: The indentations in a YAML configuration are done by using the space key and not the *Tab* key. Any indentation made by using the *Tab* key will result in errors.

2. **Indentations**: Indentations are extremely important in YAML configuration, as without them the correct Python dictionaries will not be formed, resulting in wrong data being loaded. In most cases, wrong indentations will cause the Salt run to fail without any data processing.

3. **Booleans and other data**: Boolean values `True` and `False`, and other values such as `Yes`, `No`, `On`, and `Off` are treated as Salt-specific values and not as string values as they are treated if they are not enclosed in quotes. Always remember to put quotes around these values if you are using them in configurations such as pillar data.

4. **Integers and dates**: If integers and dates are used in Salt as string values, and are not put in quotes, they will be passed on to Salt as integers and will automatically convert to the `datetime` Python object. These types of data should also be put in quotes in order to get the desired result.

See also

► `http://docs.saltstack.com/en/latest/topics/troubleshooting/yaml_idiosyncrasies.html`, to learn more about YAML problems

► The *Troubleshooting the Salt master* and *Troubleshooting the Salt minion* recipes, to learn how to troubleshoot master and minions

Index

A

a2enmod binary 170
alternatives
configuring 159-162
apache_module state module
about 170
URL 170
apache-repo
URL 156
Apache Tomcat
files 185-190
Java, setting up for 180-184
packages 185-190
services 185-190
WAR file, deploying in 191, 192
Apache web server
about 164
packages 164-167
services 164-167
archive files
handling 105-108
attributes, cmd state
creates 98
cwd 98
env 98
group 98
user 98
attributes, pkg module
fromrepo 141
hold 141
refresh 141
version 141

C

CentOS
Salt master, installing on 3
Salt minion, installing on 15
cloud maps
configuring 240-242
cloud operations, Salt
/etc/salt/cloud file 231
/etc/salt/cloud.map file 231
/etc/salt/cloud.profiles.d directory 232
/etc/salt/cloud.profiles file 231
/etc/salt/cloud.providers.d directory 231
/etc/salt/cloud.providers file 231
cloud profiles
configuring 234-237
extending 237-240
cloud providers
configuring 232-234
extending 237-240
URL 255
CloudWatch alarms
about 274
configuring 274-277
URL 277
cmd state
attributes 98
code repositories
managing, with Git 153-156
managing, with svn 156-159
command line
pillar data, setting at 35
commands
running 94-97

Thank you for buying
Salt Cookbook

About Packt Publishing

Packt, pronounced 'packed', published its first book, *Mastering phpMyAdmin for Effective MySQL Management*, in April 2004, and subsequently continued to specialize in publishing highly focused books on specific technologies and solutions.

Our books and publications share the experiences of your fellow IT professionals in adapting and customizing today's systems, applications, and frameworks. Our solution-based books give you the knowledge and power to customize the software and technologies you're using to get the job done. Packt books are more specific and less general than the IT books you have seen in the past. Our unique business model allows us to bring you more focused information, giving you more of what you need to know, and less of what you don't.

Packt is a modern yet unique publishing company that focuses on producing quality, cutting-edge books for communities of developers, administrators, and newbies alike. For more information, please visit our website at www.packtpub.com.

About Packt Open Source

In 2010, Packt launched two new brands, Packt Open Source and Packt Enterprise, in order to continue its focus on specialization. This book is part of the Packt open source brand, home to books published on software built around open source licenses, and offering information to anybody from advanced developers to budding web designers. The Open Source brand also runs Packt's open source Royalty Scheme, by which Packt gives a royalty to each open source project about whose software a book is sold.

Writing for Packt

We welcome all inquiries from people who are interested in authoring. Book proposals should be sent to author@packtpub.com. If your book idea is still at an early stage and you would like to discuss it first before writing a formal book proposal, then please contact us; one of our commissioning editors will get in touch with you.

We're not just looking for published authors; if you have strong technical skills but no writing experience, our experienced editors can help you develop a writing career, or simply get some additional reward for your expertise.

Learning SaltStack

ISBN: 978-1-78439-460-8   Paperback: 174 pages

Learn how to manage your infrastructure by utilizing the power of SaltStack

1. Execute commands and enforce the state of your entire infrastructure in seconds.

2. Make managing your servers as easy as visualizing the end goal – let SaltStack do the heavy lifting through the state system.

3. Learn by doing in this step by step guide to getting started with SaltStack.

Desire2Learn for Higher Education Cookbook

ISBN: 978-1-84969-344-8   Paperback: 206 pages

Gain expert knowledge of the tools within the Desire2Learn Learning Environment, maximize your productivity, and create online learning experiences with these easy-to-follow recipes

1. Customize the look and feel of your online course, integrate graphics and video, and become more productive using the learning environment's built-in assessment and collaboration tools.

2. Recipes address real world challenges in clear and concise step-by-step instructions, which help you work your way through technical tasks with ease.

3. Detailed instructions with screenshots to guide you through each task.

Please check **www.PacktPub.com** for information on our titles

Mockito Essentials

ISBN: 978-1-78398-360-5   Paperback: 214 pages

A practical guide to get you up and running with unit testing using Mockito

1. Explore Mockito features and learn stubbing, mocking and spying dependencies using the Mockito framework.

2. Mock external dependencies for legacy and greenfield projects and create an automated JUnit safety net for building reliable, maintainable and testable software.

3. A focused guide filled with examples and supporting illustrations on testing your software using Mockito.

Learning scikit-learn: Machine Learning in Python

ISBN: 978-1-78328-193-0   Paperback: 118 pages

Experience the benefits of machine learning techniques by applying them to real-world problems using Python and the open source scikit-learn library

1. Use Python and scikit-learn to create intelligent applications.

2. Apply regression techniques to predict future behavior and learn to cluster items in groups by their similarities.

3. Make use of classification techniques to perform image recognition and document classification.

Please check **www.PacktPub.com** for information on our titles

CPSIA information can be obtained at www.ICGtesting.com
Printed in the USA
LVOW02s2026030815

448654LV00010B/547/P